The Power of the
Early Tudor Nobility

The Power of the Early Tudor Nobility

A Study of the Fourth and Fifth Earls of Shrewsbury

G.W. Bernard
Lecturer in History
University of Southampton

THE HARVESTER PRESS · SUSSEX
BARNES & NOBLE BOOKS · NEW JERSEY

First published in Great Britain in 1985 by
THE HARVESTER PRESS LIMITED
Publisher: John Spiers
16 Ship Street, Street, Brighton, Sussex

and in the USA by
BARNES & NOBLE BOOKS
81 Adams Drive, Totowa, New Jersey 07512

© G.W. Bernard, 1985

British Library Cataloguing in Publication Data
Bernard, G.W.
    The power of the early Tudor nobility.
    1. England—Nobility—History 2. Great
    Britain—Politics and government—1485-1603
    1. Title
    305.5′223′0942   HT653.G7

    ISBN 0-7108-0991-3

Library of Congress Cataloging in Publication Data
Bernard, G. W.
    The power of the early Tudor nobility.

    1. Nobility—England—Shrewsbury (Shropshire)—
History—15th century—Case studies. 2. Talbot, John,
Earl of Shrewsbury, 1383-1453. 3. Talbot, John, Earl
of Shrewsbury, ca. 1413-1460. I. Title.
HT653.G7B47   1985   305.5′223′0942454   84-16757
ISBN 0-389-20525-7

Typeset in 11/12 Baskerville by Witwell Limited, Liverpool
Printed in Great Britain by
Whitstable Litho Ltd, Whitstable, Kent

TO MY PARENTS

Contents

Preface

My greatest debt is to my parents without whose support and confidence I should never have embarked upon this study. I am grateful to the Department of Education and Science for the award of a Major State Studentship and to St Catherine's College, Oxford, for financial assistance. My appointment as a Lecturer, first at The Polytechnic, Wolverhampton, then at the University of Southampton, has made possible the completion of this book. I am particularly grateful to Mr R.A. Revell, Deputy Head of the Department of Arts, The Polytechnic, Wolverhampton, for giving me the greatest opportunities to pursue my research. I must also thank The Polytechnic for allowing me a term's study leave and The British Academy for a grant which enabled me to deepen my knowledge of mid-Tudor politics, some of the fruits of which are presented here. I am very grateful to my colleagues at Southampton for making the Department of History so stimulating and agreeable an environment for research. I have also gained much from the stimulus of teaching my students.

I am indebted to the kindness of those who have allowed and enabled me to read and to cite manuscripts in their possession: Garter King of Arms and the Chapter of the College of Arms for permission to consult the Talbot Papers and Mr M. Maclagan, Richmond Herald, Dr C. Swan, York Herald, and his secretary Mrs M. Chorley for making it possible for me to work in the College of Arms; the Duke of Norfolk for permission to consult manuscripts at Arundel Castle and in Sheffield City Library, and the late F.W. Steer, archivist to the Duke of Norfolk, for arranging for me to visit Arundel and Miss R. Meredith, city archivist, for valuable assistance at Sheffield; the Duke of Devonshire and the trustees of the Devonshire settlement for

permission to consult manuscripts at Chatsworth, and the late
T.S. Wragg for arranging access; and the Marquess of Bath for
permission to consult manuscripts at Longleat. The staff of many
record offices and libraries have been helpful: I should wish to
thank especially those of the Manuscripts Room of the British
Library and of the Upper Reading Room and of Duke Humfrey
in the Bodleian Library, Oxford.

I owe a debt to many historians, not least to those whose books,
theses, articles and seminar papers are cited in my notes. Mr
F.H. Terry, Head of History at Reading School, showed me by
his example how rewarding the study of history could be. I must
also thank my tutors at St Catherine's College, Oxford, Dr G.A.
Holmes and Dr P.G.M. Dickson. As one of my tutors Mrs J.
Loach deepened my interest in sixteenth-century history and has
been a valued source of references and practical assistance since. I
learned much from the comments of Professor J.J. Scarisbrick
and Dr P.H. Williams on an earlier version of this study. I have
gained much from many who have given me references and
discussed early Tudor history with me: Dr S.L. Adams and Dr
C.W. Brooks (whom I must thank for reading an earlier version),
Dr J.D. Alsop, Mr C.H.D. Coleman, Mr A.C. Duke, Mr S.J.
Gunn (to whom I am grateful for giving me a copy of an
unpublished paper), Dr M.A. Hicks, Mr G. Hill, Mr R.W.
Hoyle (whom I must especially thank for informing me of his
discoveries at Chatsworth and in the Masters' MSS, and for
scrutinising parts of Chapter 2), Mr H. James, Mr S.E. Kershaw,
Dr D.N.J. MacCulloch, Dr D.M. Palliser, Dr D.R. Starkey, Miss
A. Talbot, Mr G. Walker, and many others. Versions of Chapter
2 were read as papers at St John's College, Oxford and at the
University of Sheffield; a version of Chapter 4 at the History
Faculty Library, Oxford; and versions of my Conclusion to
seminars at the Universities of Birmingham, Bristol and
Reading, at the Institute of Historical Research, University of
London, and to Historical Association branches at Southampton
and Wolverhampton: I am most grateful for the comments made
on those occasions. Dr A.T. Thacker has given me much
encouragement and many helpful suggestions. I have benefited
greatly from innumerable conversations with Dr K.M. Sharpe
since we first met as freshmen at St Catherine's: he has also read
and commented on earlier drafts of my Introduction and

Conclusion. Mr P.J. Gwyn has allowed me to read draft chapters of his forthcoming study of Cardinal Wolsey: I am most grateful to him for this and for many stimulating discussions. My greatest intellectual debt is to Mr C.S.L. Davies. For his unfailingly painstaking, generous and inspiring guidance I am more grateful than I can say.

G.W.B.
Southampton,
April 1984

Abbreviations

APC	*Acts of the Privy Council*, ed. J.R. Dasent (1980-)
BL	British Library
Cal. Pat. Rolls	*Calendar of Patent Rolls*
Cal. S.P.	*Calendar of State Papers*
DNB	*Dictionary of National Biography*
HMC	*Historical Manuscripts Commission*
LJ	*Journals of the House of Lords 1513–1800* (42 vols). vol.i
LP	J.S. Brewer, J. Gairdner and R.H. Brodie, eds, *Letters and Papers, Foreign and Domestic, of the reign of Henry VIII* (21 vols in 36, 1862–1932)
PRO	Public Record Office

Introduction

The claim of this book is that in early Tudor England—the reigns of Henry VII, Henry VIII, Edward VI and Mary—the nobility was the most important, the most influential and the most powerful segment of society. To some this may seem surprising. Were not nobles by this period merely ornaments of the court? Were not nobles powerful only in the middle ages? And were not the middle ages passing in this period, dealt mortal blows by the renaissance and reformation, as we have learned in our textbooks? Had not the English nobility committed collective suicide in the Wars of the Roses—those civil wars in the mid-fifteenth century in which noble factions strove to put their leaders on the throne? Was the age of Henry VII and Henry VIII not the heyday of the 'new monarchy', when determined rulers established strong royal government at the expense of their greater subjects? Did the Tudors not rely on new men, drawn from social categories below the nobility (who were in any case too stupid and uneducated to govern?) Did not the Tudors greatly strengthen the monarchy by exploiting all possible sources of revenue in the manner of Henry VII? Did they not allow their servants, such as Thomas Cromwell, to promote administrative change, producing a 'Tudor revolution in government'? And were not all these transformations reducing the power of the nobility and increasing that of the crown a 'good thing'? Were not the nobles self-seeking, while kings were the fathers of their people, ruling not in their own interests but for the good of all? The general view of early Tudor England that these questions imply is of course a caricature and no modern historian openly holds it. Yet there are hidden assumptions here that do remain tenaciously influential, even among historians who have studied the nobility. Two recent writers are affected at least in

1

part by such misinterpretations. Henry VII and Henry VIII
were 'innately suspicious. . . of the English baronage as a whole';
'that Henry VII deliberately set out to restrict the power and
independence of his most eminent subjects is now beyond
question'; Edward Stafford, third duke of Buckingham, who was
executed for treason in 1521 'was the victim of a conscious plan to
curb the aristocracy as a class'; by 1521 'the nobility as a class had
undoubtedly been weakened and its resolution undermined'.[1]
Another writer, for all his sensitive awareness of the general co-
operation between monarchs and nobles, can nonetheless still see
the early sixteenth century as 'an abnormal period in the
relations between the crown and its greater subjects' in which the
reigns of Henry VII and Henry VIII witnessed 'a determined
policy by the crown to undermine the power of the Stanleys and
of other leading magnates'.[2]

Such misconceptions have arisen for various reasons. Often
literary sources have been accepted unquestioningly. Much, for
example, has been made of John Skelton's emphasis, in his satires
against Cardinal Wolsey, on the cowardice of the nobility. But
given that he was portraying Wolsey as a tyrant, he faced a great
problem in explaining why his power was allowed to continue. It
was very useful for him to show the nobility as weak: it would
have been very damaging for him to have to admit that most
noblemen were for most of Wolsey's career (except, perhaps, at
its beginning) quite contented with his executive activity as the
king's chief servant.[3] Isolated contemporary remarks have
similarly been taken uncritically. Edward Stafford, third duke of
Buckingham, for instance, complained that nobles were undone
and that they did not dare combine together, but the truth was
that Buckingham's discontent was personal: others did not join
him not because they were afraid but because they did not share
his discontent.[4] The Pilgrims of Grace complained about low
born counsellors and the lack of noblemen advising Henry VIII:
not only were their particular points inaccurate, as Henry
pointed out, but they were simply exploiting a political
convention in order to criticise Cromwell and policies that they
hated, a minister and policies that in 1536 were fully supported
by the king.[5] Again the nobility are often seen as in decline
because their behaviour is implicitly compared to a model of
politics in which nobles club together to resist kings, ministers

and their policies;[6] but that mistakenly assumes that the nobility were a coherent group and that in normal times they wished to control executive government. A further important cause of these misapprehensions is the preoccupation of many historians with royal government, and especially with royal administration, in itself not improper, but liable to lead to an unfocussed view of the nobility. It is also possible that the abundance of ambassadors' despatches in this period, may, if read uncritically, underplay the role of noblemen: it was common for ambassadors to attribute too much influence to a great minister, who was usually their most frequent interlocutor, and too little to the monarch or to great nobles.[7] The fashion for county studies often gives misleading emphasis to gentry families at a time when noblemen could dominate a wider region, as is shown by the contemporary use of the word 'country' to designate not a county but a nobleman's sphere of influence. Much more is known about the gentry in the Tudor, especially the later Tudor, period, but it is important for the historian to remain vigilant, when drawing conclusions about the influence of gentry, for the 'optical illusions' created by changes in the nature and volume of evidence. Excessive weight is often placed on examples of weak noblemen. Some were indeed weak. Richard Grey, third earl of Kent (d.1524), for example, who succeeded to his earldom in 1503, was in debt by 1506, and in the next two years he sold, often for small sums, or gave away, most of his estates to courtiers and royal administrators. Despite efforts made on his behalf to recover his patrimony, by 1521 he was reduced to pawning a satin gown. Earl Richard, 'as vnmeet to governe his estate as a naturall Ideott', 'a praye sett open to the spoyle of all men', leading an 'vnstayed and disorderyd lyffe', was clearly a wasteful nobleman who destroyed his inheritance.[8] But that the colourful lives of such men are often unusually well documented does not prove that they were typical. The full study of the fourth and fifth earls of Shrewsbury presented here, showing that over two generations one of the leading earldoms was in competent hands, offers grounds for questioning the assumption that weak noblemen were the rule rather than the exception, and raises the possibility that it was noblemen like the earls of Shrewsbury who were the more typical.

Another cause of the misconceptions about the nobility is the

failure of many historians of the Tudor period to apply to the
sixteenth century the insights of historians working on earlier
periods. Yet it is fruitful to examine the early Tudor nobility in
the light of the reinterpretation of the nobility of the fourteenth
and fifteenth centuries by K.B. McFarlane. McFarlane
emphasised that there was a community of interest between
crown and nobility, that noblemen were not necessarily either
rapacious landlords or treasonable subjects and that service to
the crown was a characteristic feature of the lives of noblemen.[9]
This raises related questions about the early sixteenth century.
How significant was the role of noblemen in politics? How and
with what success were they involved in major political
issues—succession disputes, factional struggles, opposition to
crown ministers? What did a nobleman seek from politics—did
he seek to participate actively in court politics or were his
principal interests elsewhere? How far was political service seen
as a obligation, how far as a means to preserve, or to extend, local
influence? How important were noblemen in warfare? How
significant was their provision of men? How much depended on
the military abilities that noblemen displayed during a
campaign? How much land did a nobleman possess? How could
a nobleman benefit from the dissolution of the monasteries?
What was a nobleman's income and from what sources was it
derived? What was the nature of the local power of noblemen?
How important were their marriages and their connections with
each other and with other landed families? How well did they
live? It is with such questions that this book deals.

The sources for any study of the nobility are fragmentary and
tantalising. In this sense, as in many others, early Tudor history is
still medieval history. This means that any attempt to study
every noble family in a single volume would inevitably be
superficial. Such an approach moreover might succumb to the
temptations of statistical analysis, with all the consequent risks of
deriving results from fragile evidence and of merely measuring,
rather than attempting to explain, the actions of noblemen. The
most effective way of tackling these questions is rather to begin
with the detailed study of individual families. Only on such a
scale is it possible to search thoroughly a range of manuscript and
printed sources and to wrest the greatest significance from
materials whose sense, especially when read in isolation, is far

from clear. Here the Talbots, earls of Shrewsbury, have been chosen. The surviving records, while difficult, are among the fullest available for a Tudor family, although their value has been obscured by the dispersal of the papers, described in the note on sources. The briefest consideration of the role of the fourth earl of Shrewsbury in the Pilgrimage of Grace or of the fifth earl of Shrewsbury in the faction fighting of the reign of Edward VI, in which the imperial ambassador described him as 'one of the most powerful men in the kingdom',[10] suggested that these men, largely neglected in the past, were not only worthy of study in their own right, but that a full examination of their political, military and economic actions could offer a firm basis for wider conclusions about the early Tudor nobility.

Both George Talbot, fourth earl of Shrewsbury, and his son and heir Francis Talbot, fifth earl of Shrewsbury, were capable and determined. Both possessed sufficient intelligence to exercise power in their country, and to give service locally and nationally to the crown. Born in 1468, the fourth earl served Henry VII in Yorkshire in 1486 and at the battle of Stoke in 1487, after which he was installed in the order of the garter. During the conspiracies around Perkin Warbeck, there was no unrest in the Midlands, an area in which Talbot influence was considerable. In 1492 Earl George served in the short-lived French campaign. He was frequently involved in court ceremonial, at royal weddings, at the creation of Prince Henry as duke of York in 1494 ('So well horssed an soo richely ... that it was a tryhumphant sight'),[11] and in 1502 was appointed Lord Steward of the royal household, with nominal responsibility for the household below stairs. He played a significant part in the consolidation of the Tudor dynasty. On the accession of Henry VIII he received several offices on the lands of the Duchy of Lancaster. He served as lieutenant of the vanguard in the French campaign of 1513 and as lieutenant-general on the Scottish borders in 1522. He played a crucial part in suppressing the Pilgrimage of Grace in 1536. Outspoken in language, decisive in action, Earl George appears the archetype of the bluff soldier. His son, who succeeded him in 1538, served on the northern borders in 1544–5, 1548 and 1557, closely involved not just with military strategy but with the administrative minutiae of victualling, soldiers' pay and munitions. From 1549 to 1560 he was lord president of the council in the north, taking his responsibilities seriously. Although not without personal emotion, as his love for Lady Pope in the last year of his life shows, he was by temperament more restrained than his father, showing caution as a commander on the Scottish borders, and compromising quickly, though never at all costs, as governments changed in the 1540s and 1550s.

What is offered here is both a full study of the Talbots, earls of Shrewsbury, and a contribution to the general history of the early Tudor nobility. In dealing with the earls of Shrewsbury what is presented is a series of complementary studies rather than biography (there is too little material for any extended assessment of character or of motivation which must usually be inferred from actions) or a chronological account (the survival of evidence is too uneven to allow more than a dry list of facts and in any case the earls were more often simply being earls and enjoying their wealth rather than pursuing a developing career). The first part deals with politics to show and to discuss the behaviour of the fourth and fifth earls in times of difficulty (1516) or emergency (the Pilgrimage of Grace) and over a longer period (the reigns of Edward VI and Mary) in which noble involvement in turbulent court politics was considerable. The second part examines the part the earls played in war. A third part discusses the 'economy' of the earls: their estates, residences, income, domestic life, marriages, servants, connections. While concentrating on the Talbots, earls of Shrewsbury, I have throughout also exploited my detailed work on other noble families, notably Sir William Compton, founder of the fortunes of the marquesses of Northampton, the Greys, earls of Kent, the Percies, earls of Northumberland, the third duke of Buckingham, Lord Darcy, Sir Thomas Seymour and several others. The final part of this book draws on my detailed studies of the Talbots, earls of Shrewsbury, and of other noble families, to offer some conclusions on the sources of noble power, contemporary attitudes to the nobility and, finally, the relative importance of the nobility in early Tudor society.

Notes

1   C. Rawcliffe, *The Staffords, earls of Stafford and dukes of Buckingham 1394–1521* (Cambridge, 1978), pp. 99, 184, 190, 186.
2   B. Coward, *The Stanleys, lords Stanley and earls of Derby 1385–1672: the origins, wealth and power of a landowning family, Chetham Society*, 3rd series, xxx (1983), pp. 142, 146; cf. pp. 147, 149, 159.
3   I owe this point to my graduate student Mr G. Walker who is studying the poetry of John Skelton as a source for the politics of the 1520s: G. Walker, '"Baytyng the Bocher's dogg"': John Skelton's poetic attack upon Cardinal Wolsey', paper read to History graduate seminar, University of Southampton, 15 March 1983.
4   See below, pp. 199–200.
5   *LP*, XI 902, 957.
6   This underlies eg. M.E. James, 'English politics and the concept of honour 1485–1642', *Past and Present, Supplement*, iii (1978), pp. 37–41.
7   I owe this point to Mr P.J. Gwyn.
8   G.W. Bernard, 'The fortunes of the Greys, earls of Kent, in the early sixteenth century', *Historical Journal*, xxv (1982), pp. 671–85.
9   K.B. McFarlane, *The Nobility of later medieval England* (Oxford, 1973); *England in the fifteenth century* (1981).
10 *Calendar of State Papers, Spanish*, eds. G.A. Bergenroth, P. de Gayangos, M.A.S. Hume, R. Tyler and G. Mattingly (1862–   ), ix. 457.
11 J. Gairdner, ed., *Letters and Papers illustrative of the reigns of Richard III and Henry VII*, Rolls series, vols., 24a and 24b (1861–63), i. 64–67.

PART ONE: POLITICS

1 The fourth earl of Shrewsbury and political faction in 1516

The year 1516 was the eighth in the reign of Henry VIII. Three years had elapsed since the successful campaign in France. It was one of the earliest years of the ascendancy of Cardinal Wolsey. The chance survival of some correspondence between the fourth earl of Shrewsbury, then resident at his lodge at Worksop, and his chaplain Thomas Alen in London allows a recreation of those dealings between a nobleman and the court that are usually obscure.[1]

Shrewsbury's principal aim in that year was to marry his daughter Mary to Henry Percy, son and heir of the fifth earl of Northumberland. He had what seems like a deliberate policy of marrying his children into leading northern families. He married his eldest surviving son and one of his daughters to a daughter and a son of Thomas, lord Dacre; another daughter was married to the heir of the earl of Cumberland. Such a marital strategy reflected the shift in the centre of gravity in the Talbot patrimony from Shropshire and the Welsh marches to South Yorkshire and Derbyshire and was both cause and effect of the establishment of the Talbots as leading northern midlands magnates.[2] A marriage alliance with the Percy family was an obvious part of such a strategy.

The earls of Northumberland were traditionally the greatest northern lords. Their power was based on their extensive estates, service in royal office on the borders and the influence of their household.[3] In 1516 Henry , fifth earl of Northumberland was thirty-eight years old. He had succeeded his father, murdered in a tax riot in 1489, when still a minor. Although brought up at court under Henry VII, he was evidently mistrusted by that suspicious king who never gave him border office and imposed large recognisances and obligations on him. Like Shrewsbury he

had been prominent in the reaction of 1509–10 to the harshness
of the later years of Henry VII's rule and in the French campaign
of 1513. There was a degree of friendship between
Northumberland and Shrewsbury, as well as, on Northumberland's part, the respect of a younger man for one ten years his
senior, as the tone of his request to Shrewsbury to intercede on his
behalf for exemption from royal service in 1517 shows.[4]

By spring 1516 negotiations for a marriage alliance were
almost complete. The intermediary between Northumberland
and Shrewsbury was Christopher Urswick, dean of Windsor,[5]
who reported in mid-May that Northumberland continued in
the same good mind as when Shrewsbury had left him, and
'callys faster for an end to be concludit then yor lordship dose'.
Several courtiers had asked Northumberland to whom he would
marry his son: he had replied firmly, 'I have concludit with my
Lord of Shrouesbury', and added of his son that 'when he is
better lerned and well acoynted with his wife, shortly after he
shall com to the court'. This conversation in itself 'pricks hym
mor hertly forwards then euer he was'.[6] But it is clear from this
that Shrewsbury was not yet certain of success. His anxiety that
his marriage plans should not be disturbed is apparent in his
troubled reaction to the marriage proposals made to him by
Edward Stafford, third duke of Buckingham.

Buckingham was related to the king and also to Shrewsbury
whose mother was a Stafford. A substantial landowner in the
Welsh marches, he was quite a prominent courtier in the early
years of Henry VIII's reign.[7] In 1516 he made his offer to
Shrewsbury through Sir Richard Sacheverell, a close acquaintance of the Talbots. Buckingham told Sacheverell that when he
had recently been alone with Wolsey they had discussed his son,
whom Wolsey and the king desired to come to court. The risk of
infection made Buckingham unwilling to send him there until he
was married and had got an heir. Wolsey then suggested that
Buckingham should marry his son, naming the daughters of the
countess of Salisbury and the earl of Shrewsbury. The following
conversation, said Buckingham, then ensued:

Wolsey:- What saith he be my Lord Steward's? [Shrewsbury's] Else I know
none within these parts.
Buckingham:- Nay, my Lord, I know my Lord Steward's mind, that he will

never marry his son without the advice of the king's grace, and there as shall be his pleasure.
Wolsey:- Why my lord . . . this dare I promise you, that if my Lord steward were here, the king's grace would speak to him with all his heart. It were both to the king's honour and surety to see you two knit together. And this shall I say, that if ye vary in anything the king shall give the stroke betwixt you himself.

On the strength of Wolsey's encouragement, Buckingham then suggested to Sacheverell two cross marriages: one between Buckingham's son and Shrewsbury's daughter and one between Shrewsbury's son and Buckingham's daughter. From Shrewsbury Buckingham would ask a thousand marks less than he would from anyone else.[8]

Shrewsbury was not pleased by this proposal. 'It pleased him', he wrote of Buckingham,

in the first yere of the kynges reigne to speake to me to haue my lord his son promysing that I shulde haue hym better chepe by a thousand marks than any other man. Howbeit when it came to the poynte that I desired to know what som he wolde ask it was so great that I never durste speike of the mater sens. For I trust with a little helpe to mary all my daughtors with that he asked with oon of theym.

Shrewsbury was sure that Buckingham was sincere, and wished him to be thanked, but nonetheless rejected his offer outright. At the same time he asked Christopher Urswick to do his utmost to keep Northumberland favourably inclined towards Shrewsbury. Shrewsbury feared that if Buckingham 'shuld here of this matier it myght fortune he wolde doo the best he coulde to withdraw my saide Lord of Northumberlandis good mynde'.[9]

An even greater difficulty for Shrewsbury was Northumberland himself. At the beginning of May Northumberland was examined before the king and council in star chamber, acknowledged his guilt in unspecified charges, submitted himself to the king and was then imprisoned in the Fleet for reasons that remain obscure. Shrewsbury was worried lest 'he wol take no distemper nor thought for the same whiche shuld hurte hym self for if he so shuld doo it wolde be to his frendes grettest discompfort'.[10] Shrewsbury did not doubt that Henry would be 'good lord', as he wrote, to Northumberland, but he clearly feared that Northumberland might exacerbate his situation by a tactless or a petulant reaction. Northumberland was eventually released after about twelve days in the Fleet.[11]

It is clear that at this time Northumberland was not in royal favour but that Buckingham was. It is also clear that Shrewsbury was reluctant, ostensibly because it would be costly, to ally his family with the Staffords. He wished rather to marry one of his daughters to the heir of the earl of Northumberland. It has been suggested that if Shrewsbury and Buckingham had reached an agreement, this would have created 'an alliance of two of the greatest noblemen before whom even Henry VIII might have trembled'.[12] This manifestly fails to fit the circumstances of 1516. Wolsey evidently did not see it as a threat to the king. Buckingham moreover was in 'great favour' with the king.[13] He was by no means an overmighty subject but was rather the epitome of the courtier-noble. His inheritance had been greatly weakened by the disastrous failure of his father in 1483, and his long minority had been exploited by Henry VII. The financial demands that Buckingham exacted from his tenants would have made it impossible for him to have appealed to them for support in any quarrel that he might have had with the king.[14] Polydore Vergil ingeniously claims that Wolsey pursued a vendetta against Buckingham as soon as he was able to do so, and that in order to further this aim, he provoked a quarrel over wardship with Northumberland in order to frighten Northumberland into submission when Buckingham was later tried for treason. While Northumberland was being intimidated, Buckingham would obviously be in favour.[15] It has been suggested that this describes the situation of 1516.[16] But there is no evidence connecting the troubles of Northumberland in that year with any disputed wardship. Moreover since Buckingham did not fall until 1521 such a view would attribute to Wolsey a barely credible far-sightedness, accepting (and it is a questionable assumption) that Wolsey wished to bring Buckingham down.[17] It is much more likely that Buckingham was genuinely in favour in 1516 and indeed in the next years, as is suggested by his marrying his son to the daughter of the countess of Salisbury in 1518, as suggested by Wolsey. It is misleading to read back into the mid-1510s knowledge of his ultimate fate, which was sudden, and it is mistaken, as has been shown, to see Henry VIII as pursuing a consistent, long-term policy against anyone of royal blood.[18]

There is, however good evidence to support the view that the earl of Northumberland was not especially trusted by Henry VIII in the early and mid-1510s. This is not, it must be emphasised, to argue that the Tudors were seeking the downfall of the family but rather to assert the importance of personal relations between a king and his leading subjects, relations subject to all the vagaries of human character. Northumberland was never close to Henry VIII. Claims made on his behalf by one of his servants in 1509, that his master 'shulde rewlle all from Trent northe and haue Berwic and the Marches' and that 'if ther lord hade nott rowmes in the north as his fader hade, it shold not long be well' cannot have improved relations.[19] Northumberland may well have inspired, or failed to control, disturbances on the borders in 1513–14. There was no love lost between him and Lord Dacre, the king's warden in border regions traditionally under Percy rule: certainly his appointment of the borderer Heron as constable of his castle at Alnwick was not a tactful move.[20] Wolsey showed the government's distrust of him in November 1515 when he struck out the names of the three men proposed for the office of sheriff of Northumberland and substituted his own nominee.[21]

It has been argued that Northumberland followed two distinct approaches to politics. One was to ally himself with Buckingham, his brother-in-law, and, by implication, other noblemen, in the hope that this would convince the king that he deserved proper consideration; the second was to be the model of the obsequious courtier while strengthening his position in the north in order to show the government just how indispensable he was there. These approaches are not contradictory: evidence can be found for both.[22] What is clear is that Northumberland was not especially successful, notably in 1516. And what all this points to is the determination of Henry VIII and Wolsey to prevent a marriage alliance between Northumberland and Shrewsbury in that year.

It is significant that when Northumberland was asked about his plans for his son, it was Sir William Compton who was named particularly as a questioner: as Compton, groom of the stool, was Henry's closest servant, and at this time also 'marvelous gret' with Wolsey, the use of Compton may be taken as evidence of the king's and Wolsey's direct interest and interference in

Northumberland's and Shrewsbury's marriage plans.[23] In fact
the marriage between Henry Percy and Mary Talbot did not
take place until 1524. It has been surmised that this was because
'personal acquaintance does not ... appear to have produced a
favourable effect upon either of the parties most concerned in the
project'.[24] But this, in the absence of evidence, is to read into the
events of 1516 the later dramatic outcome of the marriage. If
personal dislikes prevented the marriage in 1516, it is difficult to
see why these should have changed by 1524. What had altered
were the political circumstances. Buckingham was dead;
Northumberland was more conspicuously loyal;[25] and in 1524 a
marriage between Henry Percy and Mary Talbot must have
seemed greatly preferable to Henry and Wolsey to any further
association at court between Percy and Anne Boleyn. In 1516,
however, the marriage did not have the blessing of Henry and
Wolsey, and the loyalty of Shrewsbury was such that he did not
defy the royal veto. He nonetheless did succeed in avoiding a
marriage alliance with the duke of Buckingham. If this
reconstruction is correct, it shows the potential and the
limitations of crown and magnate power: both crown and
magnate could reject a marriage proposal but neither could
impose an unwanted marriage alliance on the other.

Shrewsbury's plans for a marriage alliance with
Northumberland were his preoccupation in spring 1516. But the
difficulties he encountered in this matter are not in themselves a
sufficient explanation of the tensions revealed in his
correspondence. Clearly Shrewsbury did not wish to go up to
London. Repeatedly Alen reported the tactics he had been using
at court in order to delay Shrewsbury's arrival and attempted to
predict their success. On 23 April Alen said that he had informed
Wolsey of the sickness affecting Shrewsbury and his servants, that
Wolsey had been convinced the matter was unfeigned and that
Thomas Babington, one of Shrewsbury's officers, thought he
would have respite (from what he does not say) until the
Michaelmas term.[26] On 28 April Alen reported how he had seen
Wolsey and given him a letter containing details of Shrewsbury's
illness. Wolsey had said that the king wished to see Shrewsbury at
Whitsun but Alen had replied that this was impossible. A further
meeting had been arranged for 2 May.[27] On that day Alen and
Babington met Wolsey again and gave him further details of

Shrewsbury's illness. Babington saw Wolsey again later. By 6 May Alen was convinced that unless Shrewsbury was directly commanded to come up to court his excuse would be sufficiently strong to allow him to remain at home till the autumn.[28] A superficial reading of these letters would suggest the simple explanation that Shrewsbury and a large number of his servants were ill and that nothing more sinister was involved. But this is not convincing.

Certainly Shrewsbury and his household were troubled by sickness for some time in spring 1516.[29] But there are ample grounds for suspicion. Constantly Shrewsbury was warned by his friends and servants not to come up to court for reasons that were palpably not medical. On 16 May Sir Richard Sacheverell warned, 'My lord, I beseech you, come no more there this summer. Your lordship is wise, and if ye should go thither again many would speak of it.'[30] On 31 May Christopher Urswick and Sir Edward Poynings, an important royal diplomat, advised Shrewsbury not to come up that term if he might conveniently do otherwise.[31] On 8 June Alen wrote[32]

Hit is thought by some of your frends yf your Lordship can make your excuse to the Kynges grace better to tarry at whom then to come hether; for ther be som thinges comys not so well to pass (wherin few were of cousell) as the begynners of the same thought they wold have done.

Furthermore by early May the sickness was past. At that time Babington appointed 14 May for a meeting between Shrewsbury and the prior of Mountgrace to settle a landed transaction. Evidently Shrewsbury must have been recovering by early May at least to such an extent that full recovery could have been counted upon by 14 May.[33] On 16 May Sir Richard Sacheverell expressed his joy that Shrewsbury and his family had so well escaped the foul sickness.[34] In a letter that Shrewsbury wrote himself at this time he said that none of his servants had been sick for five or six days and that none had died for over three weeks, leading him to trust that the danger from this plague was now over.[35] Yet at the same time as he was apparently restored to health Shrewsbury was writing to Alen that he had spoken with Babington who thinketh best that you be not to hasty in knowying my lord cardynallis pleasure tochyng my comyng up to London, except he speike unto you hymself of the same, and then ye may make myn excuse and best ye can; for I am nowe at this tyme ferr oute of all good ordre.

Shrewsbury added instructions that Alen was not to mention this to Wolsey unless Wolsey raised the matter first, although at the same time Alen was to keep in Wolsey's sight as often as possible.[36] Conclusive evidence that Shrewsbury was using his illness as a cover appears in Alen's report of 28 May. Wolsey had inquired the previous day how Shrewsbury fared, 'knowing it not the contrary but that your lordship as yet is veray ill troubled and full unmete to come up'.[37] Illness does not, then, explain the efforts that Shrewsbury was making to stay at home. Those efforts continued. On 28 May Alen assured Shrewsbury that Poynings and Urswick had heard that a bill had been drawn up by the council, lacking only the king's signature, commanding Shrewsbury to come up. They suggested that he should write to Wolsey and to Sir Richard Sacheverell to make his excuse to the king, which Alen thought should be sufficient. In this letter Alen seemed to absolve Wolsey of any ill-will towards Shrewsbury, but on 8 June he advised Shrewsbury to write directly to the king as he feared Wolsey would not make the best excuse he could for him. Wolsey had told Alen that the king wanted Shrewsbury at court and Wolsey for his part advised Shrewsbury to come up.[38] At this point the series of letters from Alen to Shrewsbury ends. There is no evidence that Shrewsbury was soon back at court so it may be inferred that his manoeuvres were successful.

The question remains, why was Shrewsbury so reluctant to come up to court? The answer is to be found within the context of the three aims then being pursued by Henry VIII and Cardinal Wolsey.

The first concerned foreign affairs. The king and Wolsey were pursuing foreign policies that were unpopular and unsuccessful. An Anglo-Habsburg agreement had been reached in October 1515 but the consequent attempt to finance Swiss mercenaries to drive the French out of Milan had proved disastrous, not least because of the unreliability of England's Habsburg allies.[39] It may be that this policy was more subtle and had greater chances of success than was apparent to counsellors and diplomats who counted the cost and saw no immediate benefits[40] but what is important here is to emphasise its unpopularity. In July 1516 the Venetian ambassador noted that Bishop Fox and Archbishop Warham, two leading counsellors, had 'for many months' withdrawn from court on account of the assistance given to Emperor Maximilian against France and Venice. These lords, he wrote, see their treasure spent in vain and consequently loud murmurs and discontent prevail throughout the land.[41] In October he wrote how Wolsey 'perceived that all the grandees of England were opposed to his policy and that the people complained extremely of the new imposts' and that certain counsellors 'who usually discussed state affairs' had not been present at a discussion at which money had been voted for foreign expeditions, absences which had not passed unnoticed. These counsellors included Fox and Warham.[42] It is significant that they had earlier been involved in plans for war.[43] Of course all this depends on the Venetian ambassador, who might have wished to exaggerate opposition in England to a policy directed against Venice and who was probably mistaken in attributing that policy to Wolsey alone rather than to the king and Wolsey in partnership.[44] But the ambassador is more likely to have exaggerated the extent of opposition and its chances of becoming effective than to have invented it altogether. In that light it is possible to read Bishop Fox's comment of 23 April, as he declined to leave his diocese, 'And so the Emperor and the Swiss speed well (whereof I have as great desire to hear as of any matter) I trust ye shall haue no great troublesome matters', as ironic, as showing his doubts about the likely success of the policy.[45] There is no direct evidence that Shrewsbury had any strong feelings about foreign policy and none to suggest that the various enterprises either pleased or dismayed him. But there are some details that suggest that he was at least interested and possibly opposed. On 31 May Alen sent Shrewsbury a copy of a letter sent to Wolsey from Italy 'which Master Urswick wold after the syth therof, your Lordship shuld brake or brenne hit'. It is difficult to imagine what such a letter might contain other than details of the abortive military campaign of that spring.[46] More obscurely still, on 9 May Alen reported that Urswick 'showed vnto me at such time as Mr Poynings and Dr Tunstall [who had been treating with Charles of Castile in Brussels] come home your lordship

shall know more': on 30 May Alen saw Poynings and Urswick.[47]
In another letter Alen reported to Shrewsbury Urswick's news
that the prince of Castile would not be coming to England that
year.[48] It may well be that Shrewsbury did not accept the need
for the continued costly support of unreliable allies pursuing their
own interests, and that Henry and Wolsey suspected that he was
critical, even if silently, of their plans.

More directly relevant to Shrewsbury was the beginning of
Wolsey's vigorous conciliar enforcement of the laws of the realm.
On 2 May 1516 Wolsey delivered 'a notable and Elegant
oration' before the king and several leading noblemen,
announcing what has been seen as 'policy to impose "indifferent
justice" upon the king's realm'.[49] Too much should not be made
of this: a new broom was very self-consciously sweeping clean.
But the immediate impact was considerable. Hall wrote of this
year that Wolsey 'punyshed also lords, knyghtes, and men of all
sortes for ryottes, beryng and mayntenaunce in their countreyes,
that the poore men lyued quyetly, so that no man durst beare for
fear of imprisonment'.[50] Northumberland, as has been shown,
was examined before the king and council in star chamber and
briefly committed to the Fleet; the marquess of Dorset, Lord
Bergavenny, Lord Hastings, Sir Edward Guildford and Sir
Richard Sacheverell 'by informacion put ynto the kyngs bench
ar like to be yn gret danger for reteynyng of servands'.[51]
Shrewsbury was as guilty of retaining as any of those accused.
Alen warned him: 'At the reverens of God, my lord, take heed to
hit: for Bulkley wiche is . . . commaunded to Flete at his first
comyng (unto such tyme as som of . . . spyed hit and gaf hym
warnyng of the same) wore your bage upon. . .'.[52] Shrewsbury
may have feared that his presence at court would make him
vulnerable to prosecution for retaining.

Also of immediate concern to Shrewsbury was the general
turbulence of court politics in 1516. In his introduction to
Volume 2 of the *Letters and Papers of Henry VIII* J.S. Brewer, after
devoting the bulk of it to a discussion of foreign policy, wrote that
'in England there was no trouble or dissension . . . a court where
nothing seemed to rule except an unbroken round of pleasure'.[53]
The vigorous enforcement of the law described above does not
confirm this. Nor do two of Alen's letters. On 31 May he wrote
'her is gret snerling among diverse of them yn so muche my lord

cardynall sayd unto Sir Henry Marney that the same Sir Henry had done more displeasur unto the kynges grace by reason of his cruelnes ayenst the gret estates of this realm then any man lyving'. The marquess of Dorset, the earl of Surrey and Lord Bergavenny had been expelled from the council.[54] Later Alen reported that 'her is gret troble betwix the Lord Markes, the Lord Hastings and Sir Richard Sacheverell'. 'I her some things', concluded Alen cryptically, 'wiche are not to be wrytten.'[55] This struggling was dangerous for Shrewsbury because, as Alen wrote, 'I fer me som ther be wold take a thorn out of theyr own fote and put hit yn yours.'[56]

The explanation of this political turbulence is to be found in the efforts of Wolsey, no doubt with the support of the king, to strengthen his position. His had been a rapidly rising star. Dean of Lincoln and royal almoner in 1509,[57] he played an important part in the ill-fated invasion of Guienne in autumn 1512.[58] He was greatly involved in the French campaign of 1513 and bore the bulk of the responsibility for the organisation of victuals and military supplies.[59] His considerable administrative skills earned him the bishoprics of Lincoln and of the captured city of Tournai.[60] In the peace of 1514 'English affairs ... daily prospered and in this prosperity Thomas Wolsey gloried exceedingly'.[61] In September 1514 he was appointed Archbishop of York and two months later was showing ambitions to be cardinal.[62] 'His authority was now supreme', wrote Vergil.[63] Hall wrote that 'at that tyme he bare all the rule about the kyng and what he sayd was obeyed in all places'.[64] He became a cardinal in September 1515, Lord Chancellor in December 1515.[65] So swift an ascent could not but provoke tensions. By 1516 his influence was enormous, 'howbehit', as Alen wrote, 'everything goeth not forwards as he wold have hit'.[66] Moreover in furthering his ambition Wolsey was deliberately consolidating his position by reducing the influence of those who held high office or had earlier possessed much influence. This is evident in his relations at this time with Archbishop Warham, who resigned the Lord Chancellorship in December 1515, and with Bishop Fox, who was Lord Privy Seal until May 1516 and whose behaviour in spring 1516 parallels that of Shrewsbury.

It has been suggested that both men 'willingly made way' for Wolsey 'by retirement' and that 'the truth is that both were

anxious to escape from secular affairs and turn to other things'.[67]
Thomas More wrote that Warham had been trying to shed the
burden of the chancellorship for years, that he had given up the
office willingly and that he was now enjoying his leisure and his
books.[68] But More might have been reading his own passionate
desire for a life of cultivated leisure into the mind of another man.
Polydore Vergil wrote that Warham 'voluntarily withdrew'
from the chancellorship but then suggests that he left court in
disgust at the way in which Wolsey was monopolising power.
Wolsey, said Vergil, conducted all business at his own pleasure,
and 'it was certainly as a result of this that several leading
counsellors, when they saw so much power coming into the hands
of one man, withdrew gradually from court'. Warham and Fox
were specifically named. Before they left court they had an
interview with Henry VIII in which 'they earnestly urged the
king not to suffer any servant to be greater than his master'.[69]
Hall strongly hinted that Warham was elbowed out by Wolsey:[70]

The archbishop of Cantourbury perceauyng that the archebishop of York
medled more in his office of chauncelourship then it became him to suffer except
he would aduenture the kynges displeasure, and seynge also that the sayd
bishop of Yorke coueted to bear all the rule and to haue all the whole authoritie,
considerynge also his owne great age, gave up into the kynges handes his rowme
of chauncelor.

Cavendish wrote that Wolsey, 'remembryng as well the tauntes
& chekkes byfore susteyned of Caunterbury (whiche he entendyd
to redresse), hauyng a respecte to the auauncement of worldly
honour promocion and great benefites, ffound the means with
the kyng that he was made Chauncelour of Englond and
Canterbury thereof dismyssed'.[71] One of the charges against
Wolsey in 1529 was that 'we took away from my lord of
Canterbury, the chauncellorship, and to take therefor the fee,
notwithstanding our great livelihode'[72] A reasonable conclusion
is that harrassed by Wolsey and lacking the king's favour,
Warham had no option but to resign the chancellorship and to
find the best use for his leisure.

A similar explanation may be offered for the resignation of
Bishop Fox from his office of Lord Privy Seal. According to
Vergil he, like Warham, withdrew from court when he saw so
much power gathering in the hands of one man.[73] It is significant

that his post went to Bishop Ruthal of Durham who 'sang treble to Wolsey's bass'.[74] Fox's letter to Wolsey of 23 April has been taken as evidence that 'he wished wholeheartedly to devote his remaining years to the duties of his spiritual office, especially within his diocese'.[75] Yet it is possible to read this letter at something other than face value, especially, perhaps, Fox's advice to Wolsey not to work so hard and not to work at all after supper. It would be more eloquent testimony of the sincerity of Fox's wish to retire if he had indeed given up his involvement in secular affairs. But this he did not do. Pressed for his opinion on the defences of Calais, Fox wrote to Wolsey that he did not think about these matters any the less because he was not daily attending upon him in the council.[76] Moreover he returned to court, as the Venetian ambassador noted, in November.[77] It would be more convincing to argue that in the spring he had wished above all to stay away from court because he was unhappy at what was happening there. On 8 June Alen noted that he had not come up to court and in the same letter gave details of the appointment of Ruthal to Fox's office.[78] What is striking is the close parallel between the reluctance of Fox and that of Shrewsbury to come up to court. This similarity suggests a further explanation for Shrewsbury's behaviour in 1516, in terms of the attendance of magnates, lay and ecclesiastical, at court.

The presence of noblemen at court has long been a matter for brief and conventional generalisation. It is often held that the presence of the nobility at court prevented efficient administration at the centre and weakened social cohesion in areas whose lords were non-resident and that, because of this, early modern governments preferred noblemen to stay in their country. As noblemen on this view preferred life and influence at court, royal councils were alternatively swamped by and purged of high-born counsellors who owed their position to birth rather than to ability. But such an interpretation would totally fail to account for the behaviour of Shrewsbury—or of Fox, or Warham—in 1516. It would leave unexplained both the reluctance of Shrewsbury to come up and the desire of Henry VIII and Wolsey to have him at court. On this view they should have been delighted that Shrewsbury was living on his estates and Shrewsbury should have been anxious to exchange the duties of a local lord for the pleasure of the courtly life in London.

Evidently these judgments do not properly apply to the service nobility of later medieval England. The two-fold role of the nobility of early Tudor England, to rule their countries, and to give support and counsel to the king, demanded regular but temporary attendance at court. Local government by means of landed delegation would succeed only if noblemen did not seek to establish a quasi-regal authority in their own countries that might pose, or appear to pose, a challenge to royal power, and if they continued willingly to give military support and political counsel to the king when required. Furthermore noblemen, especially those who held offices in the royal household—Shrewsbury was Lord Steward—were expected to attend court at times of important ceremonial: this was one of the most effective ways in which the early Tudors buttressed their authority.[79] In May 1516 the Queen of Scots was at court and a number of foreign ambassadors were present: at such times kings were keen to display the support they received from their leading subjects. Alen reported Wolsey as saying that the king wished to have Shrewsbury with him at Whitsuntide 'for that ye were the great officer of the king's household'.[80] Alen feared that some still more stringent measures were likely: 'my lord, the saying is, such as be head officers of the king's household shall give attendance and be nigh the king daily'.[81] The greatest problem of the later medieval council has been seen as the difficulty of persuading men of genuine ability and suitable rank to remain with any degree of constancy in the king's council.[82] Much of J.F. Baldwin's evidence is admittedly for the troubled decade of the 1450s when the government of the most incompetent king in English history finally collapsed, but the recurrent nature of the problem is striking. The Eltham ordinances of 1526 contained several provisions relating to the attendance of councillors, including the lord steward, for whom permanent lodgings were provided at court.[83] In August 1520 Sir William Compton asked Ruthal to attend the king as there were but few counsellors with him.[84] In 1522 Wolsey was informed that the king wanted 'some personages about him, as well to receive strangers that shall chance to come, as also that the same strangers shall not find him so bare without some noble and wise personages about him'.[85]

In the light of these points, the events of 1516 may be summarised from the point of view of Henry and Wolsey on the one hand and of Shrewsbury on the other and some conclusions drawn. As Henry and Wolsey saw it, Shrewsbury was attempting to secure a marriage alliance with the less than trustworthy Northumberland; he was reluctant to come up to court at a time when the king required the presence of the nobility to impress both the Queen of Scots and foreign ambassadors in a testing diplomatic conjuncture; he was possibly suspected of sympathy towards those men whom Wolsey had ousted from the highest offices and of a critical attitude to some of the king's and Wolsey's actions, notably in foreign policy. Shrewsbury would have seen the situation rather differently. A highly desirable marriage alliance was being attacked, and plans were being laid to marry one of his daughters to the son of the duke of Buckingham which he feared would be very expensive. If he were to come up to court he might face prosecution for retaining and be expected either to remain near the king for a long period or to give up his office as Lord Steward. If he were to come up to court at this time he would risk running into royal disfavour should he question the growing dominance of Wolsey. The very fact of his physical presence at court would deprive him of the possibility of silence and evasion—the only safe means of dissent in a society in which the desirability of unanimity is universally accepted—when such issues as the payment of subsidies to Maximilian were discussed by the council.

A magnate unsympathetic to royal policies or court politicians would have little alternative if he rejected the dangerous course of rebellion but to prevaricate, and to avoid, if possible, putting himself in a position in which definite answers would have to be given to direct questions or lack of open opposition would be taken as tacit consent. Absence from court was the best way of doing this. It was because Shrewsbury's friends recognised this that they warned him against coming up and advised him to stay at home. It was because he also perceived this that Shrewsbury remained at Worksop and employed every stratagem to avoid a royal summons to come up. His absence was a quiet warning that the delicate balance of politics was in danger, that the king and Wolsey were by their actions endangering the unity and stability of the political nation. Refusal to come up might be interpreted as disaffection. It is significant that Fox defended himself against charges of disloyalty: 'As I haue said to your selve and to soom other also', he wrote to Wolsey, 'I hade neuer better wyll to serve the kyng that was my maker (whos saule God pardone) then I haue to serve the kyn his soon, my soueraigne lord that nowe is.'[86]

It is significant that Shrewsbury intended no more than a warning. He was a Tudor loyalist who did not wish to upset the political balance himself. Throughout the spring of 1516 he was working with his chaplain and his friends within accepted political conventions to secure royal acquiescence in his absence. But he would never force the issue into an outright defiance or royal commands for that would be treasonable and morally blameworthy. If necessary, if a royal summons were actually sent to him, he would obey, as Buckingham obeyed in 1521, as Northumberland did in spring 1516. Shrewsbury would follow his own advice to Northumberland not to react in a petulant fashion against the king or Wolsey. Skelton later jeered at the nobility:[87] 'Our barons be so bolde/ Into a mouse hole the wolde/ Runne away and creepe.' But it was not 'For drede of the Mastyffe cur/ For drede of the Bochers dogge' that they offered no resistance, but because silent absence was often the most plausible course of action open to them. Shrewsbury recognised an underlying unity of interest between himself and the crown. Only in a period of incompetent or excessive governance would a nobleman resist openly, and then only if he possessed the support of a large number of his peers. Firm rule, unpalatable policies and an increasingly dominant minister were not, however disagreeable, sufficient ground for revolt. What was within the capacities of a magnate, however, was to exploit to the utmost any opportunities to exert pressure which contemporary conventions allowed. And that is what Shrewsbury, with seeming success, did in the spring of 1516. His problems and his attempts to solve them provide an illustration of the possibilities and limits of magnate power in early Tudor England.

Notes

1 Talbot Papers A 27, 29, 31, 35, 37, 39, 41; P 11, 13, 24, 25, 27, 33. They are summarised in *LP*, II i; listed in G.R. Batho, ed., *Calendar of Talbot Papers in the College of Arms* (1973); and some are printed (not accurately) in E. Lodge,

Illustrations of British History (3 vols, 1791), vol. i.

2 *See below,* pp. 114, 153-4.

3 E.B. de Fonblanque, *Annals of the House of Percy* (2 vols, 1887), pp. 345-76; J.M.W. Bean, *The Estates of the Percy Family 1416-1538* (Oxford, 1958); M.E. James, 'A Tudor magnate and the Tudor state', *Borthwick Papers,* xxx (1966); M. Weiss, 'A power in the north? The Percies in the fifteenth century', *Historical Journal,* xix (1976), pp. 801-9; M.A. Hicks, 'Dynastic change and northern society: the career of the fourth earl of Northumberland, 1470-89', *Northern History,* xiv (1978), pp. 78-107.

4 Talbot Papers A 51.

5 *DNB.;* T.A. and W. Urswick, *Records of the Family of Urswyck, Urswick or Urwick* (St Albans, 1893); Talbot Papers A 59.

6 Talbot Papers P 33.

7 *DNB.,* xviii. 854-5; *see below,* pp. 199-200, 215.

8 Talbot Papers P 13. I have used the transcription of this particularly faded and illegible letter in *LP,* II i 1893.

9 Talbot Papers P 11, 27.

10 Talbot Papers A 31; BL Cotton MS, Vespasian C XIV ii fo. 226ᵥ; Lansdowne MS 639 fo. 45ᵥ.

11 Talbot Papers P 25, A 35.

12 L. Stone, *The Crisis of the Aristocracy 1558-1641* (Oxford, 1965), p. 254.

13 Talbot Papers P 11.

14 T.B. Pugh, *The Marcher Lordships of South Wales 1415-1536* (Cardiff, 1963), pp. 239-43, 260; K.B. McFarlane, *The Nobility of Later Medieval England* (Oxford, 1973), pp. 210-11; C. Rawcliffe, *The Staffords, Earls of Stafford and Dukes of Buckingham 1394-1521* (Cambridge, 1978), pp. 62-4, 100, 129-33.

15 D. Hay, ed., *The Anglica Historia of Polydore Vergil, Camden Society,* 3rd series, lxxiv (1950), p. 265.

16 James, 'A Tudor magnate', p. 25.

17 *See below;* pp. 199-200, 215.

18 The 'little trouble' that Buckingham had over the office of constable, which he claimed in 1514, was very slight: it was the office, not Buckingham's claim to hold it through inheritance, that troubled Henry VIII. (J. Dyer, *Reports of Cases ...* (3 vols, 1794), iii. 285b). M.L. Bush, 'The Tudors and the royal race', *History,* lv (1970), esp. p. 40. Rawcliffe, *Dukes of Buckingham,* p. 40, notes the marriage of Buckingham's son but treats it as an exceptional favour.

19 P.S. and H.M. Allen, *Letters of Bishop Fox* (Oxford, 1929), pp. 43-4.

20 James, 'A Tudor magnate', pp. 29-30; de Fonblanque, *Annals,* i. 349, 357.

21 *LP,* II i 1120.

22 James, 'A Tudor magnate', pp. 25-6.

23 Talbot Papers A 39, 57; G.W. Bernard, 'The rise of Sir William Compton, early Tudor courtier', *English Historical Review,* xcvi (1981), p. 757.

24 de Fonblanque, *Annals,* i. 347.

25 James, 'A Tudor magnate', p. 25.

26 Talbot Papers A 29.

27 Talbot Papers A 27.

28 Talbot Papers A 31.

29 Talbot Papers A 27, 31, 29; P 13, 24, 25.
30 Talbot Papers P 13.
31 Talbot Papers A 39.
32 Talbot Papers A 29.
33 Talbot Papers A 41.
34 Talbot Papers P 13.
35 Talbot Papers P 27.
36 Talbot Papers P 25.
37 Talbot Papers A 37.
38 Talbot Papers A 39, 41.
39 P.J. Gwyn, 'Foreign policy, 1515-1518' (I am most grateful to Peter Gwyn for showing me this unpublished paper); J.J. Scarisbrick, *Henry VIII* (1968), pp. 59-62; J. Wegg, *Richard Pace* (1962), pp. 69-94; R. Brown, ed, *Four Years at the Court of Henry VIII* (2 vols, 1854), i. 252, 307.
40 Gwyn, paper cit.
41 Brown, *Four Years at the Court of Henry VIII*, i. 252, 264.
42 *Ibid.*, i. 307-8, 320, 326.
43 *Ibid.*, i. 164, 150, 143.
44 Gwyn, paper cit.
45 *Letters of Bishop Fox*, pp. 82-4 (*LP*, II i 1814).
46 Talbot Papers A 39.
47 Talbot Papers A 35, 29; *LP*, II i 1706, 1755, 1764, 1784.
48 *LP*, II i 1941.
49 J.A. Guy, 'Wolsey, the council and the council courts', *English Historical Review*, xci (1976), pp. 482, 485 (reprinted in J.A. Guy, *The Cardinal's Court: the impact of Thomas Wolsey in Star Chamber* (Hassocks, 1977), pp. 27. 30-1.)
50 E. Hall, *Chronicle* (1809 ed.), p. 585.
51 Talbot Papers A 39, 41.
52 Talbot Papers A 41. This MS is badly damaged.
53 *LP*, II i p. cxciii.
54 Talbot Papers A 39.
55 Talbot Papers A 41.
56 Talbot Papers A 39.
57 *LP*, I i 20, 442.
58 H. Ellis ed., *Original Letters Illustrative of British History* (3 series in 11 vols, 1824-46), 2nd series, i. 188-201. Cf. for early influence *LP*, i 880, 1260, 1419, 1329.
59 C.S.L. Davies, 'Supply services of English armed forces, 1509-1550', University of Oxford D.Phil. thesis, 1963, ch. 7.
60 *LP*, I ii 2635-6.
61 Vergil, *Anglica Historia*, p. 225.
62 *LP*, I iii 3330-1, 3496.
63 Vergil, *Anglica Historia*, p. 225.
64 Hall, *Chronicle*, p. 583.
65 *LP*, I i 780, 940, 960, 1335.
66 Talbot Papers A 39.
67 Scarisbrick, *Henry VIII*, p. 42; contrast A.F. Pollard, *Henry VIII* (1950 ed.), p. 73 and *Wolsey* (1929), p. 109.

68 E.F. Rogers, ed., *St Thomas More: selected letters* (Yale, 2nd. ed., 1961), p. 68;
   T. Stapleton, *Tres Thomae* (Douai, 1588), pp. 205-6.
69 Vergil, *Anglica Historia*, p. 231.
70 Hall, *Chronicle*, p. 583.
71 G. Cavendish, *The Life and Death of Cardinal Wolsey*, ed. R.S. Sylvester, *Early
   English Text Society*, ccxliii (1959 for 1957), p. 17.
72 *LP*, IV iii 5750 (ii).
73 Vergil, *Anglia Historia*, p. 231.
74 *Ibid.*, p. 235; *Calendar of State Papers, Venetian*, 1509-19, no. 75, pp. 310-11.
75 *Letters of Bishop Fox*, pp. 82-4.
76 *Letters of Bishop Fox*, pp. 96-9.
77 Brown, *Four Years at the Court of Henry VIII*, ii. 9-11, 17, 28, 32.
78 Talbot Papers A 41.
79 S. Anglo, *Spectacle, Pageantry and early Tudor policy* (Oxford, 1969).
80 Talbot Papers A 27.
81 Talbot Papers A 39
82 J.F. Baldwin, *The King's Council in England during the Middle Ages* (Oxford,
   1913), pp. 44-5.
83 *LP*, IV i 1939 (5, 6, 7, 15).
84 *LP*, III i 957.
85 *LP*, III ii 2317.
86 *Letters of Bishop Fox*, p. 83.
87 J. Skelton, *Poetical Works* (1843 ed.), ii. 36 ('Why come ye nat to court?').

2 The fourth earl of Shrewsbury and the Pilgrimage of Grace

On 4 October 1536 George Talbot, fourth earl of Shrewsbury, residing at his lodge in Sheffield Park, received news that five days previously three thousand men had assembled about Horncastle, Lincolnshire. They had taken prisoner certain subsidy commissioners and surveyors of monasteries. They had threatened to pull Shrewsbury's informant, Lord Borough, out of his house in Gainsborough if he did not agree to become their captain. Borough, terrified, fled to a friend's house in Nottinghamshire,[1] and implored Shrewsbury to prepare his forces against the rebels 'to mak them a brekefast'.[2] This Shrewsbury did, sending a circular letter to the local nobility and gentry, calling on them to raise as many men as possible and to meet him at an appointed time and place.[3] The Lincolnshire rising, the first of a series of rebellions known collectively as the Pilgrimage of Grace, had begun: and so had the resistance to it.

These rebellions have now received the attention that their central importance in any assessment of Henry VIII's reign demands.[4] Several reinterpretations emphasise the Pilgrimage of Grace as a demonstration of discontent, in which the higher social groups retained their usual predominance, directed against the members and policies of a regime with which they were out of sympathy.[5] A general sense of grievance arising from the suppression of the smaller monasteries, the dominance of Thomas Cromwell, the spread of heresy, the attacks on regional liberties and the increasing and apparently inexorable intrusion of central government into the localities was expressed in a mass movement of protest involving the capture of representatives of central government, the occupation of regional capitals and strongpoints and the formulation of programmes of demands. But the leaders of the movement strove hard to avoid any battles or protracted sieges and attempted to make fruitful contacts with influential figures at court.[6] A far from convincing variant of such views has been the claim that the troubles in the north were largely a crisis at court played out in the provinces by discontented courtiers who deliberately stirred up the commons and imposed their own grievances upon them.[7] Henry VIII and those who chose to serve him against the rebels saw the Pilgrimage in a very different light. Henry regarded it neither as a non-violent demonstration nor as a safety-valve releasing dissent in a closed society nor as a courtiers' conspiracy: he believed that he was confronted by an armed rebellion posing a real threat to his throne that had to be appeased and repressed by a judicious combination of political concessions and military force. Over-confident one day, fearful the next, Henry remained in the south throughout the insurrection, sending out unrealistically brutal orders.[8] Thus the tasks of raising and of leading the royal army and of negotiating with the rebels fell to his principal noblemen. In the defeat of the rebellion the fourth earl of Shrewsbury, appointed one of the king's lieutenants against the rebels, played a leading part.

Shrewsbury's loyalty to the crown was immediate and unhesitating. As soon as he knew of the disturbances he raised his men and ordered others to raise theirs and to join him. Given that he first heard of the rebellion on 4 October, it seems ungenerous to say that 'on 5 October he *finally* set out to suppress the insurgency'.[9] But he had to make his loyalty known to the king, as to levy men without first receiving a command from the king might be construed as treason. Holinshed relates how Shrewsbury petitioned the king for a pardon. Asking the knights and gentlemen of his council whether or not his actions were treasonable, he was assured that his intentions were good and that therefore he could not be accused of treason. 'Ye are fooles', retorted Shrewsbury, 'I know it in substance to be treason, and I would thinke my selfe in an hard case, if I thought I had not my pardon comming.'[10] There is no other evidence that Shrewsbury either asked for or received a royal pardon but another nobleman's request to the king suggests that Holinshed's story is inherently plausible. The earl of Huntingdon, who owed his recent ennoblement to Henry VIII and was therefore unlikely to face any suspicion of disloyalty, cautiously wrote to the king on 6

October that, if he was to be commanded to raise any of the
king's subjects, he might have the king's authority to do so. Then
neither he nor any who went with him would incur 'the daunger
of your lawes which is to hevy for anny of vs to bere'.[11]
Shrewsbury was certainly careful. He wrote to the king for
instructions at once.[12] Even after he had received a royal
command to levy forces against the rebels, probably at 11 a.m. on
6 October,[13] he wished on 7 October to send Sir Arthur Darcy to
the king with a personal message that Shrewsbury would serve
him to the uttermost of his power.[14] He made and kept a copy of a
letter he sent to a suspected rebel leader, presumably in order to
be able to show that it contained nothing incriminating.[15] The
impression is that Shrewsbury feared that if the Lincolnshire
disturbances proved to be a riot of no consequence, Thomas
Cromwell might use the fact that Shrewsbury had levied a power
of armed men without the king's commission to frame a case
against him. However unfair a judgment of Cromwell's
intentions and methods this might be, that Shrewsbury, on the
evidence of his actions believed this, illustrates the atmosphere of
suspicion, watchfulness and fear that the Cromwellian regime
had produced.

Shrewsbury's loyalty emerges clearly from his vigorous
preparations. He moved from Sheffield to his house at Hardwick
so that he might be nearer Nottingham Castle where local gentry
had been appointed to meet him.[16] He wrote to Henry and
Cromwell for ordnance, artillery and money, sending one of his
friends to court with a bill of his requirements.[17] Shrewsbury
successfully mobilised his men: by 10 October he had raised an
army, 3,654 strong from his servants, tenants and friends.[18] Once
Shrewsbury was joined by two other loyalist peers, the earls of
Huntingdon and Rutland, a solid core of resistance against the
rebels had been established. Shrewsbury's swift preparations
greatly assisted the king.

At the same time Shrewsbury did Henry even more valuable
service by defusing the Lincolnshire rebellion. As M.E. James
has shown, Shrewsbury was largely responsible for ending the
part that Lord Hussey, first-generation peer, sometime courtier
and royal administrator played in it.[19] On one view Hussey was
the 'central figure' of the troubles in Lincolnshire;[20] on another
view, if he did not actually start the rebellion, he helped it to

spread, urging the rebels to take Lincoln.[21] A more plausible assessment may be that not only did he not instigate the troubles but that he was too cowardly and too weak to dare either to further or to repress the revolt. At first he failed to grasp the strength of the rebellion. Then he quickly found himself facing violent threats intended to persuade him to join in a cause with which, as chamberlain to Princess Mary and as a former confidant of Chapuys, the imperial ambassador, he doubtless sympathised.[22] However great his complicity, what Hussey would have hoped to do was to act as mediator between king and rebels, and in order to do this effectively he had to secure the support and protection of a nobleman whose sphere of influence and position at court were greater than his own. Shrewsbury was the obvious man for such a role and Hussey appealed to him in a letter written on 6 October. Referring to a letter sent to Shrewsbury by the king, he said that he had been told that 'dyvers thinges were in your lordshippes lettre which your lordship wold advertise me of'. This was a clear request to Shrewsbury to give his blessing to Hussey if he were openly to join the rebels.[23] Shrewsbury—who had been given reason to suspect Hussey's loyalty—sent an unyielding reply:[24]

I haue no oder thing in my lettre but onely commaundement to represse the kynges rebellyous whiche I dowt nat but ye woild put your helpyng hande to. My very good lord, for the olde acquientaunce & famylyartye betwyxt your good lordship & me as vnto him that I eternely loue I woild wryte the playnes of my mynd to your lordship. Ye haue allwayes bene an honourable and true gentylman and so shewed your selff, and I dowt nat but now so woll prove your selff according to your bounden dutye. And in my poore mynde there is no man may do the kyng hygher nor truear seruice in thise parties then you may.

This letter terrified Hussey: commanded unequivocally to serve the king, or else be regarded as a traitor, he fled to Shrewsbury, arriving at Nottingham on 9 October.[25] His flight deprived the Lincolnshire rebels of local noble support, and, as important, of the hope that greater magnates might encourage the rising: this contributed to its eventual disintegration.

Shrewsbury's considerable services to the king explain the tone of the letter that Cromwell sent to Shrewsbury on 9 October, probably unparalleled by any other letter from a Henrician minister to a nobleman. Cromwell thanked 'my singuler good lord' for his 'honorable' letters,

the sight whereof with the demonstracyon of your nobyll courage and trowthe
hath so comffortyd me that whylys I lyue and yf I myght after my deth I wooll
and woolde honour yow & your posteryte as the man and most woorthye erll
that euer seruyd a prynce and suche a chefftayn as ys worthye eternall glorye.

He assured Shrewsbury that he wrote this letter 'with my veray
hart' and prayed God for an opportunity 'to doo yow pleasure
whyll ye lyue and to your posteryte yf I ouer lyue yow'. He
wished Shrewsbury might know as well as he did 'how the kinges
highnes reputyth your most acceptable & loyall seruyce whiche
ye shall right well persayue by the tenour of his gracyous lettres'.
Shrewsbury would receive all the munitions and money that he
asked for. Finally Cromwell wished God would 'send your
lordshyp as long lyfe and as well to fare as I woold myself, and
then ye sholde be in goodd helthe and but xxx yeres of age'.
Cromwell was not only thanking Shrewsbury for his loyalty but
also attempting to secure its continuation by promises of favour.
No more striking evidence could be found of Shrewsbury's
loyalty and of the undiminished reliance of both king and
minister on territorial magnates in the age of the 'Tudor
revolution in government'.[26]

Although Hussey's flight contributed to the disintegration of
the Lincolnshire rebellion, it was not yet over when Shrewsbury,
Rutland and Huntingdon assembled at Nottingham on 10
October. As Henry sent the dukes of Suffolk and Norfolk
northwards,[27] Shrewsbury again made a significant intervention
in the rebellion. He sent his personal friend Thomas Miller,
Lancaster Herald, to Lincoln to read a proclamation
commanding the rebels to disperse under threat of facing
Shrewsbury and 40,000 men—a great exaggeration of the
numbers actually under Shrewsbury's command—in battle on
Ancaster Heath. Shrewsbury's menacing contained a good
measure of bluff but, as he expected, it proved highly effective
and his 'good pollycie' was warmly commended by the king.[28]

But at this point of seeming victory in Lincolnshire, the
government and loyalist commanders found themselves
confronted by a second insurrection. On 12 October Shrewsbury
received information that the commons of Beverley were risen

and sworn to one another and that their goals were first Pontefract and then York.[29] Already there had been disturbances in Northumberland and Yorkshire: on 7 October Shrewsbury had been visited by Sir Arthur Darcy who brought information about them from his father Lord Darcy.[30]

 Sir Arthur Darcy's visit is the first significant evidence of contact between Lord Darcy and Shrewsbury during the Pilgrimage of Grace. Darcy was to surrender Pontefract Castle and to become one of the principal spokesmen for the rebels. Already (if the evidence given by a witness in 1537 is to be believed) he was giving Shrewsbury grounds for doubt. Shrewsbury asked Sir Arthur 'wat nombre off mene my lord hys father myght make to serue the kynges highnes yff ned requyred & he made answer that yff abbays myght stond my lord his father myght make to serue the kynges hyghnes v thouzande mene'. Shrewsbury replied 'Goo & byd your fader stay hys contre or I will torne my bake apon yonder traytors & my fasse apone theyme.' From this time, we are told, Shrewsbury mistrusted Darcy—though he may have been worried not by fears of Darcy's disloyalty but by Darcy's defeatism.[31]

Much of the evidence concerning Darcy's involvement in the Pilgrimage is ambiguous. There is much circumstantial detail apparently against him. He had had treasonable conversations with Chapuys in 1534-5. In October 1536 he failed to mobilise his men to resist the rebels. His retreat to Pontefract Castle did nothing to halt them. His prohibition of all leets, commissions and assemblies except meetings of gentlemen and their household servants affected those loyalists who might have wished to muster forces to serve the king. His reliance on letters and persuasions of wise men to stay the countries proved ineffective. His mysterious letter (not in his letter book) addressed only to 'cousin', charging him in the king's name to come to him immediately to discuss certain 'vrgent & weghty causes' is suspicious.[32] Henry VIII mistrusted Darcy. On 13 October (responding to news sent to him no later than 11 October) Henry voiced his unease, greatly marvelling that the unlawful assembly in Holderness and Holdenshire was still unrepressed, plainly implying his belief that Darcy could and should have stopped it.[33] On 17 October Henry wondered at Darcy's failure to send reliable information about the rebellion earlier. He was amazed

that Darcy had not 'yet put your good endeuours at the
begining for the repression of the same whiche as we be
enfirmed myght than haue been easley doon and with our lesse
charge'.[34] On one occasion Henry told one of his officers that he
had no great trust in Darcy.[35] During his conversation on 23
October, the duke of Norfolk got the clear impression that
Shrewsbury's son Francis Talbot mistrusted Darcy: Talbot was
also very suspicious of the ease with which Pontefract Castle had
been captured by the rebels.[36] Two comments on Darcy's
behaviour during Bigod's rising in January 1537 are revealing of
his earlier attitudes: Shrewsbury advised him to 'follow as ye
have *at this tyme* begun in stayeng of the comons'; Henry trusted
that Darcy would *now* do his duty.[37]

But this is not conclusive. There is no necessary link between
the earlier dealings with the imperial ambassador and the
rebellion in October 1536. It is important to remember that
Darcy was much less powerful than Shrewsbury and that his area
of influence was much closer to the places in revolt. If Darcy was
actively plotting rebellion he could have done much more to
further it. If he was rebuked by the king for not dealing quickly
and firmly with the rebels, so was the unquestionably loyal earl of
Cumberland.[38] If Pontefract Castle was yielded easily, yet it is
worth noting that Shrewsbury found no ordnance at
Nottingham and that the duke of Suffolk complained about the
defences at Huntingdon and Stamford (only Newark was
strong).[39] It should not be overlooked that Darcy's sons' children
were threatened by the rebels. Darcy's relations with Robert
Aske, the captain of the Pilgrims, were by no means close or
smooth. It is also worth asking whether Darcy ever saw himself as
a rebel.[40]

None of this is to deny that Darcy sympathised with the rebels'
concerns or that his reaction to the disturbances was markedly
different from that of Shrewsbury. But however early, or
conscious, or great, his connivance in the rebellion, Darcy would
find it vital to discover Shrewsbury's intentions. If Shrewsbury
were to support the rebels, it would not only be possible for Darcy
openly to encourage them but foolhardy for him to resist. If
Shrewsbury would remain neutral, Darcy might be able to serve
in a chain of mediation running from the rebels via himself and
Shrewsbury to the king. Shrewsbury could represent the

demands of the rebels to the king and shield Darcy from the royal wrath. The importance of Shrewsbury for Darcy is similar to that of Shrewsbury for Hussey in the Lincolnshire rising. Any contact between Darcy and Shrewsbury was significant.

Darcy appealed directly to Shrewsbury through his son Sir Arthur but this served only to strengthen his son's loyalty. After speaking to Shrewsbury, Sir Arthur asked his father to send his men up to him at Nottingham: 'I shull be ther found ner to the Talbott.'[41] Darcy then appealed indirectly on 11 October. In a letter to Sir Brian Hastings, instead of responding to Hastings' suggestion that Darcy should send a force to York, he wrote in a postscript that neither the king nor Shrewsbury had answered his requests: 'iff ye haue any certaynty frome abof let me be partenor therof'.[42] It is curious that Darcy should have expected to receive 'certaynty frome abof' from Hastings as Henry VIII was sending his letters to northern noblemen and gentry via Darcy, and Hastings himself had received a letter from the king through and in the very presence of Darcy in Pontefract Castle on 8 October.[43] But Hastings was in close contact with Shrewsbury. If Shrewsbury were to decide to join the rebels, or to wink at their cause, Hastings was just the man to act as a channel for the transmission of hints.

Shrewsbury's next letter to Darcy shows that he recognised the appeal: in it Shrewsbury was emphatic that he should have no truck with rebellion. Where Darcy referred to men willing to serve God and the king—suspiciously familiar to the rebels' claim—Shrewsbury saw neighbours of Darcy who began to rise *against* the king's highness as they had in Lincolnshire. This would make Darcy understand that Shrewsbury's attitude towards the rebels in Yorkshire would be no more favourable than his uncompromising stand against the rebels in Lincolnshire had been. Shrewsbury's instructions to Darcy to remain in his country (that is, not to fly to Shrewsbury and not to shelter helplessly in Pontefract Castle) and to call together the local gentry to publish an enclosed proclamation were an implicit rebuke.[44]

Darcy—unlike Hussey—was a man of courage and made no attempt at flight. The speed with which he surrendered Pontefract Castle and the enthusiasm with which he then defended the rebels' demands suggest that his decision to ignore

Shrewsbury's advice was deliberate and clear-cut. But it is worth
raising the possibility that he may still have hesitated before fully
throwing his lot in with that of the rebels. Perhaps he did now
think of resisting them but was forced to yield because his earlier
inactivity had allowed the rebellion to grow and made resistance
increasingly dangerous. Despite the evidence of Shrewsbury's
firmness, Darcy may have continued to hope that his old friend
would eventually join him or that (and here his hopes were not
wholly unfounded) he would at least try to protect him from any
charge of treason. Shrewsbury could do nothing but hope that
Darcy would yet remain loyal. He sent him polite warnings and
full information about the collapse of the Lincolnshire troubles,
endeavouring to deflect Darcy from a fatal total commitment to
the rebellion and offering him every opportunity (short of
promising him the king's favour) to rectify his mistakes. But in
practice Shrewsbury no longer placed much trust in Darcy as a
bulwark against the rebels.[45]

Shrewsbury's suspicions of Darcy must have affected his
reaction to the news from Yorkshire. On 18 October he learned
that

parte of the rebelles of Yorkeshire came yestirnyght to Dancastre and ther ronge
the common belle and swere the mayre and comons of the same who right
gladly received their othe, and, as he sayith that was their present, that never
shipe [sheep] came fastir in a mornyng oute of their folde then they did to
receive the said othe.

Not only had men in Doncaster been sworn but the king's letters
could no longer be delivered to Darcy in Pontefract Castle.[46] On
receiving this news Shrewsbury determined to march
northwards as quickly as possible in the hope that the duke of
Norfolk would soon join him and that meanwhile the duke of
Suffolk would be strong enough to crush any remaining
resistance in Lincolnshire.

At this point Holinshed's account of how Shrewsbury swore his
loyalty to the king before his men may best be inserted. In
Shrewsbury's army there were 'diuerse speaches amongst the
soldiers vttered by some not altogither happilie well disposed'
suggesting that the earl had such 'good liking' for the northern
men's cause that 'when it came to the point of triall he would

surely ioine with them against that part which he yet pretended to mainteine'. Shrewsbury called a large number of his soldiers together and told them that he had heard of 'lewd talke' among them suggesting that he favoured the rebels. He declared to them that 'whatsoeuer their colourable pretense may be, true it is, that traitors they are in this their wicked attempt'. His loyalty to the monarchy was grounded on that of his ancestors and he did not intend to stain his blood by joining with traitors. He aimed rather 'to liue and die in defense of the crowne if it stood but vpon a stake'. Those who would take his part in the quarrel he thanked; those who were otherwise minded he asked to depart. He then swore an oath of loyalty to the king in the presence of all his men.[47]

There is no direct evidence to confirm this. But there were others who expected that Shrewsbury would take the rebels' side. Hussey and Darcy both hoped for Shrewsbury's support. Chapuys, the imperial ambassador, believed that Shrewsbury would at least remain neutral.[48] The rebel William Stapleton said that his men were 'sore amased' when they learned that Shrewsbury was coming with a great power to give them battle.[49] Similarly there are other suggestions that Shrewsbury's men were not wholly united behind the royalist cause. Norfolk had doubts about Shrewsbury's men: never, he wrote, had a prince had a company of truer nobles and gentlemen, 'yet right few of soldiers but that thought and think their quarrels to be good'.[50] Henry was disturbed at the possible unreliability of Shrewsbury's men.[51] Darcy and some rebel captains believed they could have fought Norfolk and Shrewsbury with their own men.[52] Holinshed's account is then by no means implausible.

This militates against any mechanistic interpretation of the rebellion in terms of the commons slavishly following their masters and casts doubts on the arguments that 'there was a correlation between the geography of revolt and the pattern of territorial leadership'[53] and that the failure or inability of a lord to resist rebels in his country was in itself evidence of his complicity in rebellion.[54] The commons who formed the bulk of the armed forces of late medieval magnates were certainly unsophisticated and easily swayed by 'forged tales' and 'wicked surmises'.[55] Alone the commons could usually, and ultimately, be repressed, as Shrewsbury pointed out when he asserted that if the gentlemen and men of substance could be persuaded to withdraw from the Lincolnshire rebellion, the commons could do small hurt. The commons were also vulnerable to financial temptation: 'money is the thyng that euery poor man woll call for', Shrewsbury wrote to Henry VIII early in the campaign.[56] But there was a chance, however slight in normal circumstances, that popular discontent would degenerate into class conflict, especially if the upper classes would not admit the commons' grievances. The commons might be induced, Holinshed recorded, not only to forget their allegiance to the king, but also their 'souldior-like obedience to their leaders'.[57] The commons were not mere puppets: their relationship with their masters was more complex than that. En masse they constituted in some sense a 'public opinion' which had to be won. Moreover systematic leadership was especially necessary if the commons were to follow their lords in a campaign against their own sympathies for the rebels.

The Pilgrimage of Grace was neither a 'feudal' revolt in which noblemen or dissident courtiers carried into the field their unthinking followers nor a popular rising deliberately stirred up by the nobility and gentry nor a simultaneous and spontaneous outburst by a mass of oppressed commons. It was rather a more complex series of risings inspired by various small groups of discontented, frightened or ambitious men—most especially clergy and ex-religious, yeomen, *coqs de village*, prosperous artisans, the legally trained officials of greater men, acting sometimes on more or less precise instructions or more usually on their own initiative, and, possibly, although here the evidence is ambiguous, a very few gentry and noblemen. At a moment when the religious policy of Henry VIII and Cromwell appeared particularly intrusive and destructive,[58] the rumour-mongering, largesse and organisation of these activists succeeded in drawing together large and angry mobs, producing a situation in which most noblemen and gentlemen had to decide quickly and often under real pressure whether they would resist, attempt to ignore, accept reluctantly or encourage enthusiastically an already existing movement. Many went in partly out of fear, partly out of sympathy for the rebels' cause, partly in the hope of controlling the rebellion and minimising the risks it posed to the social order. Shrewsbury chose to resist but this decision by their lord was not in itself sufficient to impose it upon the men whom he intended to command. The earl of Cumberland displayed magnificent loyalty to the king but this did not deter his retinue from deserting him and his commons from besieging him in his castle at Skipton.[59] Shrewsbury was more successful, partly because (if Holinshed is to be believed) he swore an oath which assured his men that he would not betray them, partly because he gave careful attention to the payment of wages. If Cumberland's difficulties were due to the fact that he had been a harsh landlord to gentry and commons alike, the principal reason for Shrewsbury's success in keeping his country free from rebellion was the respect he had won over the years, 'the favour which the commons bare towards him and the opinion they had conceiued of his high prowesse', a matter in which the unimproved rents on his estates may have played some part.[60] If Cumberland's difficulties arose rather from his relative weakness as a first-generation earl and as a smaller landowner, the contrast is between the authority of a new and an old nobleman.[61] Either way, in Shrewsbury's case that traditional feudal reverence for great and ancient families which has sometimes been taken as explaining the revolt is here seen working to repress it.

Strengthened by the loyalty of his men, Shrewsbury advanced to Scrooby on 21 October and (after the failure of Lancaster Herald's mission to the rebels) to within a mile of Doncaster on 22 or 23 October.[62] Norfolk, at Newark on 24 October, was not coming forward as fast as Shrewsbury had hoped: so concerned was Norfolk that Shrewsbury would fight the rebels before he arrived that he was making contingency plans for Shrewsbury's defeat.[63] At one point a skirmish took place between a group of rebels and thirty loyalist horsemen who had been sent to view their camp.[64] But by 25 October, before Norfolk arrived, Shrewsbury agreed to talk to the rebels and arranged a meeting for 27 October.[65] Meanwhile Norfolk asked Henry to take in good part whatever he might promise the rebels for he would not observe it longer than necessary.[66] On 27 October the two commanders first addressed and then met the rebels: agreement was reached and both sides 'sparpled' their forces. No details survive but Norfolk and Shrewsbury clearly promised that if the rebels dispersed they too would disband their forces. They would then sue to the king for the rebels' pardon and ensure that two of their representatives were safely escorted to petition the king.[67]

The agreement was a defeat for the government: in Lincolnshire the rebels had yielded without receiving any concessions. Why then did Shrewsbury and Norfolk decide to negotiate? They justified their actions on 28 October. They described how they successfully strengthened the defences of Rossington bridge and how heavy rain flooded what would normally have been an easily fordable river. But if they kept the rebels out of Doncaster they were nonetheless too weak to fight them. The rebels were 30,000 strong and 'well trymed having with them all the lords and gentlemen from hence to Scotland sawe the Earles of Westmorland and Cumberland and the Lord Dacre'. They were determined 'in a great fury' to attack the loyalists' camp. They dominated the surrounding country. If it came to a battle they would have the initiative in choosing the time and place. By contrast the loyalist forces, some 10,000, were not yet all assembled; they lacked victual and money; plague was in their army.[68] Norfolk justified what he had agreed on 31 October. They had been compelled by adverse conditions to disband their army. The weather was cold; there was insufficient fuel for fires; only a third of the army could be suitably housed; plague was raging at Doncaster; victual was short and no hay, oats, peas or beans could be obtained within five miles; there were insufficient horses. Furthermore he had doubts about the loyalty of Shrewsbury's men.[69] If Shrewsbury explained his earlier action in agreeing to talk to the rebels, nothing survives. Perhaps it was the realisation that his swift advance had failed to frighten them into submission that persuaded him to treat.

Norfolk blamed Shrewsbury for advancing recklessly without attending to victual and supply. Already on 25 October he had regretted Shrewsbury's advance.[70] On 29 October he was more emotional:[71]

Alas that the valiaunt heart of my lord steward would not suffer him to have taried about Trent, but with his fast hastening forwards to bring us into the most barren country of the realm, whereof hath ensued the effect that I saw long afore would ensue . . . woe! woe! woe worth the tyme that my lord steward went so far forth, for an he had not, ye shuld have heard other news.

In December Norfolk repeated his criticism: Shrewsbury and his company would have been in great danger on 26-7 October if the rebels had taken their advantage like men of war.[72]

There would have been some force to Norfolk's criticism if the frightening of the rebels into submission had been Shrewsbury's only motive for advancing northwards. But Shrewsbury's first aim was clearly to halt the rebel advance. As soon as he was encamped a mile outside Doncaster he sent 1,200 men and six pieces of ordnance into the town and to Rossington Bridge 'to kepe the passages ther soo that the rebelles shal enter no further but to ther paynes'.[73] Shrewsbury recognised the crucial importance of preventing the rebellion from spreading geographically. Much of the area between Nottingham and Doncaster was Shrewsbury's country and he would not have wished to watch on helplessly while the rebellion drifted southwards. Shrewsbury's presence would itself be a guarantee of the quietness of that area. It is significant that it was the news of the swearing of certain townsmen of Doncaster that determined Shrewsbury's advance. There is little doubt that Doncaster would have fallen to the rebels if Shrewsbury's army had not been within striking distance: Aske believed he could have won it even against the loyalists' army.[74] Henry VIII had no doubts that Shrewsbury had acted wisely in advancing: 'we see nowe', he wrote to Norfolk in early December, 'that onles he had soo doon, a greate cuntrey had been clerly ouer runne, and a greate nombre of our subgiettes thereby corrupted, oppressed and spoiled, which nowe remayn in quiet and be ready to serue vs against the rebelles.'[75] Shrewsbury's advance resulted in an enforced compromise with the rebels, but if he had not hastened forward, matters would have been much worse for the government.

After the agreement Shrewsbury doubtless hoped that the rebels' representatives, who had been accompanied on their journey to the king by Norfolk and Shrewsbury's son Lord Talbot, would return with a pardon and a reasonable answer to their demands. That would allow the rebels to pursue their grievances within a more conventional framework. Meanwhile Shrewsbury was deeply concerned by the restoration of order in the north. For example, soon after the truce, he was asked by Darcy to persuade the earl of Derby not to attack the commons at Whalley Abbey as was his reported intention; Shrewsbury wrote to Derby; Derby called off his forces; Darcy believed that Shrewsbury (together with Aske and himself) had been the clear saving of Derby's life.[76] As the rebellion degenerated into the pursuit of long-standing feuds between northern landowners, Shrewsbury attempted to exercise a restraining influence. He did so particularly in the quarrel between the loyalist Sir Henry Savile, who now sought reparation for the damage done to some of his tenants, on the one hand, and Sir Richard Tempest and Thomas Gryce, a servant of Darcy, on the other, who attempted to seize Savile in November and forced him to leave his house and flee to Shrewsbury.[77]

The rebels, however, were not satisfied by hopes of royal favour and continued to assemble in large numbers. Shrewsbury was closely involved in Henry's preparations to contain them. Henry was considering a military campaign should negotiations fail; for example, Shrewsbury and the king exchanged correspondence about which river would make the best natural defensive barrier against the rebels.[78] But the main feature of these preparations was to be a further meeting between Norfolk and Shrewsbury and the rebel leaders at Doncaster, at which the loyalist commanders would answer in the king's name to 'certen articles lately presented by his subjects in the north' and treat and conclude with the principal noblemen involved in the Pilgrimage of Grace.[79] But there were significant differences between the instructions given to Norfolk and those sent to Shrewsbury.

Norfolk was warned not to complain against other loyalist commanders and was reminded to remember the king's honour. He was to write to the rebels, reproaching them for their ingratitude and for the arrogance they had shown in raising a great force at a time when the king had sent a number of the noblest men in the realm to talk with them. He was not to proceed with the meeting until he had raised enough men for his own security. At the meeting he was first to deal with the violations of the earlier agreement: the rebels' new assembly, the seizure of a royal ship, the attempts to foment disorder in Cumberland. He was then to offer a pardon excepting certain ringleaders. If this were refused, and the rebels insisted upon a general pardon without exception, Norfolk should explain that his commission did not run that far but nevertheless offer to make suit to the king for them, asking for a truce of six or seven days in which to do this. He should then pretend to send for and await the king's pleasure. At the end of that period he should say that the king had graciously granted their petition and had asked Norfolk to present a general pardon. Norfolk should then produce the pardon that Henry was enclosing with these instructions. If this also failed to satisfy the rebels, Norfolk was to offer a further truce of twenty days, which he would employ to levy all the forces that Shrewsbury and he could make.[80]

The rather different instructions that Henry sent Shrewsbury throw some light on the intentions of the king and in particular on the purposes of that six or seven day truce that Norfolk was to offer if his opening bid failed. Henry had formed the impression from Shrewsbury's letters that Darcy had been 'of some bettre sorte thenne he hath been reaported and that he wold be content and gladde to com in and to vse him selfe in all thinges like our good and faithful subgiett'. Henry therefore wished to extend his royal mercy towards him and for that reason was sending Sir John Russell (who had previously marched northwards with Norfolk) to Shrewsbury with an individual pardon for Darcy. Shrewsbury was asked to give this to Darcy if Darcy agreed to come in. If Darcy could persuade Robert Aske to come in, he too would be given a pardon. They were to be assured that the king would be good lord to them. If Shrewsbury and Russell could win over others, they too were to be promised pardons. What is especially significant is that Henry was asking Shrewsbury and Russell to practise with Darcy *after* the Doncaster meeting, that is, during the six or seven days' truce, and without informing any of the other loyalist commanders. This strongly suggests that Henry did not seriously expect that the offer to be made by Norfolk of a pardon with exceptions would prove effective but that he hoped that he might still be able to avoid granting a general pardon, which he saw as greatly injuring his honour, if Shrewsbury could use the great credit he had among the noble leaders of the rebellion to divide them from the commons and the more committed gentlemen.[81] Henry was clearly keeping all his options open. Involvement in such negotiations was potentially dangerous. It is not difficult to imagine how a charge of treasonable dealing with rebels might have been framed against Shrewsbury on the grounds of his contacts with Darcy. When a

little earlier Shrewsbury asked Cromwell to get him excused
from continuing as lieutenant as he was very feeble and weak and
to allow him to serve under some other nobleman—a request
that was quickly refused—he may conceivably have been
attempting to avoid such dangerous responsibilities as were being
planned for him.[82]

The hopes that Henry placed in the influence that Shrewsbury
exercised over Darcy must have been encouraged by
Shrewsbury's repeated efforts to win over Darcy and Darcy's
family. At the Doncaster meeting in October, Darcy, if his later
account may be trusted, asked Shrewsbury to promise him the
king's favour: but this Shrewsbury was unable to do.[83] In
November Shrewsbury frequently thanked Darcy for his good
service and assured him of his friendship. On 1 November
Shrewsbury wrote to Darcy that he had seen how Darcy had with
great pains stayed the commons after the Doncaster agreement.
If Darcy kept the commons stayed they would be able to meet
merrily together to both God's and the king's pleasure.[84] Several
times in November Shrewsbury assured Darcy that he would do
nothing contrary to the appointment taken at Doncaster.[85]

Even more significant were Shrewsbury's attempts to detach
Sir George Darcy, Lord Darcy's eldest son, from the rebels. Sir
George was a Flodden knight who had made his name in the
Scottish wars.[86] He had been a knight of the body in the royal
household.[87] He was steward of several important monastic
manors.[88] His estates included Aston, a few miles east of the
centre of the Talbot patrimony at Sheffield.[89] His second son,
Thomas, had been contracted to Shrewsbury's daughter Anne,
although there was no subsequent marriage, in 1530.[90] In 1536
Sir George was sheriff of the West Riding, which made his
attitude during the rebellion important: it would be his
responsibility to arrest anyone committing treason.[91] But his
conduct was not worthy of his duty. His attitude was ambivalent.
To say that he only joined the commons under compulsion[92] or
that he showed coolness towards the rebels[93] is to credit him with
too much consistency of behaviour. On hearing of the rising from
Thomas Mansell, vicar of Brayton (the church in which Sir
George was ultimately to be buried),[94] Sir George simply sent
him to his father at Pontefract.[95] Sir George could have done
more: in January 1537, during Bigod's rising, Mansell and other

servants stayed the country.[96] It is possible that Sir George found courage later: under interrogation the following year, Aske said that he had once been warned that Sir George would take him if he tarried where he was.[97] By mid-October Sir George was probably at Pontefract Castle: he was certainly there after it had been surrendered to the rebels. When Aske was given an interview by Darcy just before the yielding of the castle, 'ther was deliuered for pledge the eldest sonne of Sir George Darcye'.[98]

From a letter that Sir George Darcy wrote to Shrewsbury on 2 November (which survives in late seventeenth century and later copies and has not previously been noticed) it is clear that soon after the Doncaster agreement Shrewsbury had accused him of treason against the king and disloyalty towards himself. Probably Shrewsbury supposed that Sir George might be open to threats and promises of assistance: it was at this time that Norfolk described him as a true knight.[99] On 2 November Sir George wrote an abject reply to Shrewsbury:

humbly thenckyng your Honourable Lordship for your Honourable Council & surely my very good Lord, it is no more grievous to no man living then to me that I should do the thing to the Kings Majesty my sovereign Lord & Prince & my good Lord I had lever have dyed then to beare Arms agin his Graces person, & that I uttered afore my Lord Archbishop my lord my father the Captein & Mr Magnus ... Also my very good Lord besides my duty to my Prince there is nothing more grieveth me then that I should have been ageinst you ... my sorrowfull wife which is your poore Beadwoman humbly recommendeth her vnto you whose trust is only in your Lordship. And my Lord next vnto God what your Honorable council & pleasure is I shall be ready ... Desiring your Lordship that this be kept private & secret between my father in law & your Lordship for I my wife & children are clerely vndone if it be known as the Holy Ghost knoweth who keepe your good Lordship This All Soules Dey.

Sir George denied that he had committed treason, claimed that he had declared his abhorrence of treason to the leaders of the rebellion in Pontefract Castle, obsequiously protested his allegiance to Shrewsbury, offered to do whatever Shrewsbury suggested and implored Shrewsbury to keep the matter secret.[100]

Two undated letters confirm the implications of this. William Mansell informed Sir George's brother Sir Arthur that Sir George[101]

doyth most hevelye take this matter that evr dyde any mane of lyke and sore

doyth repentt that he went with them ... the commonaltye doyth nott trust
hym for he hath oppenlye spoken that to deye he wyll take the kynges parte & if
he & others were sure that his grace wold accepte theyr servyce & hole intente,
he & a greate nombr wold sure me to his grace, which be men of high worshipe.

John Bulmer informed William Bulmer that 'Sir George Darcy
hath accused my lord his father and Sir Robert Constable'.[102]
Clearly Sir George had dithered and then vaguely gone along
with the rebels. Shrewsbury's forceful accusations had made him
realise the significance of what he had done. He then somewhat
recklessly changed his attitude. His behaviour during the
Pilgrimage largely bears out Lord Darcy's observations, made a
decade earlier, on his son's character: 'Cunyng wytte experience
and specially humanite with the moost parte of all other good
vertues surely he lakkes, good wyll to the best of his power and
trawith I trust he shall shew at all tymes.'[103] An anxiety to do the
right thing, if only he could know what that was, rather than any
steadiness of purpose or understanding of what he was doing,
characterises Sir George's letter to Shrewsbury.

   This letter also illuminates some dark aspects of other
correspondence of mid-November, making possible a
reconstruction of events and relationships. Shrewsbury was
attempting to detach Sir George from the rebels. He responded
to Sir George's reply by writing again and making him an offer.
This letter Sir George received thankfully; Shrewsbury was in
turn right glad to hear that. Meanwhile Shrewsbury had written
to Sir Brian Hastings, a loyalist who was to succeed Sir George as
sheriff, asking him to warn all his friends and servants in
Shrewsbury's name to come to the earl on the sight of his letter
and to ask for the king's pardon. Sir Brian warned Sir George,
assuring him that 'the king haith mayd my said lord
[Shrewsbury] his leiffe tenantt general to gyve pardon for lyffe
landes and gooddes', promising Sir George that 'if it pleas you to
cume I shall go with you & be yor sayff cundytte.'[104] Describing
this (or possibly a similar) letter, Sir Brian said that he had
advised Sir George to submit himself to Shrewsbury and to ask
the king's pardon.[105] What Shrewsbury was offering to Sir
George, and to others, was a pardon for past misdeeds in return
for co-operation with the crown in future. Significantly the first

surviving royal pardon is dated 2 November.[106] The importance of these negotiations may be seen from the fact that Sir Brian made a copy of his letter. A few days later Shrewsbury received a letter which he sent on to the king: 'which I beseche your highnes may be kept secret for and yf it shuld be knowne it wold be to the danger of his lyf that sende it'. Almost certainly this was a letter from Sir George offering to co-operate in return for a pardon.[107] Unfortunately Shrewsbury's endeavours were spoilt. Sir Brian Hastings sent a servant with his letter to Sir George: 'certayn of the lord Darcyes folkes that met with hym & so ryped hym & founde the lettre vpon hym & toke bothe the said master Darcye & the letter & brought theym bothe to the lord his father'.[108] As Shrewsbury informed the king, 'I perceyve that of lykelyhode he [Hastings] hath put Sir George Darcy knight in great danger.'[109]

Henry VIII had no doubts about the value of Shrewsbury's attempts to divide the rebels. He had read Shrewsbury's letters and heard the evidence of their bearer 'by the contynew and discouyrs whereof we doo right well perceyve aswel your loyal and noble hart and courage holly bent and given to serue vs, as your wisedome forsight and good circumspection howe you may best doo the same'. Henry, it should be noted, thanked Shrewsbury not only for his loyalty but also for the skilful means by which he expressed it.[110] Shrewsbury's attempt to win over Sir George by means of a pardon anticipates precisely, and may have suggested, the policy that Henry asked Shrewsbury to follow if there was no satisfactory agreement at the second meeting at Doncaster.

At that meeting in December Norfolk and Shrewsbury were compelled by fear of the strength and determination of the rebels to concede far more than had been envisaged, notably a general pardon without exception and the promise of a parliament to be held in York.[111] Thereafter Shrewsbury continued to work for the preservation of order, endeavouring to combine loyal service to the king with greatest possible conciliation of the former rebels. During Bigod's rising in January 1537 Shrewsbury made no attempt to raise his forces but he did maintain close contact with Darcy and his influence does seem to have restrained any temptation Darcy may have had to join in or to tolerate the new rebellion.[112] Shrewsbury was not involved in the seizure of Darcy, Constable and Aske after its failure and also took no part in the subsequent repression in the north undertaken by Norfolk.

Throughout the Pilgrimage of Grace Shrewsbury showed an impeccable loyalty to Henry VIII. No statement why he chose this course of action survives and any explanation of his loyalty must ultimately rest on an assessment of the balance of reasons that might have swayed him. It was by no means unthinkable that he would join the rebels. Several observers would not have been surprised if he had done so. Holinshed's account of the oath that Shrewsbury swore to convince his men that he would remain loyal suggests that there were suspicions: Shrewsbury's anxiety that there should be no doubt about his position implies that some doubt existed.[113] Shrewsbury had many grievances that might have led him to participate in rebellion.[114] He had been reluctant to support Henry VIII's divorce. In March 1531 Shrewsbury (according to Chapuys, the imperial ambassador), referring to his right to hold the crown at the coronation of a queen, declared that as neither he nor any of his family had anything to reproach themselves with, he would now take care not to fall into dishonour by placing the crown on any other head but that of the present queen. Chapuys thought Shrewsbury would not waver: he was a man of honourable and upright principles and showed sincere affection towards the Queen.[115] But for Shrewsbury, Chapuys reported in June 1531, a deputation of counsellors that went to Catherine of Aragon to persuade her to abandon her appeal to Rome would have used stronger language to her than they did.[116] His absence from the coronation of Anne Boleyn on 1 June 1533 was surely deliberate but the presence of his son, Francis, lord Talbot, who bore the sceptre and supported the queen's right arm as his father's deputy, made it less provocative.[117] A religious conservative, Shrewsbury was building a chantry chapel for himself in the parish church at Sheffield in the 1530s; he had attended the trial of a lutheran in 1531 and was to imprison two men for heresy in 1537; and in his will he provided for a thousand priests to say mass for his soul.[118] He was steward of eleven monasteries, joint steward of another, and he was concerned by the fate of at least two others: in early 1537 he made efforts to save Flanesford Priory, Herefordshire, from dissolution.[119] He could not have had any sympathy with the religious articles and injunctions of 1536. The trial of Lord Dacre in 1534 may well have angered

Shrewsbury: Dacre had married one of Shrewsbury's daughters and Shrewsbury twice interceded with Cromwell on her behalf to help her sue to the king for her husband.[120] In May 1536 Shrewsbury lost his Irish lands in Wexford to the king: the letter he wrote to Cromwell in June shows that he did not regard this as a trivial loss.[121] He was also under some pressure to pay certain debts to the king: in October 1535 he had strengthened an earlier commitment and granted his Hallamshire manors to trustees to secure the annual payment of 200 marks to the king. Moreover he evidently felt that he was being asked to repay more than was due.[122] It is a formidable list of grievances.

Nevertheless Shrewsbury remained loyal. He already owed much to Henry VII and Henry VIII. In 1509 he had been appointed steward of Tutbury, Newcastle-under-Lyme, Ashbourne, Wirksworth and other Derbyshire and Staffordshire estates of the Duchy of Lancaster, constable of the castles of Tutbury, Melbourne and High Peak, and master forester of Duffield Frith and Needwood Chase.[123] In 1529 Shrewsbury's son and heir, Francis, lord Talbot, had been appointed to succeed him on his death.[124] In 1525 Shrewsbury and Talbot had been granted a number of Welsh offices in the former earldom of March.[125] Royal service had brought rewards to Shrewsbury. If he assisted in the suppression of rebellion he could expect further grants and indeed he and his son not only received considerable areas of lands in the years from 1537 to 1541 but they were allowed to consolidate their holdings around Sheffield.[126] Shrewsbury's career had been based on loyalty and while he was prepared to defend his interests and to avoid unpalatable commitments, as in 1516, he was not prepared to run the risks of rebellion. His actions in 1536 show that he felt an underlying unity of interest between himself and the crown. His opposition to the divorce, and to religious change, did not extend to Henry VIII himself, to whom there was in any event no alternative, and he was not sufficiently embittered to be led into rebellion. He was not the victim of direct royal oppression. He was allowed to dominate his regional society without any attempt to deprive him of offices or influence traditionally held by his family. There was no royal or ministerial spy in his household. He never spoke with Chapuys or became involved in any intrigue during the break with Rome. His experience on the northern borders in

1522 may have given him a real fear of Scottish intervention
during a rising in the north of England. It is, of course, possible
that Shrewsbury may have calculated that it was not necessary
for him to join the rebellion for its aims to be accomplished: in an
age in which political theory emphasised that rebellions were
divine punishments for wicked rulers, a rebellion that required
Shrewsbury and Norfolk to suppress it was an unequivocal
warning to the king that his ministers and policies were
endangering the unity of the realm. Against this, unlike Norfolk,
Shrewsbury was never suspected of using the rebellion, and the
need to crush it, to improve his position at court. A further
influence on Shrewsbury may have been his ill-health and great
age—he was about 68 years old and within two years of
death—and therefore his desire to do nothing that might
prejudice his duty of leaving his son a strong and untainted
inheritance. But these rationalisations may be wide of the mark.
Ultimately Shrewsbury's attitude was instinctive, determined by
his lifelong loyalty to the Tudors. Once he had decided not to join
the rebels, he would not resort to half-measures or prudential
hesitancy: that might be fruitful during a disputed succession,
but in a rebellion playing a waiting game and making promises
to both sides might have led to his losing control over much of his
country (as the earl of Derby did in much of north and east
Lancashire), especially when many of Shrewsbury's men had
sympathies for the rebels. Shrewsbury's loyalty was rewarded by
the grant of a commission of lieutenancy during the rebellion,
continuing royal favour which permitted the consolidation of his
patrimony, and, in the long run, the reliance of later governments on his son the fifth earl as the premier representative of
central authority in the north in the offices of lord president in the
council in the north and of lieutenant-general during border
campaigns.

The importance of Shrewsbury's loyalty emerges clearly from
a study of his actions during the Pilgrimage of Grace. He
mobilised his forces immediately. His 'dangerous discretion'[127] in
so doing kept his own region free from rebellion and helped to
prevent the reported sympathy of the inhabitants of Bedfordshire
and Cambridgeshire (and possibly also Huntingdonshire) from
issuing in united insurrection.[128] His uncompromising refusal to
mediate between Lord Hussey and the Lincolnshire rebels on the

one hand and the king on the other was of crucial importance in the demoralisation of the rising. His skilful employment of Lancaster Herald led to the dispersal of the Lincolnshire commons. His swift northward march prevented the Yorkshire rebels advancing beyond Doncaster. His conciliatory dealings with the rebels after the first agreement contributed to the avoidance of a renewal of major insurrection. His attempts to restrain and to win over Lord Darcy and his son Sir George divided the rebels and facilitated their eventual repression. Above all the very fact of Shrewsbury's loyalty was of decisive importance, for three reasons. First, the vast size of his estates and their proximity to the areas infested by rebellion made developments in them crucial. Secondly, the veneration that Shrewsbury inspired among his peers no doubt meant that his stand stiffened the resolve of the Henrician earls of Rutland and Huntingdon and helped to remove any temptation that the duke of Norfolk or the earl of Derby might have felt to join the rebellion. Thirdly, the presence of Shrewsbury among the loyalists gravely damaged the claim of the rebels' leaders that they were protesting against evil counsellors of low birth and small reputation and so cooled their ardour to fight the royal armies. In this light the influential comment that 'the king was saved not so much by the loyalty of his friends as by the loyalty of the rebels' may be modified.[129] Shrewsbury's loyalty confronted the rebels with the dilemma that Aske noted when he said that any outcome of a battle would have harmed the rebels. Obviously if the rebels lost, all the gentlemen involved would have been undone. But if the rebels won, if the duke of Norfolk, the earls of Shrewsbury, Rutland, Huntingdon and Surrey, Lord Talbot and others had been defeated and killed, 'what grete capitains, counsailles, noble bloodes, dredde persons in foren realms & catholique knyghtes had wantid & ben lost in this realme, what displeasur shulde this haue ben to the king & publique welthe & what comforth to thauncient enemies of this realme'.[130] The loyalty of Shrewsbury deprived the rebels of any hope that a military victory could serve their purpose. If Shrewsbury had supported the rebels Henry VIII and Cromwell would undoubtedly have been faced by a much greater threat. Cromwell's astonishing eulogy and Henry VIII's many letters of thanks testify to the value that they attached to Shrewsbury's

attitude. A rare consensus of historians highlights the crucial role
played by Shrewsbury. Froude argued that Shrewsbury's
'courage and fidelity on this occasion perhaps saved Henry's
crown'.[131] 'With his support', wrote R.B. Smith, 'they [the
rebels] might have won the day. Without it they had only a
slender chance of success'.[132] M.E. James saw Shrewsbury as 'the
man whose support could have taken the rebellion a long way
towards its transformation into a broad movement of political
opposition which the king himself could scarcely have
resisted'.[133] Current interpretations of the Pilgrimage have
emphasised the tremendous significance of the decisions taken by
a small number of key individuals.[134] Because of the extent of his
power, the location of his estates and the respect in which he was
universally held, Shrewsbury must be seen as the most important
of that group. Holinshed was perceptive as well as pithy when he
wrote of Shrewsbury 'which way he was inclined, it was thought
verily the game were likely to go'.[135]

Notes

1 PRO SP1/106/fo. 252 (*LP*, XI 536).
2 PRO SP1/106/fo. 248 (*LP*, XI 533).
3 BL Egerton MS 2603 fo. 20 (*LP*, XI 537).
4 The most important recent discussions are: A.G. Dickens, 'Secular and
   religious motivation in the Pilgrimage of Grace', *Studies in Church History*, iv
   (1967), pp. 39-64 (reprinted in A.G. Dickens, *Reformation Studies* (1982),
   pp. 57-82); J.J. Scarisbrick, *Henry VIII* (1968), pp. 339-48; C.S.L. Davies,
   'The Pilgrimage of Grace reconsidered', *Past and Present*, xl (1968), pp.
   54-76 (reprinted in P.A. Slack, ed., *Popular Protest and the Social Order in
   Early Modern England* (Cambridge, 1984), pp. 16-38); C. Haigh, *The Last
   Days of the Lancashire Monasteries and the Pilgrimage of Grace*, Chetham Society,
   3rd series, xvii (1969); M.E. James, 'Obedience and dissent in Henrician
   England: the Lincolnshire rebellion, 1536', *Past and Present*, xlviii (1970),
   pp. 3-78; R.B. Smith, *Land and Politics in the England of Henry VIII: the West
   Riding of Yorkshire, 1530-46* (Oxford, 1970), ch. v.; M. Bowker,
   'Lincolnshire 1536: heresy, schism or religious discontent?', *Studies in
   Church History*, ix (1972), pp. 195-212; A.J. Fletcher, *Tudor Rebellions* (2nd
   ed. 1973, 3rd. ed. 1983); C. Haigh, *Reformation and Resistance in Tudor
   Lancashire* (Cambridge, 1975), pp. 118-38; M.E. James, 'English Politics
   and the concept of honour 1485-1642', *Past and Present Supplement*, iii
   (1979), pp. 37-41; M. Bowker, *The Henrician Reformation: the Diocese of
   Lincoln under John Longland 1521-1547* (Cambridge, 1981). For more

general discussions of rebellions see C.S.L. Davies, 'Les révoltes populaires en Angleterre (1500–1700)', *Annales, ESC,* xxiv (i) (1969), pp. 24–59; 'Peasant revolt in France and England: a comparison', *Agricultural History Review,* xxi (1973), pp. 123–34; P.H. Williams, 'Rebellion and revolution in early modern England', in M.R.D. Foot, ed., *War and Society,* (1973), pp. 225–40; *The Tudor Regime* (Oxford, 1979), ch. x, esp. pp. 316–23.

5 Especially Davies, 'The Pilgrimage of Grace', James, 'Obedience and dissent', Haigh, *Reformation and resistance,* Smith, *Land and Politics.*

6 James, 'Obedience and dissent', p. 7.

7 G.R. Elton, 'Tudor Government: the points of contact. II The Council', *Transactions of the Royal Historical Society,* 5th series, xxv (1975), p. 222; *Reform and Reformation* (1977), pp. 260–71; 'Politics and the Pilgrimage of Grace', in B. Malament, ed., *After the reformation: essays in honour of J.H. Hexter* (Pennsylvania, 1980), pp. 25–56 (reprinted in G.R. Elton, ed., *Studies in Tudor and Stuart Politics and Government* (Cambridge, 3 vols, 1974–83), iii. 183–215). For a rebuttal see C.S.L. Davies, 'Popular religion and the Pilgrimage of Grace', in A.J. Fletcher and J. Stevenson, *Order and Disorder in Early Modern England 1500–1750* (Cambridge, 1985).

8 Scarisbrick, *Henry VIII,* pp. 339–48, esp. p. 342.

9 Smith, *Land and Politics,* p. 176; cf. R. Holinshed, *Chronicles,* (6 vols, 1807–8 ed.), iii. 800–2.

10 Holinshed, *Chronicles,* iii. 800–2.

11 PRO SP1/106/fo. 282 (*LP,* XI 560).

12 PRO SP1/106/fo. 252 (*LP,* XI 536).

13 Longleat, Nathaniel Johnston, MS Lives of the early lords of Sheffield ... p. 210; G.A.J. Hodgett, *Tudor Lincolnshire, History of Lincolnshire,* vi (Lincoln, 1975), p. 30.

14 PRO SP1/107/fo. 74 (*LP,* XI 592); PRO SP1/110/fo. 38 (*LP,* XI 929 (ii)).

15 PRO SP1/107/fo. 71 (*LP,* XI 589).

16 PRO SP1/107/fo. 65 (*LP,* XI 587).

17 PRO SP1/107/fo. 70 (*LP,* XI 588).

18 PRO SP1/110/fos. 73–76 (*LP,* XI 930).

19 James, 'Obedience and dissent', pp. 52–5, 57–62, 64–5.

20 Ibid., pp. 52, 58–61.

21 Elton, 'Politics and the Pilgrimage of Grace', p. 36.

22 I intend to write elsewhere on the role of Hussey and on the reality of popular violence in the Lincolnshire rising.

23 PRO SP1/106/fo. 283 (*LP* XI 561).

24 PRO SP1/107/fo. 67 (*LP,* XI 587).

25 PRO SP1/107/fo. 71 (*LP,* XI 589).

26 Talbot Papers A 61 (printed in R.B. Merriman, ed., *Life and Letters of Thomas Cromwell* (Oxford, 2 vols, 1902), ii. 33) (*LP,* XI, 612).

27 *LP,* XI 642, 656.

28 PRO SP1/108/fo. 39 (*LP,* XI 694); *LP,* XI 854. Cf. PRO SP1/107/fos. 99, 118 (*LP,* XI 615, 625); PRO SP1/108/fo. 92 (*LP,* XI 771).

29 PRO SP1/108/fo. 7 (*LP,* XI 673); PRO SP1/107/fos. 138, 154 (*LP,* XI 647, 662).

30 PRO SP1/110/fo. 38 (*LP,* XI 565).

31 *Ibid.*; PRO SP1/117/fo. 191 (*LP*, XII i 783). (I owe the last suggestion to Mr R.W. Hoyle).
32 PRO SP1/107/fos. 85, 88 (*LP*, XI 605, 606).
33 PRO SP1/110/fo. 45 (xvii) (*LP*, XI 687).
34 PRO SP1/108/fo. 149 (*LP*, XI 749).
35 PRO SP1/108/fo. 185 (*LP*, XI 768 (i)).
36 BL Cotton MS App. L fo. 63 (*LP*, XI 846).
37 *Ibid.*; PRO SP1/119/fo. 235 (*LP*, XII ii 226).
38 Chatsworth, Clifford Letters, 13. I owe this reference to Mr R.W. Hoyle: I am most grateful to him for showing me his transcript of this document and of that cited in note 62.
39 *LP*, XI 588, 615, 621, 808 (but cf. 846).
40 I hope to explore these points further elsewhere.
41 PRO SP1/107/fo. 74 (*LP*, XI 592); PRO SP1/110/fo. 38 (*LP*, XI 929 (ii)).
42 PRO SP1/110/fo. 40 (vii) (*LP*, XI 604).
43 PRO SP1/107/fo. 154 (*LP*, XI 662).
44 PRO SP1/110/fo. 47 (xxi) (*LP*, XI 675).
45 PRO SP1/108/fos. 39, 129 (*LP*, XI 694 (i), 740).
46 PRO SP1/108/fo. 197 (*LP*, XI 774).
47 Holinshed, *Chronicles*, iii. 800-2.
48 G. Mattingly, *Catherine of Aragon* (1942), p. 288.
49 J.C. Cox, 'William Stapleton and the Pilgrimage of Grace', *Transactions of the East Riding Antiquarian Society*, x (1903 for 1902), pp. 80-106 (*LP*, XII i 392 p. 190). Cf. PRO SP1/113/70 (b) (*LP*, XI 1046).
50 PRO SP1/109/fo. 96 (*LP*, XI 864).
51 PRO SP1/109/fos. 214-29 (*LP*, XI 884); *LP*, XI 1024.
52 PRO SP1/118/fo. 189. See also *LP*, XII i 944 (2).
53 Smith, *Land and Politics*, p. 197. Cf. criticisms by F.W. Brooks, *Journal of Ecclesiastical History*, xxiii (1972), pp. 280-1.
54 Williams, *Tudor Regime*, p. 320.
55 Holinshed, *Chronicles*, iii. 800-2.
56 PRO SP1/106/fo. 65 (*LP*, XI 587).
57 Holinshed, *Chronicles*, iii 800-2.
58 Davies, 'Popular religion and the Pilgrimage of Grace'.
59 M.E. James, 'The first earl of Cumberland (1493-1542) and the decline of northern feudalism', *Northern History*, i (1966), p. 47.
60 *Ibid.*; Holinshed, *Chronicles*, iii. 800-2.
61 R.W. Hoyle, 'The first earl of Cumberland: a northern peer reassessed', paper read at the Institute of Historical Research, University of London, 6 February 1984.
62 *LP*, XI 826; PRO SP1/109/fos. 62-7 (*LP*, XI 850); Chatsworth, Clifford Letters, 41 (I owe this reference to Mr. R.W. Hoyle).
63 BL Cotton MS App. L fo 63 (*LP*, XI 846); PRO SP1/109/fo. 62 (*LP*, XI 850).
64 PRO SP1/115/fos. 253-4 (*LP*, XII (i) 393).
65 This may be inferred from PRO SP1/109/fo. 96 (*LP*, XI 864).
66 *Ibid.*
67 PRO SP1/109/fos. 221, 252 (*LP*, XI 887, 901).

68 Bodleian Library, MS Jesus c. 74 fo. 323v. (Cf. Lord Herbert of Cherbury, *Life and Reigne of Henry VIII* (1649), pp. 414-5). I am most grateful to Mr R.W. Hoyle for following my vague suggestion of searching this volume (my knowledge of which I owe to Mr P.J. Gwyn) for information about the Pilgrimage of Grace and for bringing to my attention his discovery of fos. 322-27v therein, a series of notes and transcripts of letters most probably once part of the Cotton MSS and now lost, which he is editing for *Northern History*.
69 PRO SP1/110/fos. 6-7 (*LP*, XI 904).
70 PRO SP1/109/fo. 96 (*LP*, XI 864).
71 PRO SP1/110/fos. 6-7 (*LP*, XI 904).
72 PRO SP1/112/fo. 131 (*LP*, XI 1241). Cf. M.H. and R.H. Dodds, *The Pilgrimage of Grace 1536-37 and the Exeter Conspiracy 1538* (2 vols, 1915), i. 116.
73 PRO SP1/109/fo. 62 (*LP*, XI, 850).
74 PRO SP1/120/fos. 35-6 (*LP*, XII i 1175).
75 PRO SP1/112/fo. 47 (*State Papers*, i. 518; *LP*, XI 1226).
76 PRO SP1/109/fos. 251-2 (*LP*, XI 900-1); PRO SP1/110/fo. 35 (*LP*, XI 928); PRO SP1/111/fos. 211, 224, 233 (*LP*, XI 1134, 1140, 1153); PRO E/36/121 (*LP*, XI 947); *LP*, XI 922.
77 Smith, *Land and Politics*, pp. 147-50, 193-4.
78 PRO SP1/110/fos. 73-6 (*LP*, XI 930); PRO SP1/111/fos. 41, 111-18, 216 (*LP*, XI 1028, 1063, 1136 (2)).
79 PRO E/36/118 (*LP*, XI 1064).
80 PRO SP1/112/fos. 85-105 (*State Papers*, i 511; *LP*, XI 1227).
81 PRO SP1/112/fos. 79-82 (*State Papers*, i 519; *LP*, XI 1225).
82 PRO SP1/111/fo. 43 (*LP*, XI 1029).
83 *LP*, XII i 944 (2).
84 PRO SP1/110/fo. 101 (*LP*, XI 949).
85 PRO SP1/111/fos. 94, 225, 233 (*LP*, XI 1058, 1141, 1153).
86 *LP*, I ii 2246 (4 ii), 2740.
87 *LP*, II i 2735.
88 Smith, *Land and Politics*, p. 67.
89 J. Hunter, *South Yorkshire: the History and Topography of the Deanery of Doncaster* (2 vols, 1828-31), ii. 162-3.
90 PRO SP1/122/fos. 62-84 (*LP*, XII ii 186 (40)).
91 Smith, *Land and Politics*, p. 194.
92 Dodds, *The Pilgrimage of Grace*, i. 294.
93 Smith, *Land and Politics*, p. 194.
94 Hunter, *South Yorkshire*, ii. 162-3.
95 PRO SP1/113/fo. 62 (*LP*, XI 1042).
96 *LP*, XII i 81.
97 PRO SP1/118/fo. 192 (*LP*, XII 946 (108)).
98 PRO SP1/119/fo. 4v (*LP*, XII 1022) (very faded MS); *LP*, XI 729.
99 PRO SP1/110/fos. 6-7 (*LP*, XI 909).
100 Sheffield City Libraries, Bacon-Frank MS 3/1 fo. 315, and fair copy Bacon-Frank MS 3/2; Chatsworth and Longleat, fair copies in N. Johnston, MS Lives of the early lords of Sheffield; eighteenth-century copies in BL Add.

MS 18446 pp. 28-9 and BL Egerton 3402. (I owe the last reference to Mr R.W. Hoyle).

101 PRO SP1/111/fos. 74-5 (*LP*, XI 1047).
102 PRO SP1/113/fo. 78 (*LP*, XI 1408).
103 PRO SP1/31/fo. 223 (*LP*, IV i 541).
104 PRO SP1/111/fo. 40 (*LP*, XI 1027).
105 PRO SP1/111/fos. 97-9 (*LP*, XI 1059).
106 A.G. Dickens, 'Royal pardons for the Pilgrimage of Grace', *Yorkshire Archaeological Journal*, xxxiii (1939), p. 401.
107 PRO SP1/111/fo. 41-2 (*LP*, XI 1028).
108 PRO SP1/111/fos. 97-9 (*LP*, XI 1059).
109 PRO SP1/113/fo. 121 (*LP*, XI 1067).
110 PRO SP1/111/fos. 111-18 (*LP*, XI 1063).
111 Bodleian Library, MS Jesus c. 74 fos. 325-6; PRO SP1/109/fos. 253-4 (*State Papers*, i 496; *LP*, XI 902 (miscalendared)); PRO SP1/112/fos. 116, 180-1, 184-9 (*LP*, XI 1223-4, 1271-2, 1267); P.L. Hughes and J.F. Larkin, *Tudor Royal Proclamations* (3 vols, 1964-9), i. 246-7.
112 PRO SP1/114/fos. 152, 186, 214, 233, 235 (*LP*, XII i 104, 135, 141, 169-70); PRO SP1/115/fos. 51, 75 (*LP*, XII i 226, 247).
113 Holinshed, *Chronicles*, iii. 800-2.
114 James, 'Obedience and dissent', pp. 62-3.
115 *Calendar of State Papers, Spanish, 1531-33*, no. 646, p. 80 (*LP*, V 120).
116 *Ibid.*
117 *LP*, V 601, 701, 396, 562.
118 *LP*, V 148; XII ii 436; PRO PROB 11/26.
119 *See below*, pp. 142, 148; BL Add. MS 11042 fo. 92.
120 *LP*, VII 927, 897.
121 *LP*, X 1198.
122 *See below*, pp. 149-50; Sheffield City Libraries, Arundel Castle MS SD 112; PRO SP1/85/fos. 72-3 (*LP*, VII 991); *LP*, VII 1047.
123 See below, p. 146.
124 See below, p. 146.
125 See below, p. 146.
126 See below, pp. 141, 175-6, 178.
127 Herbert, *Life and Reigne of Henry VIII*, p. 412.
128 Bodleian Library, MS Jesus c. 74 fos. 322-2v.
129 Scarisbrick, *Henry VIII*, p. 342.
130 PRO SP1/120/fo. 36 (*LP*, XII i 1175).
131 J.A. Froude, *History of England from the fall of Wolsey to the death of Elizabeth* (12 vols, 1893 ed.), ii. 522.
132 Smith, *Land and Politics*, pp. 175-6.
133 James, 'Obedience and Dissent', p. 63.
134 Davies, 'The Pilgrimage of Grace reconsidered', p. 74.
135 Holinshed, *Chronicles*, iii. 800.

3 The fifth earl of Shrewsbury in mid-Tudor politics

The involvement of Francis Talbot, fifth earl of Shrewsbury, in national political life in the reign of Henry VIII was limited. He attended some sessions of the Reformation Parliament. He assisted his father in the repression of the Pilgrimage of Grace. After his father's death in 1538 he was an infrequent attender at court. He was a leading military commander on the Scottish borders in 1544-5. Military service, the putting down of rebellion, local government and occasional appearances at court are the principal themes here. This should not be surprising. It was unnecessary for noblemen of ancient standing and possessed of large landed estates to serve the king constantly at court.[1] In this light the prominence in early Tudor politics of men newly ennobled and of lesser gentry origin with estates to build up is something of an illusion. It does not support generalisations about a 'rise of the gentry' or a 'middle-class government' or a 'decline of the nobility'. The death of Henry VIII in 1547 and the accession first of a boy king and then by a woman after a disputed succession produced a different political situation in which noble involvement was much greater. In such times noblemen would not only wish, but see themselves as bound, to take an unusual interest in matters of state. The contrast is not an absolute one: in September 1549, in the month after large commons' rebellions and just before the downfall of Protector Somerset, Shrewsbury still invited the earl of Huntingdon to join him 'to kyll a stagg or too'.[2] Nevertheless it was in the years after 1547 that Shrewsbury emerged from relative obscurity and realised his latent political influence. He became a privy councillor and lord president of the council in the north in 1549, the year in which the imperial ambassador described him as 'one of the most powerful men in the kingdom'.[3]

Although not an executor of Henry VIII's will and not yet a councillor, Shrewsbury was much involved in ceremonial in the weeks after Henry's death, most significantly at the creation of Edward Seymour, marquess of Hertford, as duke of Somerset: in this way old nobles such as Shrewsbury accepted the new. Moreover Shrewsbury's participation in these ceremonies suggests that he approved of Somerset's advancement at the expense of his rival, Thomas Wriothesley, earl of Southampton.[4] Shrewsbury's active service in the most important aspect of Somerset's rule, war against Scotland, and his assiduous attendance of the House of Lords modifies the view that these years saw 'the eclipse of the ancient peerage'.[5] It is not wholly accurate to claim that in these years, and especially in 1547–8, Somerset assumed quasi-regal power—'effectively Somerset was king'—and behaved in a high-handed, autocratic manner.[6] Somerset's dominance was illusory: his power appeared great in 1547–8 because it was largely accepted. The men whom he sharply rebuked were not great men. In any serious matter, such as the imprisonment of Bishop Gardiner, he took care not to act alone. In 1549 he defended himself by claiming that the earl of Warwick was as responsible for the errors of the government as he had been, a reply that Warwick did not take as self-evident nonsense.[7] Any important political struggle would soon visibly involve most noblemen and politicians. Such a matter was the downfall of Thomas Seymour, Somerset's brother, in early 1549.[8] It was then that Shrewsbury was first sworn in as a councillor: his first recorded attendance was on 6 January.[9] He was soon regarded as one of the most influential councillors: when Seymour's associate Sir William Sharington wrote begging for his life on 20 February, he addressed his letter to the earl of Southampton, the secretary (William Cecil) and Shrewsbury.[10] Shrewsbury took part in several of the dealings that the council had with Seymour and was one of the signatories of his death warrant.[11] Seymour had never expected anything from Shrewsbury. In his efforts to recruit support Seymour had encouraged the earl of Rutland to see himself as Shrewsbury's equal and implied that Shrewsbury was Rutland's enemy: Rutland testified that Seymour 'thout me to be so frended in my contry, as I was able enhowe to matche with my Lord Shrosbery; I seyd I coulde not tell; how beyt, I thowte my lord wolde do me no wronge'. It is not surprising that Shrewsbury was brought on to the council at this time and that he acquiesced in the destruction of Seymour.[12]

After spending much of the spring at court, Shrewsbury may well have been despatched home following reports of popular unrest in southern England: on 3 July the imperial ambassador reported that the earl of Arundel and Lord Russell and others had been sent to speak with the commons, 'each one in that part of the country to which he belongs'.[13] It is possible that Shrewsbury resorted to Arundel's technique of inviting the rebels to his castle, providing an abundance of food and drink, especially beer, of no small importance in years of high grain prices, listening to their complaints, ordering enclosing gentlemen to change their ways and setting ringleaders up by their heels.[14] However this may be, Shrewsbury's area of influence—Derbyshire, southern Yorkshire, Nottinghamshire, Shropshire—remained quiet, which was to his credit. On 19 July he was asked by the council to inform the commons that they would be 'partakers of all suche things as have byn, or shalbe, graunted to any of them that be in any parte of the realme in this unlawfull maner assembled', a remarkable admission of weakness.[15] In early August he was asked to prepare captains and men to be ready to march at an hour's notice if necessary against the rebels in Norfolk. By beginning the letter with news of the deaths of Lord Sheffield, Sir John Clere and another gentleman called Cornwallis, the councillors were showing Shrewsbury just how dangerous this rising was for men of property and making it clear how irresponsible it would be for men like Shrewsbury to think of tacitly encouraging risings that (in so far as they were directed against the upper social groups) were against new landowners on the make rather than against old-established families.[16]

During the rebellions and most probably prompted by the disorders of government which they revealed, the earls of Warwick, Southampton and Arundel and Sir Richard Southwell and Sir Thomas Arundell began plotting against Somerset.[17] Shrewsbury does not seem to have been involved. The tone of his letter to the earl of Huntingdon in September, inviting him to hunt with Shrewsbury, does not suggest much concern, unless his invitation is taken as a covert appeal.[18] It may

well be that the counsellors who overthrew Somerset in October
were originally intending merely (as they claimed on 21
October) to have sought the 'reformacion of thynges' and
'mynded quyetlye to haue communed with him' but were then
provoked into firmer measures by Somerset's efforts to raise
forces and to hold on to the young king Edward.[19] Somerset
certainly attempted to recruit Shrewsbury, appealing to him on
6 October to join him at Hampton Court.[20] As Shrewsbury
reached London the following day, the imperial ambassador
called him 'one of the most powerful men in the kingdom'.[21]
Clearly his attitude would be important. If he had decided to join
Somerset, the Protector might have delayed disbanding the four
thousand men that he was alleged to have raised to defend
himself.[22] But Shrewsbury joined the large majority of
counsellors that was opposed to Somerset, attending their
meeting at the Mercers' Hall on 6 October, and those at which
Somerset's abduction of Edward to Windsor was discussed and
letters to Somerset, and Paget and Cranmer, both influential
with Somerset, were framed.[23] He was also present at Windsor
between 13 and 15 October when Somerset and his supporters
were sent to the Tower.[24]

It is possible to do no more than speculate why Shrewsbury did
not join Somerset. He had been poorly treated by Somerset
during the Haddington campaign in 1548.[25] He probably
blamed Somerset for the disturbances of 1549. He very likely
sympathised with plans to limit his authority and was provoked
by his resistance in October. He may well have sympathised with
the religious conservatism of some of his leading critics and with
their hopes of making Princess Mary regent. That is what the
earls of Arundel and Southampton attempted to achieve. One
chronicler saw them as so incensed against Somerset that they
wished to have him, and Warwick, whom they saw as his
accomplice, executed. But Warwick, aided by the earl of
Wiltshire and by Archbishop Cranmer, managed to turn the
tables. Arundel and Southampton lost their influence: both were
expelled from the council and Arundel was certainly put under
house arrest.[26] It may be significant that it was in early
December, before these struggles were resolved, that Shrewsbury
was appointed lord president of the council in the north (the first
reference is 8 December and he was in his country just before 10

December).[27] His departure may have been sudden: on 20 November he had been named one of a group of councillors two of whom would have to sign financial warrants, which does not suggest an early departure.[28] The timing of Shrewsbury's appointment and his disappearance from court strongly suggest that Warwick and his friends were making use of the need for strong rule in the north to remove from court one of the conservatives and potential supporters of Southampton and Arundel. Shrewsbury replaced Robert Holgate, archbishop of York, as lord president. Holgate had proved unable to deal effectively with the Seamer rebellion in August 1549. But he later claimed (although with some inaccuracies in dating) that it was Warwick who 'touke such displeasure with me that . . . he put me furth of the rowme of the President'.[29] As Holgate's religious views were protestant, his replacement by Shrewsbury may well have been welcomed by catholic councillors even though it deprived them of an immediate ally on the council. Perhaps they did not yet realise what Warwick had in store for them.

In order to confirm his victory over Southampton and Arundel, Warwick attempted to repair his relations with Somerset, and in the early months of 1550 there was a gradual reconciliation, which went further than self-interest alone would have dictated.[30] It was ceremonially emphasised by the celebration on 3 June (followed by prolonged festivities) of the previously arranged marriage between Warwick's son Lord Lisle and Somerset's daughter Anne.[31] Yet even then mistrust lingered. Warwick did not attend the marriage: he 'suspecteth he should haue ben betraied there and therfore cam not thither'.[32] Gradually Warwick and Somerset quarreled, largely, it seems, Somerset's fault. Warwick attempted to prevent a renewed rift by warning Richard Whalley, Somerset's steward, on 25 June that by taking up the cause of Bishop Gardiner (then imprisoned) and Arundel, Somerset would provoke his own ruin. Above all Warwick cautioned that Somerset was not 'in that credit and best opinion with the kings majesty as he believeth . . . and by some fondly persuaded'.[33] As Warwick's influence increased in the autumn so discord between him and Somerset grew.[34] By mid-February 1551 rumours that Somerset and Warwick 'shulde not be in full and perfecte amytie' were current.[35] At this time Whalley was examined 'for perswading divers nobles of the realme to make the duke of Somerset protectour at the next parleament'.[36] On 1 March Warwick and Somerset were reported in competition to marry a daughter to the young duke of Suffolk.[37] Early that month they 'fell into dispute in open council', although the matter was soon calmed down. Later, when a gentleman from Somerset's household claimed that Somerset was better qualified to govern than Warwick, Warwick had him imprisoned.[38] It was in this climate that Gardiner was deprived of his bishopric.[39] On 28 April the imperial ambassador cited reports that Somerset had rebelled against the king's counsellors.[40]

It is against this background that the actions and attitudes of Shrewsbury must be appreciated. Immediately after his appointment as lord president of the council in the north Shrewsbury seems to have been on good terms with the new conciliar government. He willingly sent his son Lord Talbot to France as one of a number of hostages in April 1550 while peace terms were being negotiated.[41] Moreover the council excused Shrewsbury from attendance at the annual celebrations of the order of the garter on St George's day and licensed him to retain a hundred men.[42] But such amity was short-lived and relations between Shrewsbury and the council became increasingly strained in mid-1550. Possibly Shrewsbury was angry at the way that fortunes had swung at court after his departure northwards in early December 1549. R.R. Reid suggested that Warwick distrusted Shrewsbury from the start, having 'no mind to allow all civil and military power in the north to be concentrated in the hands of the catholics'. Shrewsbury, she claimed, was forced to give up the lieutenancy, 'which remained in abeyance despite the troubled state of the country', to admit to the vice-presidency of the council in the north Warwick's ally, Wharton, and to allow Warwick to take for himself the wardenry of the east and middle marches and a substantial grant of lands from the confiscated Percy estates in Yorkshire and Northumberland, then in the crown's possession. Some of these assertions are incorrect—the lieutenancy was usually a temporary military command that went into abeyance during periods of peace; Shrewsbury was apparently given the chance to veto Wharton's appointment if he wished—but there was clearly an atmosphere between Warwick and Shrewsbury.[43] Writing to Shrewsbury on 25 June,

Humfrey Bentley, one of Shrewsbury's servants, mentioned 'the truth of the matter betwixt th'erle of Warwyk & your Lordeshypp'. What 'the matter' was was not specified but 'for answer off the sead matter' Warwick, it had been (wrongly) rumoured, was going to travel north.[44] Possibly connected with this was the rough handling that James Clarke, one of Shrewsbury's auditors, experienced at the hands of Warwick's men that spring. Clarke had been connected with one Dunche, a former auditor of the mints at York who had been imprisoned in the Tower and then bound in 1549. Clarke reported that he had just spent some time imprisoned in the Fleet. While he had been there

> by comaundement of my lorde of Warwyke, my closett was broken up and all my bokes so handled and tossed together with thos bokes which were in the bagge, which yor lordship sent up to the counsaill, with wett and yvell handlying ar so evell and rent, that I shall be forced not onelie to make your lordships bokes newe agayne but also provide newe bokes as the statutes and iiii partes of the byble whiche thing shalbe done out of hande.

He saw himself as 'one tastyng the force of cloked malyce and therebye dryven to the shore'.[45] It is not fully clear what this amounts to: it may be reasonably assumed that Shrewsbury would be annoyed by such treatment of one of his servants. Moreover he would have been further annoyed at this time by the peremptory request to him and other officers of the council in the north to choose a residence nearer the borders.[46]

Shrewsbury's dissatisfaction fused with that of another nobleman, the earl of Derby. Already on 17 August 1550 Derby had been reported as refusing to go to Newcastle to meet Warwick for discussions, fearing that he might be tricked.[47] On 1 September it was reported that Shrewsbury and Derby had a quarrel and Warwick and Paget over the boundaries of their countries with the extent of their jurisdiction. Derby was summoned to appear at court but refused to come before the next parliament. 'It is feared that some disorder may follow on his appearance at that season, because the said Lords Derby and Shrewsbury are powerful lords, of ancient lineage, faith and religion, and beloved of the people.' They were reported to be intending to propose in the next parliament that Henry VIII's will be strictly observed—especially in religion— until Edward came of age.[48] The earl of Arundel was said to be supporting them. At the same time the council was recalling five hundred footmen from Boulogne and Scotland to go north and west against Derby and Shrewsbury to remove any obstacle that they might set in religious matters. No more was heard of this until the new year—although it may be significant that there was no parliament until early 1552. In January 1551 the imperial ambassador reported that the councillors feared that religious disunity and popular dissatisfaction would lead to disturbances. They had decided to impose one form of religion and to ensure that it was strictly observed. 'This will also provide a weapon', he added, 'to be used against certain great lords still holding the old religion like Derby and Shrewsbury.'[49] On 1 March certain persons had told the ambassador that if there were no war against France, the English would turn their arms against some of the great lords in the north and other parts who were still of the old religion, naming Shrewsbury and Derby.[50] Some interpreted the appointment of the marquess of Dorset as the king's lieutenant in the north as directed against these lords: Dorset was said to be about to surround them or at least to keep an eye on them.[51] On 19 April the council sent a clerk to the north to request Derby and Shrewsbury to come to court.[52] It was rumoured that fifteen to twenty well-manned ships in the Thames were to be sent north to make a further attempt to attack Derby and Shrewsbury.[53] On 21 April the imperial ambassador wrote that the council was frightened of Derby and Shrewsbury, who were powerful and popular not only among the people but secretly with many prominent personages. The councillors had failed to have them surprised and arrested. They had ordered them to come to court. But Shrewsbury and Derby had excused themselves on the grounds that the times were suspicious and said that they thought it better for the king's service not to leave their lands yet. If the council (they added) was governing the kingdom well, they were very glad to hear it, and if not, they would not say what might hereafter come to pass. It was believed that these two lords could raise very large armed forces.[54] By mid-May these stories were current abroad. It was bruited that 'betwixt the noblemen of the realm is like to be a great sedition, especially in the north ... the marquess of Dorset with a great company is sent thitherward, and to be immediately followed by the earl of Warwick with all his power'. Shrewsbury was said to have been deprived of his office and Derby commanded to give up his title in the Isle of Man. Lurid rumours predicted 'the ruin of the king'.[55] On 12 May the council issued express orders to the constables to seize and to make an example of any man who said that there was discord between Shrewsbury and Derby on the one hand and the council on the other.[56] The weight of evidence convinces beyond doubt that there was a serious and growing difference between the council and its representatives in the north and north-west. It was a state of affairs pregnant with risks of civil war.

Up to March-April 1551 there is no sign that this quarrel had any connection with the increasing animosity between Warwick and Somerset at the centre. Indeed Shrewsbury refused to give his support to either. On 17 February he wrote to Huntingdon that he was convinced that rumours of dissension between them were untrue. Moreover he roundly declared 'I never intended to take partie with any noble man agaynst other but to my power to increase there frenshippes and to serue the kinges majestie according to my dutye.'[57] But this attitude was to change, probably prompted by religion. On 9 April the imperial ambassador reported that people were beginning to whisper that Somerset would not object to abandoning the new religion, although its introduction had been his responsibility, and taking up the old again.[58] Somerset's revised religious ideas may well have been seen sympathetically by Shrewsbury and Derby, especially after the deprivation of Bishop Gardiner in March 1551. The imperial ambassador repeatedly emphasised their conservative religious views.[59]

Whatever their reasons, Shrewsbury, Derby and Somerset reached an agreement in March-April, marking the fusion of the differences between Somerset and Warwick with those between Shrewsbury and Derby and the council, especially Warwick. The evidence for this is circumstantial, but telling. One of the charges made against Somerset by Sir Thomas Palmer in October 1551 was that 'the duke once minded and made him prevey to raise the north' on St George's day.[60] Somerset's servant Whalley appears to have been trying to enlist 'divers nobles' in February 1551.[61] Somerset made potentially dangerous contacts with Derby. A marriage alliance was arranged between Somerset's daughter Jane with Derby's son

Lord Strange, and Somerset asked Strange 'to be his spie in al mattieres of my doynges and saynges'.[62] When Somerset was arrested in October 1551 the imperial ambassador at first reported that Strange had been arrested too and that Derby and Shrewsbury had had something to do with the plot.[63] If Derby and Shrewsbury were to raise the north for Somerset they would obviously have to remain there as their efforts would be hampered if they were compelled to come up to court and stay there. On 24 March Derby had been relieved of the obligation to attend court on St George's day, significantly 'according to his request made unto the Duke of Somerset'. Was Somerset furthering the conspiracy?[64] Against this, however, on the same day the council wrote to Shrewsbury refusing him permission to come up and informing him that the council 'for the good order and quietnesse' of the north preferred him to remain there 'and attende to the good governaunce of that cuntrey with like wisedome and circumspeccion that hitherto your Lordship hath doon'. It is of course possible that Shrewsbury had deliberately applied for permission to come up in the knowledge that Somerset would see to it that the request was refused.[65] Certainly the council repeatedly summoned Derby and Shrewsbury to come up in April.[66] It is tempting here to see some collusion between Somerset, Shrewsbury and Derby. The political and religious ramifications of this alliance are clearly seen in the rumoured involvement of Princess Mary. One Benet of Ware, examined on 24 April, 'confessed that a certen talke ther was emonges them howe my ladie Marye wolde goo westwarde to th'erl of Shrewsburye'.[67] This was the sort of situation that could produce a religious civil war.

It is little wonder that Warwick countered firmly. Dorset was to go north in early April.[68] Councillors were to convince the world of their unity by banquetting in public.[69] It became an offence to mention the possibility of discord between Derby and Shrewsbury and the council.[70] Somerset's influence in the council was reduced: on 12 May he was deprived of his separate table.[71] In these precautions Warwick was successful: nothing came of the projected coup. Moreover Warwick achieved a reconciliation with Shrewsbury and Derby. Derby arrived at court on 31 May, Shrewsbury on 5 June.[72] Perhaps Shrewsbury felt that he was in some way incriminated in Somerset's plots and

wished to secure his position by openly, if superficially, co-
operating with Warwick. Loyalist sentiments remained strong in
a decade of popular rebellion and religious diversity. There was
always the prospect of a more favourable moment for political
action. It was, however, a reconciliation with reservations. Derby
arrived 'with a goodly compeny of men and horssys', Shrewsbury
with "vii˟ hors and afor hym xl welvet cotts and chynes and in
ys own leveray'.[73] No doubt they brought their men as an
insurance against any possible arrest: some believed that the
council was intending to keep them at court.[74] At a time of no
special ceremonial, these numbers were intimidatingly large.
When Shrewsbury was summoned up in late 1552 the council
thought it prudent to 'frendlye signifye vnto you that ye shall doo
well to order that at yor beinge here yor nomber may be the fewer
to attende vpon you ordinarylye here in the courte', possibly a
delayed comment on the numbers Shrewsbury brought in June
1551.[75] Meanwhile Shrewsbury was keeping his options open,
making contacts with Somerset's men and informing Warwick of
some of what he was told. On 26 October Shrewsbury was asked
'to signifie hither what talke passed this last summer betwixt Mr
Whalley and hym whereof he opened sume part to the duke of
Northumberland'.[76] The accommodation with Warwick also
had its drawbacks. Before he left court in August Shrewsbury was
a signatory of an order from the council ordering Mary to
conform in religion and one of twenty-four councillors who 'met
at Richemonde to commune of my sister Marie's matter: who at
length agreed that it was not meet to be suffered any longer'. 'At
length' suggests a heated discussion.[77] It may have been this that
induced both Derby and Shrewsbury to leave court at this time.
Shrewsbury was here associated with decisions clashing with his
known past and future opinions and actions: this emphasises how
strong the pressure for conciliar unanimity was. The peremptory
tone in which Shrewsbury was shortly afterward informed that
an office the patronage of which he had requested had already
been granted suggests that he was not held in high regard by
Warwick.[78] Another part of the reconciliation may have been a
bargain that Shrewsbury would not oppose, but would rather
assist, the trial of Somerset, and that in return Warwick would
suppress any mention of connections between Shrewsbury and
Somerset. That may explain why the references to Somerset's

plans to raise the north were so vague. Somerset was arrested in October.[79] On 16 November Shrewsbury and Derby were summoned to court to take part in Somerset's trial. Derby arrived an hour late but his son Lord Strange was an important witness against Somerset. Shrewsbury did not appear at all, explaining his absence as due to ill-health.[80] On 3 January 1552 the council invited him to come up to parliament if he could.[81] He did eventually go up, arriving on 28 January,[82] significantly six days after Somerset had been executed.[83] Evidently he wished to be involved in Somerset's downfall as little as possible. Relations between Shrewsbury and Northumberland were far from warm, despite the reconciliation. But Northumberland had managed to divide Shrewsbury and Derby, so reducing the risk of a united northern alliance against him, and he had destroyed Somerset.

Shrewsbury now had to deal with a situation in which Northumberland's power was great and increasing. A new regime was established in late 1551–early 1552. It was well supported. On 7 December 1551 'a gret muster of men of armes' was held in Hyde Park: the duke of Northumberland, the marquesses of Northampton and Winchester, the earls of Bedford, Rutland, Huntingdon and Pembroke, and Lords Bray, Cobham, Darcy and Cheyney were present.[84] The leading administrators were Cecil, Darcy and Sir John Gates, especially Cecil, 'who is the duke of Northumberland's man'.[85] Somerset's associates were purged in early 1552: Vane, Partridge, and Stanhope were executed; Beaumont, Paget and Arundell were imprisoned; and Whalley, Thynne and Holcroft lost their offices.[86] There was no obvious challenge to this regime and no likelihood that it would fall: Edward VI's death was not yet predictable. Shrewsbury adopted a subtle policy: dissent within limits in a framework of loyalty. He irreproachably linked himself to the new regime, while attempting to exploit potentially significant differences within it. This is illustrated by his relations with William Herbert, newly created earl of Pembroke. Pembroke was one of Northumberland's leading followers. His importance and his association with the regime are shown by the substantial grants of Wiltshire estates formerly held by Somerset and Thomas Arundell that he received in 1551-2.[87] But there were differences between Pembroke and Northumberland. Pembroke was so suspicious when Northumberland had a long conversation with Somerset on 27 December 1551 that he was reported to have fallen out with him.[88] On 18 April 1552 Pembroke surrendered his post of master of the horse to Warwick.[89] Rumours of disagreements continued into early 1553.[90] But there was no final rift and Pemroke remained a significant and influential figure. It was with Pembroke that Shrewsbury arranged a marriage alliance in spring 1552.[91] This gave Shrewsbury a useful foothold in the new regime and yet it strengthened those within it who were wary of Northumberland. Northumberland interpreted Shrewsbury's actions correctly. On 19 May the imperial ambassador reported some coolness between Pembroke and Northumberland. This had been increased by the marriage that Pembroke had just contracted with Shrewsbury's daughter 'which has given Northumberland pause'.[92] Accordingly Northumberland planned to go north to face Shrewsbury there, using the opportunity to assert his own authority as a northern magnate. On 22 May it was decided 'for asmuch as ther was much disordre on the marches on Scotland side ... the duke of Northumberland, general wardein thereof, shuld goe downe and vieu it, and take ordre for it, and returne home with spede'.[93] On 16 June he was reported to be setting off for the north.[94] On 29 June he arrived at York with Shrewsbury. He wrote to the council how he had found[95]

thies parties in as good order and quietnes as ever I saw yt in any plas, and as loving and as obedyient a sort of gentellemen I have found in thies parties, and as redye to do me honour and pleser for my master's sak, as Hart can wishe.

This visit cemented the reconciliation between Shrewsbury and Northumberland. Shrewsbury had already been taking some part in the political life of the new regime. He had been at court and attended council meetings from 28 January to 26 April.[96] He had been intermittently present in the House of Lords between 28 January and 15 April, significantly dissenting from the bill on the marriage of priests.[97] He had been named lord justice and lieutenant of Yorkshire and the city of York in May 1552.[98] But after Northumberland's northern progress, Shrewsbury received some grants and became more closely involved in the new regime. On 10 July 'in consideracion of seruice' he was granted the reversion of rectories in the Sheffield area originally granted to his sister in 1549 and a further package of rectories and the manor of Kimberworth on favourable tenure.[99] He also became an important noble-administrator at court. On 23 November his name was put forward for a commission.[100] On 24 November he was ordered to come to court—'certeyne matters of importance touchinge the Kinges majestes service be in hande, wherein we would be glad to haue your Lordships advise and companye'—and duly arrived by 13 December.[101] From then he was regularly present at council meetings for the rest of Edward's reign.[102] He was on a commission inquiring into financial corruption.[103] On 28 December he acted as the representative of the council to Northumberland, bringing 'a note of soche thinges as haue byn consyderyd by the same most nesesserye to be preferryd in the next parliment'.[104]

Shrewsbury had reconciled himself to Northumberland's dominance but he was not one of the most enthusiastic supporters of the regime. How would he react when that regime was imperilled by Edward VI's fatal illness and how would he look on Northumberland's attempts to perpetuate it in another form? Shrewsbury temporised. He was not willing to go into outright opposition and so risk a permanent loss of favour, and possibly a civil war. He remained at court throughout the final months of Edward VI's life.[105] He accepted lavish grants of land. A memorial of 15 April 1553 mentions 'the sute of the lorde Talbot for a fee ferme of certen lands in Yorkshire of the yerely value of one hundred pounds', and on 20 May Lord Talbot was duly granted a package of lands (including Bolsover Castle, Derbyshire, and the site of Pontefract Priory) worth £101 12s 6¼d yearly.[106] On 30 June, as the crisis approached, Shrewsbury was granted several London properties formerly belonging to the bishopric of Durham, together with some lands from Pontefract Priory and St Robert Knaresborough, worth £66 16s 1½d a year.[107] This was part of a general attempt by Northumberland to win over, or to confirm, men's loyalties by grants of land: the earls of Westmorland, Pembroke, Huntingdon and Bedford, Lords Clinton and Darcy and Sir John Gates were among others rewarded in these months.[108] The imperial ambassador reported on 4 July that the king had given in legacies lands worth some £5-6,000 annually to be distributed among the lords of the council and that Northumberland had managed to obtain yet more for the councillors independently of Edward's will.[109]

On the face of things Shrewsbury behaved as if Northumberland had indeed won his full support. He signed the engagement of the council to maintain the sucession as limited by the crown. He signed Edward's will of 21 June.[110] After Edward's death Shrewsbury was one of those who went to the Tower of London and put Clinton in command.[111] Shrewsbury was a signatory of letters on behalf of Lady Jane Grey to Mary on 9 July and to the sheriff and JPs of Kent (and presumably other counties) on 12 July.[112] Presumably he also acquiesced in the decision to cut off both ears of 'a yong man taken that tym [10 July] for spyking of serten wordes of qwen Mare, that she had the ryght tytle'.[113] On this evidence it might at first sight seem fair to conclude that Northumberland 'goverened ... with such quietness that all the other nobles of the realm have obeyed him as if he had been the true king'.[114] R.R. Reid thought that Shrewsbury 'was more loyal [to Northumberland] than most of his fellows': 'it mattered little to Shrewsbury who ruled England so long as he ruled the land beyond Trent and he was ready to swear allegiance to whomever would allow him to keep the offices he held there'.[115] That is not the whole truth. Shrewsbury undoubtedly did not run the risk of outright opposition. He did not look upon Northumberland as a monster to whom Mary was in all events to be preferred. He recognised, and was prepared to accept, the rewards of a superficial loyalty. He may well have believed, as did the imperial ambassadors, that Northumberland's chances of success were high and was therefore concerned to be on the winning side. After all, Mary might have proved a weak reed. The reaction of the councillors to her letters received on 10 July—they were greatly astonished and troubled—suggests that they had not expected her to show any courage.[116]

But the support that Shrewsbury offered Northumberland was not wholehearted. He did not have much chance to dissent from Northumberland's schemes. He was very much a captive at court. As early as 20 May the imperial ambassador noted that Shrewsbury and Lord Dacre 'are still here, and it appears they will not be allowed to leave'.[117] Northumberland did not trust Shrewsbury sufficiently to allow him to deliver the north to Lady

Jane. He attempted to marry his brother Sir Andrew Dudley to
Margaret Clifford, daughter of the second earl of Cumberland,
and sent him north as lieutenant and governor, a manifest
attempt to reduce Shrewsbury's authority.[118] Shrewsbury and
other noblemen later claimed that they had been forced to
support Northumberland and Lady Jane. Only three or four
councillors had willingly agreed to Edward's device: the rest had
been compelled and then treated almost as if they were
prisoners.[119] Chief Justice Montagu only acquiesced after
relentless pressure from Northumberland and Petre.[120] One
observer noted that 'almost all had only consented to this treason
under constraint'.[121] There is certainly much evidence of disquiet
among counsellors about Northumberland's plans. On 11 June
the imperial ambassador noted that all the nobility would rally
around Mary as Northumberland was hated and loathed as a
tyrant.[122] On 24 June he said that it was sure that several great
nobles and some councillors were opposed to Northumberland's
scheme, naming Winchester, Bedford and Cheyney.[123] On 4 July
he said that those three together with Shrewsbury and Arundel,
as well as others, had demurred and made many difficulties
before signing Edward's will.[124] On 7 July the French
ambassador mentioned 'several of the company whom I know to
be too devoted to the service of the Emperor', that is favourable
to Mary.[125] Northumberland's speech to his colleagues on 13
July shows that he expected bloodshed and feared disloyalty.
One councillor protested: 'my lorde, yf ye mistrust eny of us in
this matter, your grace is far deceaved; for which of us can wipe
his handes clene thereof? And if we should shrincke from you as
one that were culpable, which of us can excuse himself as
guiltles?'. The heart of at least one councillor was evidently not
fully in the struggle: his allegiance was based not upon principle
but simply on the fact of a recent and compromising
commitment.[126] Further evidence of the true feelings of many of
the councillors may be seen in the way that Suffolk kept them
captive in the Tower 'lest in the absence of Northumberland they
should cause a revolution'.[127] The dissatisfaction of certain
councillors, which did not diminish after Edward's death, was a
major explanation of Northumberland's failure to establish Lady
Jane Grey on the throne. Shrewsbury was clearly unhappy. 'The
earl of Shrosburye beareth hymselfe equal: God kepe hym',

wrote one anxious supporter of Mary.[128] On 18 July a young man from Grantham claimed to have learned that Mary had sent a message to Northumberland 'that hir grace wold gyve hyme his breakfast, diner and supper. And if that wold not serue, hir grace hade a talbate to byte hyme by the bake.' The reference to a 'talbate' suggests that Shrewsbury was thought to be secretly supporting Mary.[129] This is strengthened by the remarkable joy with which Shrewsbury's son, Lord Talbot, sent on the news of Mary's eventual success.[130] The earl of Arundel played a more prominent role in undermining the loyalty of the councillors to Northumberland, notably when speaking at Pembroke's house.[131] Shrewsbury's role was less glorious, characteristic of a man who, unlike Arundel, had survived coup and counter-coup without incurring a fine or sojourning in prison.

What gave substance to the grumblings of Shrewsbury, Arundel and others was the news from the provinces. Reports of support for Mary in Essex came on 12 July.[132] On 14–15 July the councillors learned of the mutiny of the crews of five or six ships off the Suffolk coast: 'but after once the submyssion of the shipes was knowne in the Tower, eche man then began to pluck in his hornes'.[133] When news that Sir John Williams was proclaiming Mary in Oxfordshire arrived, 'from that tyme forwarde certayne of the counsayll, that is, the erle of Pembroke and the lord warden [Cheyney] sought to go out of the Tower to consult in London'.[134] The lords 'after they vnderstood how the better part of the realme were enclined, and heering every day newes of great assemblies, began to suspect the sequel of this enterprice'.[135] 'Worde of a greater mischief' than the defection of the squadron of ships arrived: 'the noblemen's tenauntes refused to serve their lordes agaynst quene Mary'.[136] A striking illustration of the two-way relationship between lords and tenants, this shows how tenants anxious to preserve customary tenure were unhappy to support Lady Jane and so break the traditional laws of inheritance, an attitude reflected in Throckmorton's poetical autobiography, 'Right heires for to displace I did detest.'[137] Thanks to a discovery by Diarmaid MacCulloch in the Yelverton Papers, much more is now known of the courage and vigour with which Mary set out to raise the nobility and gentry of East Anglia, gaining the support of the earl of Sussex, Sir Richard Southwell, then Sir Thomas Cornwallis and Lord Wentworth (after they had first proclaimed Lady Jane Queen) and (later) the earl of Oxford and many lesser men.[138] It was to face this powerful challenge that Northumberland left London with his own forces.[139] But one of Arundel's most telling arguments was that Northumberland was not as strong as he looked: 'the greater part of his armie haith forsaken him'.[140] News of Mary's mobilisation and of support for her in many counties gave her supporters in the council their opportunity. On 16 July some of the councillors sent Northumberland 'lettres of discomfort' containing 'a slender answer' to his request for help.[141] On 18 July they warned Suffolk and Lady Jane of the imminent proclamation of Mary, in effect giving Northumberland a final chance.[142] On the same day the French ambassador was doubting that Northumberland would succeed.[143]

A final explanation of Northumberland's failure must be sought in the skilful diplomacy of the imperial ambassadors, especially the newly arrived Renard, who offered the councillors concessions and guarantees in return for their support of Mary.[144] In these negotiations Shrewsbury was closely involved. On 12 July Cobham and Mason had been astonished by the ambassadors' offers. They had been sent by Northumberland but significantly they reported back to Shrewsbury, Arundel, Bedford, Pembroke and Petre.[145] A day later Shrewsbury, Arundel, Bedford, Cobham and Mason indicated that they would give the ambassadors a formal audience; these again made a favourable impression.[146] On 19 July Shrewsbury and Mason went to inform them of the councillors' decision to proclaim Mary.[147]

Shrewsbury was one of those who proclaimed Mary Queen on 19 July.[148] That need not in itself have changed very much. But Northumberland had little will, and ever declining support, to continue. News of the proclamation 'made a sodaine chaunge of mindes' in his army and his campaign collapsed, saving England from a civil and religious war of 'brother against brother, unckle againste nephewe, father inlawe against sonne in lawe, cosen against cosen'.[149]

Shrewsbury had not played an heroic role. He had been prepared to acquiesce, stiffened by grants of land, and believing that there was no alternative, in Northumberland's conspiracy, but he was opportunistic in doing what he could to turn the difficulties of Northumberland's campaign to Mary's advantage. His non-committal attitude may be compared to that of the earl of Westmorland, thanked on 25 July for 'hys coldnes in prosequityng the causes of the usurpede, with a commendatyon of his indifferency towards the Queenes Majestie, with exhortatyon of a more ferventnes'.[150]

Shrewsbury was not immediately accepted by Mary. On 2 August Shrewsbury, Pembroke and Winchester went to beg Mary's pardon. She reproached them for having been against her: they had plotted and committed dishonourable and unjust things against her. While she allowed them to kiss her hands, she refused them an immediate pardon. Indeed, Shrewsbury and his son Lord Talbot are not named on the pardon roll till early October.[151] But it was impossible for Mary to dispense with Shrewsbury's services. On 10 August he was admitted to the council and was intermittently present between 17 and 31 August.[152] He attended the trials of Northumberland and Northampton on 18–19 August and was involved in various ceremonies, for example, putting on Norfolk's garter when that duke was restored to the order.[153]

By late August Shrewsbury had won his way into high favour. He was sent north 'that he might give an awe to the country by his presence, and provide against any tumults. And having settled matters there in safety, to return to her again'.[154] On 2 September Mary asked the countess of Shrewsbury after the earl. Mary prayed God to send Shrewsbury good health 'with maunye other good and comfortable words towards your Lordship to long her to wryte'. Mary also saw to the signing of the commission reappointing Shrewsbury as president of the council in the north: the patent is dated 1 September. There was more warmth here than political factors alone would have dictated but these were clearly important. Mary was anxious to see the north obedient. 'Somewhat dowteful of the quietnes of that cuntrye', she asked Shrewsbury at once to tell her how the 'new' service was taken.[155] More general political considerations that led Mary especially to favour Shrewsbury may be found in the unhappy state of affairs in August-September 1553. Men such as Derby who had always been loyal to her were complaining that they, and particularly their followers, were not being rewarded as they deserved.[156] Councillors of previously doubtful loyalty such as Pembroke were acquiescing only half-heartedly: he had brought more men to court than his licence permitted and then had left abruptly, arousing suspicions of a plot.[157] There were disturbances over religious changes in London. In September there was considerable discontent in Suffolk and Norfolk. Gardiner constantly wore 'la chemise de maille sur le dos', fearing a threatened attack from the men of Kent.[158] Mary was anxious about her coronation.[159] Considerable difficulties were looming over Mary's marriage. In such a 'volatile political atmosphere'[160] Shrewsbury's loyalty was a godsend.

From the accession of Mary in July 1553 to the death of Bishop Gardiner in November 1555 political life was stormy. This was largely the result of the conflicting ambitions of William, lord Paget, and Bishop Gardiner, both of whom aspired to be Mary's principal counsellor. But they were divided also by issues: Mary's marriage, the treatment of heretics, the question of lands once owned by the church but now in lay hands, and the problem of Mary's half-sister Elizabeth.

Over the marriage Gardiner supported the claims of the English nobleman Edward Courtenay whom he had befriended while they were both imprisoned in the Tower while Paget supported those of Philip of Spain. In September 1553 the majority of the English nobility strongly desired Mary to choose an Englishman as her husband.[161] There was not much support for a Spanish marriage, opposition to which was based on fears aroused by accounts of Spanish behaviour in the New World, Sicily, Naples, Lombardy and the Netherlands.[162] Fears of the religious and political consequences of such a match had been exploited by the supporters of Lady Jane Grey.[163] In order to counter this the imperial ambassadors had on 12 July told Cobham and Mason that Charles V 'had expressly instructed us ... to recommend her [Mary] ... to marry her within the country and obtain assurances that she would make no alterations as to religion and customs'.[164] It is quite likely that in the autumn many councillors felt that they had been tricked. Only Paget of the Queen's advisers strongly supported the Spanish marriage. His reasons were personal not political. He had been alarmed by the support for Courtenay as Courtenay had been reported as saying that if he ever became Mary's husband he would remember that Paget had proposed to put him to death in the reign of Henry VIII. Courtenay had first been imprisoned as a child in 1538: Paget was then one of Cromwell's men.[165] That strong feelings against Paget did exist among Courtenay's friends is suggested by reports that some of them, happily dissuaded by Courtenay, discussed murdering Paget.[166] Understandably Paget supported Philip of Spain and used the credit that this gave him with Mary to consolidate his personal position. General disquiet at the Spanish marriage was reflected in parliament in November 1553. A deputation that included Shrewsbury saw Mary and desired her to choose a husband in England.[167] But Courtenay had ruined his reputation with Mary 'pour avoir entendu qu'il faict beaucoup de jeunesses et mesme d'aller souvent avecques les femmes publicques et de mauvaise vie'.[168] And as Mary's determination to marry Philip became clearer, opposition among her councillors dwindled. Mary humiliated Gardiner over this in November.[169] On 28 November the council and the nobility were reported to have changed their minds.[170] By 29 November Mary was convinced that there would be no further conciliar or noble opposition to a Spanish marriage: she was intending to speak to Shrewsbury, Derby and others whom she thought she might win over to her cause.[171] Mary's judgment was correct. By 20 December Shrewsbury had assured Mary of his goodwill and fidelity.[172]

But this was not the last of trouble over the Spanish marriage. There were reports of plotting in December involving Derby (although their veracity is uncertain).[173] General noble embarrassment was reflected in the lack of volunteers to accompany the earl of Bedford and Bishop Bonner to Spain to settle the marriage and in the remarks of Windsor, Smith and Norfolk, who in their different ways put the same question, namely who would ensure that the marriage articles, which were very favourable to English interests, would be respected?[174]

Worse still, fears and resentments ultimately issued in rebellion. Wyatt's rising in January 1554 went off prematurely at half-cock but nevertheless Mary 's'est veue par l'espace de huict jours en bransle de sa couronne'.[175] 'The like stoutness of rebels was never seen or heard of, that durst enterprise to come into Southwarke and lie there so near London.'[176] There is considerable evidence that the rebels were prepared to depose Mary and it is highly probable that Elizabeth knew of and agreed with these plans. It was crucial to Mary's survival that noblemen such as Shrewsbury, Pembroke and Arundel stood firmly loyal, despite their misgivings over the marriage. They may well have hoped that the rebellion and its repercussions would suffice to deter any Spanish ruler from attempting to increase his authority at their expense. If they were to condone rebellion, this might in the long run weaken their position. A further motive for their loyalty may have been the markedly protestant nature of the rising: many of the participants had been active in government service under the protestant regime before July 1553.[177]

It has been suggested, however, that Arundel and Shrewsbury 'feigned sickness and withdrew from the court'.[178] The source of this seems to be a letter by the French ambassador Noailles dated 24 January: 'le comte d'Arondel faict encor le malade et Paget s'est absenté il y a quatre ou cinq jours. Ilz sont en grand peyne, aussy est leur maistresse, de sentir et veoir ce qui se prépare et dresse'.[179] This is not conclusive evidence of Arundel's attitude and it does not warrant drawing conclusions about Shrewsbury. There is strong evidence to the contrary. Arundel's servant, Sir Thomas Palmer, 'said ... to a friend of his that the complot betweene the Frenche king and the seid duke of Suffolk was nowe come to light'.[180] Arundel 'did then furnishe into the feilde lx great horses of his owne, owte of his owne stable, with men and all thinges fitt for service on horsemen' and 800 foot, all at his own expense.[181] Later that year when Arundel (and the earl of Pembroke and Lord Williams) were summoned to attend the queen on the arrival of Philip of Spain, they were thanked, in a letter that specifically mentioned the rebellions against the marriage, for 'the faythefull seruice ye haue heretofore done vnto vs bothe in the suppressyon of the late consperycyes and rebellyons and sundre other wayes'.[182] Conclusive evidence that neither Arundel nor Shrewsbury were assisting the rebels appears in a letter that Arundel sent Shrewsbury on 28 January (when he was supposedly feigning illness). He gave Shrewsbury full details of the risings, commenting that 'the quenes Highnes is in good helthe of her bodye, but syke in certyn naughty members of her comonwelthe'. He added that the rebels were not doing very well.[183] Shrewsbury had been ordered to go to his country by Mary.[184] On 4 February he ordered Wharton to look out for Suffolk and the other traitors in the north-west.[185] On the day that the victory was won Mary told Renard that Shrewsbury had written to her that her subjects in Wales and the north were very happy about the marriage.[186] On 18 February he was sent an imperial letter of thanks.[187] Dissatisfaction did linger on. In mid-year the French ambassador noted that since the disturbances Shrewsbury and other noblemen had continually 'tenu en leur pays quelques gens arrestez et prests à prendre les armes quand il en seroit besoing, craignans nouvelles eslevations du peuple'.[188] But the failure of Wyatt's rebellion was also the end of other, less violent, attempts to prevent the Spanish marriage.[189]

Political life continued to be stormy in 1554, especially in the important spring parliament in which Shrewsbury was involved. Before this began the quarrel between Gardiner and Paget flared up again. This was partly the result of the backwash of the coup of the previous year and of Wyatt's rebellion.[190] It was also in some part the consequence of Mary's openness: she 'chooses to give audience not only to all the members of her privy council . . . but also to other persons who ask it of her'.[191] The unusual influence exerted over her by Renard, and through him by Charles V, is important here too. Personal resentments, especially after the experiences of the first months of the reign, played their part: in November 1553 Paget claimed that Gardiner had a spite against him.[192] But 'issues' and principles (even if these were rationalisations of self-interest) were of importance as well, and factiousness alone does not explain the events of early 1554. Both Paget and Gardiner had followers and took advice from others. Naturally they looked for support from nobles, churchmen and leading administrators. These were not 'factions' in any strict party sense: but there were real divisions of opinion between different groups.

There were divisions in February–March over the treatment of the defeated rebels and over what should be done with Elizabeth. There was 'quarrelling on all sides in council'.[193] Arundel and Gardiner were said to have fallen out violently.[194] But what especially produced the intensity of feeling evident in Renard's despatches was the attempt of Gardiner, as Lord Chancellor, to drive forward his religious proposals. He wanted 'an article concerning religion and the pope's authority, establishing a form of inquisition against the heretics, setting up again the power of the bishops'.[195] He wanted to use blood and fire to re-establish

religion.[196] By 22 March 'the council had split up into two
parties'; words had been spoken 'which clearly showed how
much the chancellor is disliked'.[197] Pembroke and Paget left the
council without leave when Gardiner was putting forward
matters for the next parliament, 'it is supposed in order not to
give their consent to the articles on religion and subsequently to
make trouble for the chancellor on that score'.[198] Obviously
personal rivalries count for something here, but the bitter
resentment felt by many lords against Gardiner's proposals arose
from their fears over church lands. Gardiner lost no time in
making his intentions here plain. On 24 July 1553 he had
intimated to Pembroke that he should return certain revenues
formerly due to the bishopric of Winchester.[199] Already there had
been difficulties in parliament over the restitution of church
property, 'so much so that a conspiracy has been discovered
among those who hold that property ... who would rather get
themselves massacred than let go'.[200] The whole council—and
particularly Pembroke—was affected, Renard noted on 4
November.[201]

Shrewsbury was present at council meetings from 3 April
1554.[202] That day Mary unsuccessfully attempted a
reconciliation.[203] The clash between Gardiner and Paget spilled
over into parliament and ultimately wrecked it. On 19 April
Paget was reported very unhappy at the state of the parliament.
On 22 April Renard reported that quarrels, jealousy and ill-will
among councillors had increased: 'what one does, another
undoes; that one advises, another opposes'.[204] This does not
depend solely upon Renard. On 23 April the French ambassador
referred to 'contrarietez que de jour à aultre s'y engendrent pour
raison de la religion et mesme entre les plus grands de ce conseil,
dont le chancellier et quelques evesques font une faction; Paget,
les comtes d'Arondel et de Pembroug l'autre'.[205] Gardiner had
attempted to discredit Paget and Petre by complaining against
them to Mary who had accordingly taken a dislike to them.
Paget and Petre and their followers then openly combined in
parliament to fight certain religious bills, introduced without
their knowledge, that provided for the punishment of heretics.
Gardiner furthermore proposed the restitution of the usurped
property of the bishopric of Durham.[206] There was a half-
reconciliation on 27 April but it was short-lived.[207] On 1 May the

House of Lords rejected the bill proposing capital punishment for heretics.[208] Paget was inciting lords to vote against saying that its passage would endanger their church lands.[209] At the same time he was also stirring up difficulties over a bill extending the protection of the treason laws to Philip despite having initially agreed to it. His explanation that he was ignorant of the provisions of the bill does not carry conviction.[210] Earlier there had been difficulties over proposals for the coronation of Philip, which vanished without trace.[211] Paget understandably asked for leave of absence from court, irritating the Queen just as certain diplomatic negotiations were beginning.[212] Matters between Gardiner and Paget came to a head in mid-May. Mary was giving Gardiner great support.[213] But Gardiner and his friends were suspicious that Paget, Arundel, Pembroke, Cobham and other 'heretic peers' were weaving a plot against Mary and himself.[214] Mary found herself compelled to order the captain of her guards not to lay his hands on Gardiner.[215] Paget forcibly detained a gentleman friend of Gardiner in his own house for two days. Gardiner feared he would again be imprisoned by the 'heretics'. He urged Mary to strike first by arresting Paget, Arundel and Winchester. Mary avoided such rash counsels but took some firm decisions.[216] Paget was disgraced, 'contrainct se jetter à genoulx devant ladicte dame [Mary] avecques la larme à l'oeil, ce qui ne l'a sceu toutesfois garder d'estre fort recullé'.[217] Gardiner obtained 'the management of everything'.[218] It was decided to send noblemen back to their countries to keep them apart.[219]

One of the noblemen so despatched was Shrewsbury.[220] Though not named, he had no doubt been one of those 'heretic peers' whom Gardiner had mistrusted. He had been on the committee for the bill 'that the compassing or imagining of the death of the queen's husband, she living, be treason'.[221] His lack of favour at this time may be seen in the difficulties that his servant Robert Swyft was experiencing in financial negotiations on Shrewsbury's behalf with Winchester: Shrewsbury, under no illusions about his chances of success, asked Swyft to attend to other matters.[222] He would obviously have been upset by any threat to continued lay possession of former church lands. The Talbot patrimony had been greatly extended by the grants of lands formerly belonging to Rufford Abbey and Worksop Priory soon after the dissolution of the monasteries. In 1549 Shrewsbury had bought a package of chantry lands for over £700. In June 1552 he had been granted a number of rectories, with the reversion of several more. In June 1553 he had been granted several London properties, notably Coldharborough in Thames Street, formerly part of the estates of the bishopric of Durham. This last would have been immediately put at risk from Gardiner's proposal for the recovery of the property lost by that bishopric.[223] Clearly Shrewsbury—and Pembroke, Arundel, Sussex, Huntingdon, Rich and others—would have required little persuading to support Paget's opposition. There is a brief record of a bill that no bishop should be able to sue for abbey lands:[224] this emphasises that part at least of the secular lords' opposition to the recovery of church lands was political. These lands had formerly been held largely by monasteries, chantries, colleges and gilds with which these peers, or their ancestors, had often been associated, and in whose affairs bishops had not greatly interfered. What was being proposed by Gardiner might have led to an increase as much of episcopal as of church power. That his plans met with opposition is not surprising. Paget, it has been pointed out,[225] was trying in spring 1554 to convince Mary of his indispensability as a leading counsellor by showing her that he could bring together a group of men sufficiently powerful to frustrate many measures which she wished to implement. His power depended crucially on the continued existence of anxiety over church land. But his activities did more to safeguard the lay possession of church property than they did to further his political career. If fears over church property could be stilled, men such as Shrewsbury would again give the government full support and Paget's inconstant services might be dispensed with. The violence of the resistance to the confiscation of church lands in May 1554 convinced Mary that she would have to accede to the wishes of her nobility on this issue. On 13 May she sent a gentleman to Cardinal Pole to see whether he would agree that she should[226]

prier et requerir sa saincteté [the pope] de voulloir permettre que le bien de l'église de ce pays demourast perpetuellement à ceulx qui presentement en joyssent, qui est pour tousjours gratiffier ses subjectz et mesmement la noblesse, et par soubz main d'aultant plus faciliter son mariaige.

Shrewsbury had played his part in the agitation that had brought this to pass. Paget's services were now unnecessary and he was greatly out of favour.[227] In the last resort, the interests of a nobleman such as Shrewsbury were seen as fundamental; the political intriguing of a 'master of practices' helped him but little.

There was now no reason not to welcome Philip of Spain and to celebrate the marriage. Shrewsbury may have been more willing to accept Philip owing to the sudden resurgence of the traditional French threat. On 11 June eighty French ships sailed between Portsmouth and the Isle of Wight. 'Yf the prynce come not in shortlye I pray God save the ysle of Wuyght frome ther daunger', wrote one of Shrewsbury's correspondents.[228] In June Shrewsbury returned to court to await Philip. On 17 June he mourned Joanna, Philip's grandmother.[229] Shrewsbury's son Lord Talbot was on a boat welcoming Philip; then Shrewsbury attended Philip in a richly gilded barque that brought them ashore.[230]

Shrewsbury's subsequent absence from court again gave rise to rumours. On 10 September a story went round 'that my lorde of Westmerlande, and other kept a counsail at Yorke, and that the erle of Pembroke, therle of Sherysbury and the erle of Westmerlande were proclaymed traytours at the courte of Hamton'. This was far-fetched even by mid-sixteenth century standards. The crossing out of this passage in the manuscript may well mean that the rumour was found to be false.[231] Shrewsbury does seem to have been working to promote stability. In June-July he was listed as a recipient of a Habsburg pension of 2,000 crowns.[232] On 13 October Renard reported that royal pensioners had been doing such good work in their countries that one heard nothing but the people's gladness about the marriage.[233]

Shrewsbury returned to court for the autumn parliament: he 'came riding to London with vi$_{xx}$ horse, and of gentlemen in velvet caps thirty, to his place in Coleherber in Thames Street'.[234] He attended parliament from 12 November to 29 December and the council from 13 November to 19 January 1555.[235] On 12 November he carried Philip's 'cap of maintenance'.[236] Lord Talbot was present 'very brave with a great following but not nearly as sumptuously dressed as Pembroke's'.[237] Shrewsbury also went to meet Cardinal Pole at Gravesend, returning to

London in his barge 'with the talbot, all ys men in bluw cotes, red-hosse, skarlett capes, and white fethers'.[238] Shrewsbury's ceremonial acquiescence in the new order was highly important.

The parliament was the occasion for the ratification of the compromise on church lands on which Mary had decided in May. Pole had never been willing to agree to the secular possession of church lands.[239] He wanted the restoration of England to the papal obedience to be accomplished nobly and holily 'and how could it be so were they to reduce the business to an offer of the church property and thus make . . . a purchase of obedience?'.[240] Philip made the position quite clear to him on his arrival in England, telling him 'in short that it was impossible to effect the return to the obedience, unless the holders of this church property were allowed to retain its actual possession'.[241] The compromise was duly achieved in December 1554, the Venetian ambassador noting that 'the church property is to remain in the hands of its present English possessors'.[242] The settlement was legally imprecise and Pole continued to regard his dispensation as 'a mere permission'.[243] But political realities made the confirmation of ecclesiastical lands a matter beyond dispute. Shrewsbury and many other peers had made their feelings abundantly clear in parliament in May 1554.

The nobility were still, however, uneasy at the Spanish alliance. Renard had had to allay their fears during the coup in July 1553. The marriage negotiations had been marked by noble attempts to secure at the very least terms detrimental to Philip's long-term interests. In the parliament held in April–May 1554 there had been difficulties over proposals to extend to him the protection of the treason laws and to secure his coronation.[244] Anti-Spanish feeling was manifested in a series of affrays.[245] Some incidents involved noblemen. On 8 August 1554 Derby's son was reported to have killed two of the chief Spaniards who had come over with Philip while in return other Spaniards had wounded him and Huntingdon's son.[246] Books and 'placards' were distributed against the Spanish.[247] One of the most interesting of these is *The Copye of a letter sent by John Bradforth to the right honorable lordes the erles of Arundel, Derbie, Shrewsbury and Penbroke.* This assailed the Spanish from a catholic, not a protestant, nationalism. On the basis of his experiences in Spain, the author argued that the Spanish were lustful, proud, ambitious and lecherous. He was at pains to emphasise those arguments which his intended noble audience would find convincing. The Spanish, he claimed, threatened to destroy the earls to whom the *Letter* was addressed. Their lands, their wives, their children were vulnerable. The earls would never be trusted to stay at home but would have to follow the Spanish king in strange countries.[248] This letter may reasonably be assumed to reflect the anxieties of Shrewsbury and other noblemen, in particular their continuing reservations over Philip.

Philip repeatedly attempted to increase his chances of influencing English government in the long run. But in the parliament of November–December 1554 a new bill extending the protection of the treason laws to him was passed only after difficulties, and plans to introduce legislation permitting the coronation of Philip were shelved.[249] On 14 January 1555 the French ambassador reported his unsuccessful attempt to secure his coronation: 'despuis six jours il en avoit particulierement faict rechercher ceulx de la basse chambre du dict parlement, qui luy ont tous d'une voix rejetté'.[250] It is significant that Shrewsbury did not attend the House of Lords after 29 December although he did attend council meetings up to 19 January: Renard noted that several lords stayed away from parliament 'not to give their consent to a measure infringing upon the right hitherto exercised by the nobility to appoint a protector when need has risen'.[251]

Clearly the best hope of permanent Spanish influence in England would have been for Mary to bear a child. But by mid-1555 it was becoming less and less likely that there would be any children of the marriage. Philip was therefore more and more insistent that he should be crowned. After he left England he attempted to make his return conditional on his being crowned, exploiting Mary's loving desire to have him back.[252] Mary did what she could but she was aware of the political difficulties. She hesitated to propose Philip's coronation to the parliament of autumn 1555. 'If unable to carry this act ... she thought of effecting it on the dissolution of parliament with a number of peers and other personages of the kingdom'.[253] A council meeting discussed whether Mary could use her powers to have Philip crowned but advised against.[254] There were rumours that force might be used.[255] Shrewsbury's consent would have been essential for any extra-parliamentary coronation. On 11 May

one William Crowe confessed that he had heard that Pembroke
was going 'to fetche the crowne from the Earle of Shrewsbery to
crowne the kyng wythal'.[256] Philip might have been more
successful if he had remained in England, personally seeking
support and establishing a group of followers by patronage.
Perhaps he was hoping that the gradual restoration of catholic
order would make his coronation more feasible in due course;
perhaps he just underestimated the political problems; or
perhaps he was fearful of assassination. Related to Philip's
coronation was the treatment of Elizabeth. In May 1555, when it
was still possible to expect that Spanish influence in England
would be secured by the birth of an heir, Gardiner, Shrewsbury,
Arundel and Petre tried to persuade Elizabeth to go to Flanders.
But generally there was considerable opposition to any proposal
to exclude Elizabeth from the succession.[257]

Shrewsbury was involved in some of the most important tasks
facing the government in this period. At various times in the
years 1553–5 suggestions were made to reduce the number of
councillors. On 22 March 1554 Renard recommended a small
council which principal noblemen, such as Shrewsbury, would
be able to attend while at court. The general point here was the
belief that a smaller council would be less faction-ridden and
therefore more efficient.[258] It has been further argued that these
plans were largely Paget's and that they were designed to
eliminate Gardiner's supporters among the so-called
'Framlingham group' in Mary's household.[259] But there is no
evidence that any 'council of state' actually came into being, and
in any case such institutional reforms could not have solved
problems that were at bottom political. Moreover the continued
presence on the council of lords such as Shrewsbury would have
meant that resistance to the coronation of Philip and to any
attempt to recover church lands, issues that produced divisions,
would have continued.

The final years of Mary's reign have generally been regarded
as a period of sterility, to use Pollard's influential description, as a
frustrating and exhausting battle between the queen's policies
and her subjects.[260] More sympathetic accounts are few.[261] But
Mary's personal tragedy should not be confused with politics as a
whole. Much of the recorded dissatisfaction may well be
attributed more fairly to the serious epidemics of 1557–8 than to

Mary's governance.[262] For the nobility in general and for Shrewsbury in particular these years were characterised by political stability and military service. Admittedly there was opposition to certain crown measures in parliament in autumn 1555: noblemen were noted as opposed to Mary's attempt to return to the church properties still in crown hands.[263] But it seems that Shrewsbury may well have accepted the attitude of the government over the confiscation of the property of religious exiles who did not return within a certain time. Shrewsbury did not attend parliament because of illness: Mary's warm concern rebuts any suspicion that his sickness was diplomatic. And Shrewsbury rebuked one of his closest servants, Sir Thomas Gargrave, for his misbehaviour in parliament: he had sat still during the passing of a bill—most likely the exiles' bill—and was therefore accused of disservice to king and queen.[264] A comment by the Venetian ambassador strengthens this supposition: 'the chief nobility and principal personages ... at least show themselves very well disposed and inclined towards the Queen's demands and wishes, commending and defending her Majesty's acts by every sort of demonstration'.[265]

Understandable condemnation of the Marian persecutions should not lead to the assumption that men in the 1550s saw the burnings in the same light as those brought up on Foxeian martyrology. Their political effect was small. Noblemen were not burnt; noblemen and gentry were heavily involved in administering the persecution.[266] On 22 April 1555 Shrewsbury was present when the council issued an order for the execution of an heretic and added that 'for the more tirible example he shulde before he were executed have his right hand striken of'.[267] That he was not in disagreement with the general policy is further suggested by the off-hand tone of the report by his servant John Criche that ' I can at this tyme assertayne yor lordship of no newes, but that Mr Ryddelye and Mr Latymer be brent at Oxford, who died in like manner as others heretofore have done'.[268] The Venetian ambassador reported that 'many persons are of opinion that the example afforded by the nobility who ... showed their great readiness to assist at the thanksgiving and high mass, will do no less now to confirm the people in their obedience to the church than any sermon preached last year.[269] In August 1557 the Spanish ambassador noted that where

religion was concerned, matters were going well: many churches
and monasteries were being repaired. As far as outward
appearances went, things were as in Spain.[270]

There are many indications of order. The brevity of
Shrewsbury's attendance at court (he was present from 27
October to 15 November 1556 and from 5 January 1558 or
slightly earlier to 13 March 1558)[271] itself points to a lack of
seriously contentious issues, an impression reinforced by the
warm feelings expressed in letters that Shrewsbury wrote to and
received from men at court.[272] It is unlikely that the regime was
undermined by the profusion of hostile pamphlets.[273] There are
many references to stability. 'Everything in England proceeds in
the usual course, and without any disturbance', wrote the
Venetian ambassador in August 1555.[274] The most important
business of 1557–8 was war. This helped to reunite a ruling class
that had been divided in 1553–4 and was by no means unpopular
and unsuccessful.[275] In summer 1557 Shrewsbury played a
conscientious and largely successful part in the northern
campaign. In early 1558 parliament voted considerable sums of
money and was highly satisfactory for Mary.[276]

On 16 October 1558 Shrewsbury was among those ordered to
leave their charge and come immediately to the Queen.[277] At
court by 3 November, he took part in the essential ceremonial
after Mary's death and the accession of Elizabeth. Sworn in as a
councillor on 21 November, he remained in regular attendance
until 7 May 1559. there were even momentary rumours that his
son Lord Talbot might be a suitor to the queen.[278]

Shrewsbury did not, however, agree with the religious
settlement of 1559. In mid-March he was a member of a
committee of the House of Lords which dismantled a composite
supremacy-and-uniformity bill, removing what were probably
radical doctrinal and liturgical provisions that had been added
by a small number of extreme protestants in the House of
commons to a simpler bill that restored the royal supremacy and
permitted communion in both kinds.[279] On 18 March he
dissented from the third reading of the dismantled bill but was
absent when a further revised bill was read on 22 March.[280] Was
his opposition principally to protestant doctrine rather than to
the royal supremacy? Had he perhaps misread signs from court
and continued to oppose even after the composite bill had been

dismantled? In April he did not dissent from the revised supremacy bill but he did dissent from the uniformity bill when that was read a third time on 28 April, narrowly passing by 21 votes to 18.[281] His reasons may have been similar to those put forward in speeches by Viscount Montagu, Archbishop Heath, Bishop Scot and Abbot Feckenham, though they went beyond him in consistently defending the Pope and rejecting the royal supremacy. They emphasised the novelty of protestantism, the divisions and confusions among the protestants, the dangers of social instability that protestantism posed, the complications that the proposed changes would make in English foreign relations. They complained of the iconoclastic and blasphemous attitudes of the protestants towards the sacraments, and Bishop Scot pointed out that uniformity based on the 1552 prayer book would abolish prayers for the dead and invocations to saints.[282] Despite his opposition, Shrewsbury was reappointed president of the council in the north and reported to the council later that year that 'I do not yet perceve the contrary bot the people in thes partes receuyth the Inglyshe seruice daily and obedyently.'[283] In summer 1559 he was commissioned to hold a visitation in the Province of York: although lords-lieutenants were not expected to take an active part but merely to assist those serving under them, it is clear that once again Shrewsbury's loyalty to the crown was overcoming any religious scruples.[284] But the government was wary of showing him full confidence. When the duke of Norfolk was sent to the Scottish borders in late 1559 he was told to use the advice of Shrewsbury and Talbot whenever they were with him. In secret instructions, however, he was asked to explain to him why the Queen had not sent for him to ask his opinion of the practices of the French.[285] Interestingly, Shrewsbury returned to London on 27 January 1560: 'the sam day cam rydyng to London, and so entered at Ludgatt, the good yerle of Shreusbery, with a c men rydyng and so to Cold Herber to ys owne plasse'.[286] A few days later the Spanish ambassador recorded that 'these people are cleverly making sure of all the catholics of whom they have any suspicion by summoning them hither on various excuses'. Shrewsbury, he added, was already present.[287] He played little further part in government. He died on 21 September 1560, striking a final blow for his religious beliefs by requesting a requiem eucharist and communion for his funeral.[288]

Shrewsbury had become much more closely involved in national politics during Somerset's protectorate. He was a crucial participant in ceremonies in 1547, acquiescing in Somerset's advancement and in his dominance in 1548. Somerset depended on him *in extremis* for the repression of popular rebellion in 1549. Shrewsbury was one of the conciliar majority against Somerset in October 1549. His importance was reflected in his appointment as lord president of the council in the north, although this may have been a political manoeuvre designed to strengthen the hand of Warwick's friends. During 1550 relations between Shrewsbury and Warwick became increasingly strained, and Shrewsbury plotted, especially with the earl of Derby, to preserve his power. In spring 1551 the dissatisfactions of these nobles fused with that of Somerset and for a moment there was a risk of civil war. But Shrewsbury and Northumberland reached an understanding, so strong was the desire for stability in a decade of commons' unrest. Shrewsbury co-operated further with Northumberland in 1552–3. But here he again attempted to keep his options open, exploiting differences within the regime. During the coup of 1553 he temporised. He accepted lavish grants of land and offered Northumberland support. But his preference for Mary was revealed when the opportunity to support her arose. After initial coolness, Mary soon showed him considerable favour. He accepted the Spanish marriage, despite misgivings, after he had been convinced of Mary's determination, and he remained loyal during Wyatt's rebellion. But in the parliament of 1554 he was one of those peers who made it clear to Mary that church lands currently in lay possession could not be resumed. It is also likely that Shrewsbury never consented to the coronation of Philip. Once these decisive issues had been settled, or allowed to lapse, Shrewsbury served the regime loyally, especially during the northern campaign of 1557. After Mary's death he was well regarded by Elizabeth despite his opposition to the religious settlement. He did not take this outside parliament but by early 1560 there are hints that the government had some reservations about his trustworthiness. He died in 1560 before his loyalty to the crown could be seriously tested by his religious beliefs.

A number of conclusions may be drawn from this. Again and

again the often crucial significance of noble power is apparent. The most striking example of this was the failure of the Marian government to recover secularised church lands. More particularly, one need only consider a few possibilities to see how important Shrewsbury's decisions were: if he had supported the earl of Southampton in 1547, if he had answered Somerset's appeals in 1549, if he had plotted more vigorously against Northumberland in 1551, if he had joined in Wyatt's rebellion in 1554, political developments would have been very different. But Shrewsbury's most important attitude was his loyalty, not so much perhaps to whatever regime was in power, but to the general opinion among his colleagues. He wished to avoid disturbances and quarrels. In 1551 he wished Somerset and Warwick to be reconciled. If there was a policy with which he disagreed he attempted to deflect its impact. He continued to maintain contact with Somerset even after his reconciliation with Warwick in 1551. He never supported Northumberland wholeheartedly in 1552-3. That this was a policy for all weathers is not wholly borne out. Shrewsbury was never compelled irrevocably to decide between loyalty and principle: in this he may well have been fortunate to die when he did.

Notes

1 *Cal. S.P., Spanish*, xi. 172; G.A. Lemasters, 'The Privy Council in the reign of Queen Mary', University of Cambridge Ph.D. thesis, 1972, p. 59.
2 Talbot Papers A 415.
3 *Cal. S.P., Spanish*, ix. 457.
4 J.R. Dasent, *Acts of the Privy Council*, (32 vols, 1890-1907), ii. 1, 8, 9; J. Strype, *Ecclesiastical Memorials* (3 vols, 1721), ii. appendix A pp. 4-5, 10, 15; J.G Nichols, ed., *Literary Remains of King Edward the Sixth, Roxburghe Clube*, lxxiv (1857), pp. xcii-xciii, cclxx, ccxcvi-ccxcvii; ccxcix; R.H. Brodie, ed., *Calendar of the Patent Rolls: Edward VI*, (6 vols, 1924-9), i. 174, v. 396. For Somerset's struggle against Southampton see R. Grafton, *Chronicle; or History of England* (1809 ed.), pp. 499-500; Strype, *Ecclesiastical Memorials*, ii. appendix HH, p. 109; BL Add. MS 48126 fo. 15; BL Harleian MS 249 fos. 16-18; D.E. Hoak, *The King's Council in the Reign of Edward VI* (Cambridge, 1976), pp. 43-5, 231-9; A. J. Slavin, 'The fall of Lord Chancellor Wriothesley: a study in the politics of conspiracy', *Albion*, vii (1975), pp. 265-86.
5 M.L. Bush, *The Government Policy of Protector Somerset* (1975) *passim*, esp.

pp. 3, 129; *Lords Journal*, i. 194–311; W.K. Jordan, *Edward VI* (2 vols, 1968–71), i, 89–103.

6   Hoak, *King's Council*, pp. 103, 260–1; Strype, *Ecclesiastical Memorials*, ii. appendix GG p. 108.

7   BL Add. MS 48126 fos. 15–16.

8   I am preparing a study of the downfall of Sir Thomas Seymour.

9   Hoak, *King's Council*, p. 49 (from PRO SP61/2/fos. 4–7). Cf. R.C. Anderson ed., *Letters of the Fifteenth and Sixteenth Centuries, Southampton Record Society*, xxii (1921), pp. 56–7, 61.

10   *Historical Manuscripts Commission, Hatfield House, Salisbury MSS* (24 vols, 1883–1976), i. no. 295 p. 70.

11   *APC*, ii. 236, 238, 258 (not in *LJ*), 262–3.

12   S. Haynes, ed., *A Collection of State Papers . . . Left by Lord Burghley 1542–70* (1740), p. 81.

13   Anderson, *Letters*, pp. 62–5; N. Pocock, *Troubles Connected with the Prayer Book of 1549, Camden Society*, 2nd series, xxxvii (1884), pp. 6–8; *Historical Manuscripts Commission, 2nd report, Appendix* (1871), p. 152; *Cal. S.P., Spanish*, ix. 397.

14   J.G. Nichols, ed., 'The life of Henry Fitzallen, earl of Arundell', *Gentleman's Magazine*, ciii (1833), pp. 11–18, 118–24, 209–15, 490.

15   Talbot Papers B 115.

16   Arundel Castle, Autograph Letters 1513–85, no. 16; cf. *Cal. S.P., Spanish*, ix 432.

17   *Cal. S.P., Spanish*, ix. 445–8, 454, 457–8, 470; Grafton, *Chronicle*, pp. 521–4; A.J.A. Malkiewicz, 'An eye-witness's account of the coup d'état of October 1549', *English Historical Review*, lxx (1955), pp. 602–5; BL Add. MS 48126 fos. 6–16; BL Add. MS 48023 fos. 350–1v (I am preparing an edition of fos. 350–369v, part a would-be historian's working notes on the reign of Edward VI, part a diary-like account of the years 1558–62); J. Ponet, *A Shorte Treatise of Politke Power* (1556), sig. I iii–iiiv; J. Hayward, *The Life and Reigne of King Edward VI* (2nd ed, 1636), p. 247; Nichols, 'Arundell', pp. 14–15; Bush, *Government Policy*, p. 79; S.R. Gammon, *Statesman and Schemer: William, first Lord Paget: Tudor Minister* (Newton Abbot, 1973), p. 167. On timing see J.S. Berkman, 'A reappraisal of the coup d'état against Protector Somerset in the light of the summer rebellions', University of Oxford M.Phil. thesis, 1979, and 'Van der Delft's message: a reappraisal of the attack on Protector Somerset', *Bulletin of the Institute of Historical Research*, liii (1980), pp. 247–52.

18   Talbot Papers A 415.

19   BL Add. MS 48018 fos. 404–4v.

20   Talbot Papers B 117.

21   *Cal. S.P., Spanish*, ix. 457.

22   *Ibid.*

23   *APC*, ii. 334–6.

24   *Ibid.*, ii. 343–5.

25   *See below*, pp. 126–8.

26   BL Add. MS 48126 fos. 15–16; Ponet, *A Shorte Treatise*, sig. I iii–iiiv. Hoak, *King's Council*, pp. 241–58; cf. BL Harleian MS 523 fo. 56; *Historical Manuscripts Commission, Rutland*, i. 55; D. Hoak, 'Rehabilitating the duke of

Northumberland: politics and political control 1549-53' in J. Loach and R. Tittler, eds, *The Mid-Tudor Polity c. 1540–1560* (1980), pp. 36-8, 47-8.

27 *LJ*, pp. 355-66; Talbot Papers P 153, B 121. (The documents noticed in *Cal. S.P., Domestic 1547–1580*, ed. R. Lemon (1856), pp. 399-400 and in *Cal. S.P. Domestic: Elizabeth 1601–3 with addenda 1547–65*, ed. M.A.E. Green (1870), iii. no. 47 (PRO SP15/3/fos. 89-103; PRO SP15/2/fo. 106) are misdated at ?May 1549).

28 *Cal. Pat. Rolls, Edward VI*, ii. 250-1.

29 A.G. Dickens, 'Archbishop Holgate's apology', *English Historical Review*, lvi (1941), p. 456 (reprinted in *Reformation Studies* (1982), p. 359); *idem*, 'The marriage and character of Archbishop Holgate' *Ibid.*, lii (1937), p. 429 and n. 5; *idem, Robert Holgate: Archbishop of York and President of the King's Council in the North, Borthwick Papers*, viii (1955) (reprinted in *Reformation Studies*, p. 337); Lambeth Palace MS 709 fo. 158.

30 *Cal. S.P., Spanish*, x. 7-8, 14, 28, 63, 72, 87.

31 *ibid.*, x. 98, 109; Lambeth Palace MS 700 fo. 5.

32 BL Add. MS 48023 fo. 350; *Cal. S.P., Spanish*, x. 98.

33 *Cal. S.P. Dom., 1547–80*, p. 27.

34 *Cal. S.P., Spanish*, x. 186, 216.

35 BL Cotton MS Titus B ii fo. 29; Strype, *Ecclesiastical Memorials*, ii. 279-80.

36 Nichols, *Literary Remains*, p. 303.

37 *Cal. S.P., Spanish*, x. 230; Gammon, *Statesman and Schemer*, p. 177.

38 *Cal. S.P., Spanish*, x. 262.

39 *Ibid.*, x. 225.

40 *Ibid.*, x. 285.

41 *Ibid.*, x. 62; Nichols, *Literary Remains*, p. 262 n.

42 *APC*, ii. 428; *Cal. Pat. Rolls, Edward VI*, iv. 26.

43 R.R. Reid, *The King's council in the north* (1921), pp. 172-3; Talbot Papers B 171; Lambeth Palace MS 695 fo. 121.

44 Lambeth Palace MS 700 fo. 5.

45 *APC*, ii. 312; Talbot Papers P 185.

46 Talbot Papers B 209.

47 *Cal. S.P., Spanish*, x. 166.

48 *Ibid.*, x. 168-9.

49 *Ibid.*, x. 215.

50 *Ibid.*, x. 230.

51 *Ibid.*, x. 263.

52 *Ibid.*, x. 283.

53 *Ibid.*, x. 281.

54 *Ibid.*, x. 279-80.

55 W.B. Turnbull, ed., *Calendar of State Papers, Foreign, 1547–58* (2 vols, 1861), nos 370 and 370 (i), pp. 119-20.

56 *Cal. S.P., Spanish*, x. 291.

57 BL Cotton MS Titus B ii fo. 29 (I accept Professor Jordan's attribution of this letter).

58 *Cal. S.P., Spanish*, x. 262.

59 e.g. *ibid.*, x. 168-9, 215, 230.

60 Nichols, *Literary Remains*, pp. 71, 353, 370-3.

61 *Ibid.*, p. 313; *APC*, iii. 217.
62 Nichols, *Literary Remains*, p. 361; *Cal. S.P., Spanish*, x. 104, 300.
63 *Cal. S.P., Spanish*, x. 386.
64 *APC*, iii. 240.
65 Arundel Castle, Autograph Letters 1513–85, no. 18.
66 *Cal. S.P., Spanish*, x. 279–80.
67 *APC*, iii. 264.
68 *Cal. S.P., Spanish*, x. 263.
69 Nichols, *Literary Remains*, pp. 3–5; *Cal. S.P., Spanish*, x. 292.
70 *Cal. S.P., Spanish*, x. 291.
71 *Ibid.*, x. 301, 325.
72 J.G. Nichols, ed., *The Diary of Henry Machyn, Camden Society*, 1st series, xlii (1848), p. 6; *Cal. S.P., Spanish*, x. 300.
73 Nichols, *Machyn*, p. 6.
74 *Cal. S.P., Spanish*, x. 300.
75 BL Add. MS 48018 fo. 295.
76 *APC*, iii. 398.
77 *Historical Manuscripts Commission, Cowper, Melbourne Hall* (3 vols in 2, 1888–9), i. 1; Nichols, *Literary Remains*, p. 336 & n.; *APC*, iii. 328; *Cal. S.P., Spanish*, x. 347.
78 *APC*, iii. 354–5; *Cal. S.P., Spanish*, x. 347.
79 *Cal. S.P., Spanish*, x. 381; PRO SP46/6/fo. 127v.
80 Talbot Papers B 219; *Cal. S.P., Spanish*, x. 393, 406, 408; Nichols, *Literary Remains*, p. 361.
81 Talbot Papers B 219.
82 *APC*, iii. 464; *LJ*, p. 397.
83 *Cal. S.P., Spanish*, x. 445; *LJ*, p. 394.
84 Nichols, *Machyn*, p. 13.
85 *Cal. S.P., Spanish*, x. 611; Hoak, *King's Council*, pp. 143–4; N.P.Sil, 'The rise and fall of Sir John Gates', *Historical Journal*, xxiv (1981), pp. 929–43.
86 B.L. Beer, *Northumberland: the Political Career of John Dudley, Earl of Warwick and Duke of Northumberland* (Kent State, 1973), pp. 130–1; Nichols, *Literary Remains*, p. 410.
87 J.E. Nightingale, 'Some notice of William Herbert, first earl of Pembroke of the first creation', *Wiltshire Archaeological and Natural History Magazine*, xviii (1879), p. 97.
88 *Cal. S.P., Spanish*, x. 425.
89 Nichols, *Literary Remains*, p. 409.
90 *Ibid.*, p. 465; *Cal. S.P., Spanish*, x. 549, 565–6, 579; xi. 13, 36.
91 Talbot Papers P 219, 255.
92 *Cal. S.P., Spanish*, x. 526.
93 Nichols, *Literary Remains*, p. 418.
94 Talbot Papers P 255.
95 Haynes, *State papers*, p. 112; *Historical Manuscripts Commission, Hatfield House, Salisbury*, i. no. 387 p. 97.
96 *APC*, iii. 464 to iv. 26.
97 *LJ*, pp. 394–428 esp. 401.
98 Reid, *Council in the North*, p. 175.

99 *Cal. Pat. Rolls, Edward VI*, iv. 407; PRO SP10/19/fo. 45ᵥ; Sheffield City Libraries, Arundel Castle MS SD 268 p. 114; *see below*, pp. 142–3.

100 Haynes, *State Papers*, p. 137; *HMC, Salisbury*, i. no. 406 p. 103.

101 *APC*, iv. 177, 193; BL Add. MS 48018 fo. 295.

102 *APC*, iv. 193–289; cf. *LJ*, pp. 431–44.

103 *Cal. Pat. Rolls, Edward VI*, iv. 391–2; Nichols, *Literary Remains*, p. 469.

104 PRO SP10/15 no. 73; *Cal. S.P. Dom., 1547–80*, xv. 73 no. 49; Hoak, *King's Council*, p. 320 n. 158.

105 *APC*, iv. 193–289.

106 Haynes, *State Papers*, p. 146; *HMC, Salisbury*, i. no. 439 p. 118; *Cal. Pat. Rolls., Edward VI*, v. 70–2.

107 *Cal. Pat. Rolls, Edward VI*, v. 231.

108 Gammon, *Statesman and Schemer*, p. 185.

109 *Cal. S.P., Spanish*, x. 70.

110 J.G. Nichols, ed., *The Chronicle of Queen Jane and Two Years of Queen Mary, Camden Society*, 1st series, xlviii (1850), pp. 91. 99.

111 *Cal. S.P., Spanish*, ix. 75; M. l'abbe de Vertot, *Ambassades de Messieurs de Noailles en Angleterre* (Leiden, 5 vols, 1743), ii. 50.

112 J. Pratt, ed., *The Acts and Monuments of John Foxe* (8 vols, 1877), vi. 385–6; *Historical Manuscripts Commission, Finch*, i. 1.

113 Nichols, *Machyn*, pp. 35–6.

114 A. de Guaras, *The Accession of Queen Mary*, ed. R. Garnett, (1892), p. 85.

115 Reid, *Council in the North*, p. 180.

116 *Cal. S.P., Spanish*, xi. 82.

117 *Ibid.*, xi. 44.

118 *Ibid.*, xi. 51, 55.

119 *Ibid.*, xi. 95–6; cf. *Historical Manuscripts Commission, City of Exeter* (1916), p. 366.

120 F. G. Emmison, *Tudor Secretary: Sir William Petre at Court and Home* (1961), pp. 107–8.

121 de Guaras, *The Accession*, p. 95.

122 *Cal. S.P., Spanish*, xi. 50.

123 *Ibid.*, xi. 67.

124 *Ibid.*, xi. 70.

125 E.H. Harbison, *Rival Ambassadors at the Court of Queen Mary* (Princeton, 1940), p. 45.

126 Nichols, *Chronicle*, pp. 6–7.

127 de Guaras, *The Accession*, pp. 92–5.

128 Nichols, *Chronicle*, pp. 119–20; *The Copie of a Pistel or Letter Sent to Gilbard Potter in the Tyme when he was in Prison for Speakinge on our Most True Quenes Part the Lady Mary*, sig A viiᵥ.

129 W. K. Jordan and M.R. Gleason, 'The saying of John late duke of Northumberland upon the scaffold, 1553', *Harvard Library Bulletin*, xxiii (1975), p. 154 n. 26; F. Madden, 'Petition of Richard Troughton ... relating to the share by him in the duke of Northumberland's plot', *Archaeologia*, xxiii (1831), pp. 20, 40.

130 Chatsworth, Clifford Letters, no. 57. (I owe this reference to Mr R.W. Hoyle).

131 Nichols, *Chronicle*, pp. 1-2, 10, 119-20; 'Arundell', pp. 119-30; *Cal. S.P., Spanish*, xi. 108. Cf. BL Lansdowne MS 104 fo. 1 no. 1.
132 *Cal. S.P., Spanish*, xi. 86.
133 D. MacCulloch, ed., 'The *Vita Mariae Angliae Reginae* of Robert Wingfield of Brantham', *Camden Society*, 4th series, xxix (1984), pp. 258-9; Nichols, *Chronicle*, pp. 8-9
134 *Ibid.*, p. 9.
135 Grafton, *Chronicle*, pp. 533-4.
136 Nichols, *Chronicle*, pp. 8-9
137 *Ibid.*, p. 2.
138 MacCulloch, *Vita Mariae Angliae Reginae*, pp. 254-8, 263-4, 266.
139 Nichols, *Chronicle*, pp. 5-6.
140 Nichols, 'Arundell', pp. 119-20.
141 Nichols, *Chronicle*, p. 9.
142 de Guaras, *The Accession*, p. 96.
143 Vertot, *Ambassades*, ii. 75.
144 Harbision, *Rival Ambassadors*, p. 49; Lemasters, thesis cit., p. 30; *Cal. S.P., Spanish*, xi. 85.
145 *Cal. S.P., Spanish*, xi. 82-8.
146 *Ibid.*, xi 88.
147 *Ibid.*, xi 95-6.
148 *HMC, Finch*, i. 2-3; Nichols, *Chronicle*, pp. 12, 110; *Cal. S.P., Spanish*, xi. 95-6.
149 Nichols, 'Arundell', pp. 119-20.
150 *APC*, iv. 417.
151 M.S. Giuseppi, J.C. Walker and A.C. Wood, eds., *Calendar of the Patent Rolls: Philip and Mary* (4 vols, 1936-9), i. 421, 464; *Cal. S.P., Spanish*, xi. 150-1.
152 *APC*, iv. 315, 322-6.
153 *Cal. S.P., Spanish*, xi. 184-5; *Cal. Pat.Rolls, Philip and Mary*, i. 75, 121; Nichols, *Literary Remains*, p. ccxl; Strype, *Ecclesiastical Memorials*, ii. 432; *APC*, iv. 315.
154 Strype, *Ecclesiastical Memorials*, iii. 31.
155 Talbot Papers p. 233; Rymer, *Foedera*, xv. 337-8.
156 *Cal. S.P., Spanish*, xi. 172.
157 Nichols, *Chronicle*, p. 15; *Cal. S.P., Spanish*, xi. 228.
158 Vertot, *Ambassades*, ii. 167-69.
159 *Cal. S.P., Venetian*, v. no. 813 p. 400.
160 J. Loach, 'Opposition to the crown in parliament, 1553-1558', University of Oxford D. Phil. thesis, 1974, pp. 64-6.
161 *Cal. S.P., Venetian*, v. no. 934 pp. 559-60.
162 Loach, 'Opposition to the crown', pp. 226-30.
163 *Cal. S.P., Spanish*, xi. 82.
164 *Ibid.*, xi. 85.
165 *Cal. S.P., Venetian*, v. no. 934 pp. 559-60.
166 Vertot, *Ambassades*, ii. 245-6.
167 *Cal. S.P., Spanish*, xi. 363.
168 Vertot, *Ambassades*, ii. 219.

169 *Cal. S.P., Spanish*, xi 364–5.
170 *Ibid.*, xi. 395.
171 *Ibid.*, xi. 399.
172 *Ibid.*, xi. 443.
173 *Ibid.*, xi. 425, 431, 443; Lemasters, thesis cit., pp. 131–2.
174 Vertot, *Ambassades*, ii. 231, 317–18, 320; Harbison, *Rival Ambassadors*, p. 103; Loach, 'Opposition to the crown', p. 101; D.M. Loades, *The Reign of Mary Tudor* (1979), pp. 121–3.
175 Vertot, *Ambassades*, iii. 60.
176 *Historicial Manuscripts Commission, Buccleuch and Queensberry, Montagu House, Whitehall*, (4 vols in 3, 1899–1926), iii. 4.
177 D.M. Loades, *Politics and the Nation 1450–1660: obedience, resistance and public order* (1974), pp. 226–7; *Cal. S.P., Venetian*, v. nos. 851, 858, 934, pp. 458, 468, 560; Grafton, *Chronicle*, p. 538; P.A. Clark, *English Provincial Society from the Reformation to the Revolution: religion, politics and society in Kent 1500–1640* (Hassocks, 1977), pp. 88–90, 426–7; Mackwell, 'Sir James Croft', pp. 44–6; M.R. Thorp, 'Religion and the Wyatt rebellion of 1554', *Church History*, xlvii (1978), pp. 363–80.
178 D.M. Loades, *Two Tudor Conspiracies* (Cambridge, 1965), p. 69; *idem, Reign of Mary Tudor*, p. 127.
179 PRO PRO E/31/3/21 fo. 167; Harbison, *Rival Ambassadors*, p. 127.
180 Nichols, *Chronicle*, p. 37.
181 Nichols, 'Arundell', p. 122.
182 BL Add. MS 48018 fo. 295v.
183 Talbot Papers C 5.
184 *Cal. S.P., Spanish*, xii. 38.
185 Talbot Papers C 15.
186 *Cal. S.P., Spanish*, xxii. 87, 95.
187 *Ibid.*, xii. 118–19.
188 Vertot, *Ambassades*, iii. 265.
189 Loach, 'Opposition to the crown', p. 102.
190 *Ibid.*, p. 98.
191 *Cal. S.P., Venetian*, v. no. 934 p. 533; Loades, *Reign of Mary Tudor*, pp. 75–6.
192 *Cal. S.P., Spanish*, xii. 335.
193 *Ibid.*, xii. 77.
194 *Ibid.*, xii. 96.
195 Loach, 'Opposition to the crown', p. 100.
196 *Cal. S.P., Spanish*, xii. 200.
197 *Ibid.*, xii. 166–7.
198 *Ibid.*, xii. 167.
199 *Ibid.*, xi. 120.
200 *Ibid.*, xi. 305.
201 *Ibid.*, xi. 335.
202 *APC*, v. 8.
203 *Cal. S.P., Spanish*, xii. 200.
204 *Ibid.*, xii. 220.
205 Vertot, *Ambassades*, iii. 78.
206 *Cal. S.P., Spanish*, xi. 220–1.

207 *Ibid.*, xii. 228.
208 *Ibid.*, xii. 231.
209 *Ibid.*, xii. 238–40.
210 *Ibid.*, xii. 250–1.
211 Vertot, *Ambassades*, iii. 170.
212 *Cal. S.P., Spanish*, xii. 258.
213 Vertot, *Ambassades*, iii. 218–19.
214 *Cal. S.P., Spanish*, xii. 251.
215 Vertot, *Ambassades*, iii. 218–9.
216 *Cal. S.P., Spanish*, xii. 251.
217 Vertot, *Ambassades*, iii. 225–6.
218 *Cal. S.P., Venetian*, v. no. 934 pp. 558–9.
219 *Cal. S.P., Spanish*, xii. 251.
220 *Ibid.*
221 *LJ*, p. 455.
222 Talbot Papers P 263, 267.
223 *Cal. Pat. Rolls, Edward VI*, v. 231; PRO SP10/19/fo. 51ᵥ; *Cal. S.P., Spanish*, xi. 221; *see below*, pp. 141–3, 178.
224 Loach, 'Opposition to the crown', pp. 103–4; cf. Loades, *Reign of Queen Mary*, p. 181 n. 122.
225 Loach, 'Opposition to the crown', p. 113; Lemasters, thesis cit., p. 183.
226 Vertot, *Ambassades*, iii. 216–17.
227 *Cal. S.P., Venetian*, v. no. 934 pp. 558–9.
228 Sheffield City Libraries, Bacon-Frank MS 2/5.
229 Nichols, *Machyn*, p. 90.
230 Vertot, *Ambassades*, iii. 284–5.
231 Nichols, *Chronicle*, p. 82 & n. Cf. *Cal. S.P., Spanish*, xii. 276, 290, 295, 308; xiii. no. 2 p. 2, no. 5 p. 4, no. 7 p. 5.
232 *Cal. S.P., Spanish*, xii. 295.
233 *Ibid.*, xiii. no. 76 p. 65.
234 Nichols, *Machyn*, p. 74.
235 *LJ*, pp. 465–89; *APC*, iv. 81–91.
236 *Cal. S.P., Spanish*, xiii. no. 97 p. 81; Foxe, *Acts and Monuments*, vi. 567; Nichols, *Machyn*, p. 74.
237 *Cal. S.P., Spanish*, xiii. no. 97 p. 82.
238 Strype, *Ecclesiastical Memorials*, iii. 203; Nichols, *Machyn*, pp. 75–6; *Cal. S.P., Spanish*, xiii no. 108 p. 101.
239 *Cal. S.P., Venetian*, v. no. 952 pp. 579–81.
240 *Ibid.*, v. no. 957 p. 585.
241 *Ibid.*, vi (i) no. 14 p. 10.
242 *Ibid.*, v. no. 975 p. 598; vi (i) no. 4 p. 3.
243 *Ibid.*, vi (i) no. 14 p. 10.
244 Vertot, *Ambassades*, iii. 170; *Cal. S.P., Spanish*, xii. 230, 251.
245 Vertot, *Ambassades*, iii. 220; v. 12–13; *Cal. S.P., Venetian*, vi (i) no. 97 p. 85, no. 150 p. 126, no. 245 p. 212; Nichols, *Machyn*, p. 79.
246 *Cal. S.P., Spanish*, xiii. no. 26 pp. 23–4; no. 108 p. 102.
247 Vertot, *Ambassades*, iii. 249; *Cal. S.P., Spanish*, xiii. no. 161 p. 147; *Cal. S.P., Venetian*, vi (i) no. 297 pp. 269–70.

248 Strype, *Ecclesiastical Memorials*, iii. no. xlv for text. Cf. D.M. Loades, 'The authorship and publication of *The copye of a letter sent by John Bradforth to the right honourable lordes the erles of Arundel, Darbie, Shrewsbury and Penbroke'*, *Transactions of the Cambridge Bibliographical Society*, iii part ii (1960), pp. 155-60 (I owe this reference to Mrs J. Loach).
249 Loach, 'Opposition to the crown', pp. 132, 137.
250 Vertot, *Ambassades*, iii. 137, iv. 153-5.
251 *LJ*, pp. 490ff; *APC*, iv. 81-91; *Cal. S.P., Spanish*, xiii. no. 139 p. 134.
252 *Cal. S.P., Venetian*, vi (i) no. 245 p. 212, no. 322 pp. 299-300, no. 460 pp. 415-16; Vertot, *Ambassades*, v. 50, 131, 172.
253 *Cal. S.P., Venetian*, vi (i) no. 257 p. 227.
254 *Ibid.*, vi (i) no. 315 pp. 281-2; Vertot, *Ambassades*, v. 175, 184, 231, 242, 246, 265.
255 *Cal. S.P., Venetian*, vi (i) no. 301 p. 271, no. 464 p. 419, no. 501 p. 470.
256 *Cal. S.P., Dom. 1547-80*, p. 83.
257 *Cal. S.P., Spanish*, xiii. no. 184 p. 169; Vertot, *Ambassades*, v. 364-5.
258 *Cal. S.P., Spanish*, xii. 168; xiii no. 164 p. 151; Harbison, *Rival Ambassadors, passim;* Loades, *Reign of Mary Tudor*, p. 86.
259 Lemasters, thesis cit., pp. 162-5, 174-5, 214-15, 221; Loades, *Reign of Mary Tudor*, pp. 78-82.
260 Loades, *Politics and the Nation*, p. 225.
261 C.S.R. Russell, *The Crisis of Parliaments* (Oxford, 1971), pp. 133-45; C.S.L. Davies, *Peace, Print and Protestantism* (1976), pp. 291-316; J. Loach, 'Opposition to the crown', and reviews in *English Historical Review*, xcvi (1981), pp. 866-9, xcviii (1983), pp. 623-5; J.J. Scarisbrick 'Did Mary have a chance?', paper read to Brasenose College, Oxford, History Society, February 1979.
262 F. J. Fisher, 'Influenza and inflation in Tudor England', *Economic History Review*, 2nd series, xviii (1965), pp. 120-9; D.M. Palliser, 'The crisis of the 1550s', paper read at St John's College, Oxford, 1 March 1983.
263 *Cal. S.P., Venetian*, vi (i) no. 190 p. 168, no. 297 p. 268; see also vi (i) no. 150 p. 125, no. 256 p. 226.
264 Talbot Papers O 8; Lambeth Palace MS 704 fo. 102; Loach, 'Opposition to the crown', p. 174: *see below*, pp. 157-8.
265 *Cal. S.P., Venetian*, vi (i) no. 316 p. 283.
266 J. Loach, 'Pamphlets and politics, 1553-1558', *Bulletin of the Institute of Historical Research*, xlviii (1975), p. 38; Loades, *Politics and the Nation*, p. 237; R.A. Houlbrooke, 'Mary Tudor's persecuting justices', paper read at St John's College, Oxford, Hilary Term 1973.
267 *APC*, v. 118.
268 Talbot Papers C 175.
269 *Cal. S.P., Venetian*, vi (i) no. 305 p. 274.
270 *Cal. S.P., Spanish*, xiii. no. 338 p. 317.
271 *APC*, v. 13-17, 230-82; *LJ*, pp. 514-40; Foxe, *Acts and Monuments*, vii. 445.
272 Talbot Papers C 211; Arundel Castle, Autograph Letters 1513-85, no. 20.
273 Loach, 'Pamphlets and politics'.
274 *Cal. S.P., Venetian*, vi (i) no. 200 p. 174; *Cal. S.P., Dom. 1547-80*, v. 34 p. 67; cf. *Cal. S.P., Spanish*, xiii. no. 338. 317.

275 C.S.L. Davies, 'England and the French war, 1557-59', in J. Loach and R. Tittler eds, *The Mid-Tudor Polity c.1540-1560* (1980), pp. 159-85.

276 *Cal. S.P., Spanish*, xiii. no. 402 pp. 355-57, no. 406 p. 362, no. 413 p. 367; Loach, 'Opposition to the crown', pp. 191-4, 205.

277 *Cal. S.P., Dom. 1547-80*, xiv 2 p. 106.

278 *APC*, v. 423; *Calendar of Patent Rolls, Elizabeth* (5 vols, 1939-   ), i. 71; Talbot Papers E 15; *Cal. S.P., Spanish, Elizabeth*, i. 2; *Calendar of State Papers, Foreign*, iii. *passim; Cal. S.P., Venetian*, vi (ii) no. 1296 p. 1571.

279 *LJ*, pp. 562-3; G.W. Bernard, review of N.L. Jones, *Faith by Statute: Parliament and the Settlement of Religion* (1982) and W.S. Hudson, *The Cambridge Connection and the Elizabethan Settlement of 1559* (Durham, North Carolina, 1980) in *The Heythrop Journal*, xxv (1984), pp. 228-32. Cf. J. Loach, 'Conservatism and consent in parliament, 1547-59', in J. Loach and R. Tittler, eds., *The Mid-Tudor Polity c.1540-1560* (1980), pp. 21-2.

280 *LJ*, pp. 564-5, 567-8.

281 *LJ*, p. 574; E.J. Davies, 'An unpublished manuscript of the Lords' Journals for April and May 1559', *English Historical Review*, xxviii (1913), pp. 537-8.

282 T.E. Hartley, ed., *Proceedings of the Parliaments of Elizabeth I i. 1558-1581* (Leicester, 1881), pp. 4-32; T.J. McCann, "The parliamentary speech of the Viscount Montague against the act of supremacy', *Sussex Archaeological Collections*, cviii (1970), pp. 50-7; J.P. Moreau, 'Les discours des lords catholiques au Parlement de 1559', *Ethno-Psychologie*, xxxii (ii/iii) (1977), pp. 169-84.

283 Lambeth Palace MS 696 fo. 37; *Cal. S.P., Foreign*, iii. 55.

284 C.G. Bayne, 'The visitation of the province of Canterbury', *English Historical Review*, xxviii (1913), pp. 637, 660.

285 Talbot Papers E 41; Lambeth Palace MS 709 fo. 1; *Cal. S.P., Foreign*, lv. no. 497 pp. 233-7, no. 499 p. 237.

286 Nichols, *Machyn*, p. 224.

287 *Cal. S.P., Spanish, Elizabeth*, i. no. 85 p. 125.

288 F. Peck, *Desiderata Curiosa* (1779), pp. 252-6.

PART TWO : WAR

4 The fourth and fifth earls of Shrewsbury and military campaigns in France and on the Scottish borders

War was of the greatest importance in early Tudor England. In 1492, in 1513, in 1522–3, in the 1540s and the late 1550s, large armies were raised to fight in France or on the Scottish borders. Much of the energy of politicians and administrators was devoted to diplomacy and to the preparation of war. Most of the history of Anglo-French warfare after 1450 has been written as if English withdrawal from France was as desirable as it was inevitable and little sympathy has been shown towards the aggressiveness with which English aims were pursued against Scotland. But such judgments may be anachronistic. Apart from the isolated and ineffective sermons of Colet, Warham and Erasmus, there was little opposition to war as amoral and futile. Wars in the early sixteenth century were still in large measure the sport of kings and nobilities, another aspect of the world of tournaments, fought for honour, fought for their own sake.[1] Military service could pave the way for promotion into or within the nobility. After serving in the French campaign in 1513 Charles Somerset, Lord Herbert, was created earl of Worcester, Charles Brandon was created duke of Suffolk. After nearly a year's service on the Scottish borders, Francis Talbot, fifth earl of Shrewsbury, was elected to the order of the garter in April 1545.[2] Military service was a means of gaining a reputation. Greeting the earl of Rutland in 1549, Sir James Croft wrote 'I heare you ar come to the Borders to winne honour.'[3] In July 1548 five Englishmen complained that they had not been able to take their places among the defenders of the besieged town of Haddington, alleging that 'we thyncke we were not kept from the enterpryse for anye fere of the losse of vs but rather for envye that we new soldyours shuld take eny part of there honor that hath seruyd here before'.[4] Military service was a way of redeeming political disgrace. Lord Bray, imprisoned in 1556 for his participation in conspiracy, was released in May 1557 in response to the moving

pleas of his wife and his father-in-law, the fifth earl of
Shrewsbury, on condition that he took up residence with
Shrewsbury. This Bray was well content to do, especially as it was
thought that there would be war with Scotland.[5] In the event
Bray saw service, and lost his life, in the French war of that year, a
campaign that helped to reunite a divided ruling class: many,
like Bray, who had opposed Mary in 1553 or plotted against her
later now served loyally, including the earl of Bedford and the
three sons of the duke of Northumberland.[6] War, then, was not
an aberration. For the nobility it was usually welcome. In the
early Tudor period, as in the age of Edward III, 'war was the
supreme expression of the social purposes for which the military
aristocracy existed'.[7] Of course, noblemen might oppose war if it
required heavy taxation or placed demands of service on their
tenants and servants that these were unwilling to bear: this would
be the more likely after years of unsuccessful or inconclusive
warfare, or in times of economic difficulties. But more generally,
and particularly (as in the early years of Henry VIII's reign) after
a generation of peace, the nobility would seize the opportunity of
demonstrating its valour and its military skills, of showing the
leadership that justified its social privileges, of increasing its hold
over lesser men by a judicious use of military patronage. When
Henry VIII granted Lord Darcy his request to lead the army that
the king was sending to assist Ferdinand of Aragon against the
Moors in 1511, 'many lordes and knightes made suyte to be in the
same iorney'.[8] War was at once a demonstration and a forging of
links of common interest and experience between monarch and
noble subject. It would, however, be to credit Henry or his
advisers with too much calculation to suggest that the campaign
was a deliberately planned investment of inherited royal wealth
in the belief that nothing established a monarch, consolidated a
dynasty and discharged internal tensions more effectively than a
successful war across the sea.[9] Henry VIII's French wars were
rather a return to the policies of Henry's Lancastrian predecessors, notably Henry V. They were a renewal of the Hundred
Years' War, in the context of late medieval chivalry and
ceremony, of Henry's sponsorship of a translation of Froissart,
and of the publication in 1513 of a translation of Titus Livius' life
of Henry V, pointing the parallel with Henry VIII 'now of late
entered into semblable war against the Frenchmen'.[10]

Noblemen were the commanders of early Tudor armies. Their leadership was not just 'ritual': however chivalric in theory, wars could quickly degenerate into messy and bloody conflicts, and noblemen were always closely involved, as will be shown, in the administration of war and in the making of strategy and tactics. Noblemen were chosen as commanders for their personal abilities and experience. They were also chosen because the recruitment of Tudor armies depended on landed magnates. Whenever large armies were required, men might be raised by two methods, the 'quasi-feudal' and the 'national'. 'Quasi-feudal' forces, the most common in this period, were men raised by individual magnates on the authority of letters under the privy seal or privy signet from their own dependents, often by contract between the king and individual magnate. 'National' levies, which were attempted in the 1540s and 1550s, were raised by groups of commissioners on the authority of letters under the great seal from the ranks of the ablest men in the shire. Both methods shared in practice a dependence on the co-operation of the greater magnates. Both made it desirable that men should serve on the battlefield under their lords.[11]

George Talbot, fourth earl of Shrewsbury, served as lieutenant-general of the vanguard of the army royal which invaded France in 1513, capturing the cities of Thérouanne and Tournai.[12] He was no doubt appointed because he raised the largest single contingent, 4,437 men. The total force under his command, including the retinues of the Earl of Derby, Lords Hastings, Fitzwalter and Cobham, was some 8,000 strong.[13] A further reason for his appointment was that his name, re-calling the exploits of John Talbot, first earl of Shrewsbury, still struck the French with fear. In 1512 the Venetian ambassador had noted that the fourth earl of Shrewsbury came from a noble and ancient family called Talbot, and 'to this day in France they still their babies by threatening them when they cry with the coming of the Talbots'.[14] (A Scottish lord in 1522 was to argue for a truce with the English 'for redy coming is the lord Talbot, erle of Shrewesbury, so much drad in Fraunce, as you know well').[15] This fear may even have influenced the outcome of the only decisive engagement of the 1513 campaign, the battle of the spurs. The main French force intent on relieving the besieged city of Thérouanne came upon the English waiting for them at

Guinegate in larger numbers than they had been expecting. the English prepared to give battle but in it Shrewsbury was not taken on.

Therle of Shrewesbury with banner displaied was al daye prest in order of battayle to haue fought with the duke of Alanson and therle of Sainct Polle and the lord of Florenges which was v.M men ... were appoincted to reskewe the towne where the lord of Shrewesbury lay, and to let him come to aid the king, but how so euer that it happened, they stode still and came not down but only skirmished with Sir Rice [ap Thomas]

and then fled in disarray. Members of Shrewsbury's vanguard took four of the six French standards captured that day.[16] The battle was decisive in persuading the captain of Thérouanne to yield his city after a siege of some weeks during which the English had made little impact. That had in no way been Shrewsbury's fault. He complained of inadequate supply and had gone to unusual lengths to secure what little he had. Early in the campaign the king had accused him of having taken (above what he had been allocated) certain pieces of small ordnance and various items of harness that had been intended for the king's and Herbert's men. Shrewsbury never denied the charge, defending himself somewhat disingenuously, on the grounds that he had not known of any such allocation:

Syr, I beseche your grace bee good and gracious souerain lord vnto me soo as by noo synystre surmyse your grace take noo displeasure wuth me: for vndoubtedlye excepte the booke that Morland shewed vnto me I saw noo book of prouysyon that was assigned with you most gracious hand.

If—and only if—Henry still wanted one of the pieces of ordnance to be sent to him, Shrewsbury would not fail to obey the king's command. But even with this additional supply, Shrewsbury thought he had 'but a verraye small porcion', scarce sufficient 'to make not passed oon good abaterye' when they ought to have been able to make two on the side of the city where they lay. They had so few serpentines [lighter guns] 'that for lak of ordenance we be compelled to mak our felde strong with cartes' of which they were also in great need.[17] It is not surprising that this unpromising situation led to no swift triumphs. At least in the preparation and conduct of the siege Shrewsbury had avoided any serious mishaps. He was also prominent in the ceremonial associated with the campaign. He had sent an herald with an address to the captain and inhabitants of Thérouanne, urging them to yield.[18] He reached an agreement with the captains of the city on the terms of surrender.[19] He then entered the city, and placed the banner of St George on the highest point: after searching for hidden resistance he left, unlocking the gates of the city for the king the following day. According to the prior agreement, he then formally delivered the city to Emperor Maximilian.[20] In this campaign Shrewsbury had undoubtedly been one of the 'chief counsellors'.[21] The campaign also marked a watershed in the history of the earldom. It was the last Talbot campaign in France. In the 1520s and later the earls of Shrewsbury were to serve on the Scottish borders.

Anglo-Scottish warfare, and the significance of noble involvement in it, cannot be understood without a prior appreciation of the general characteristics of border society. The borders were forbidding mountainous areas whose people reared cattle, sheep and (possibly to a lesser extent) horses: arable cultivation, particularly of oats, was restricted to the coastal plains and to the long but narrow valleys of rivers and streams, where it might, nonetheless, be practised at higher altitudes than in modern times.[22] Some places, for example Cheviot Forest, because of 'a wete flowe mosse so depe that scarcely eyther horse or cattall may goo thereupon excepte yt be by the syde of certayne lytle broukes & waters', were uninhabitable and of little value as pasture.[23] Transhumance ('the seasonal migration of pastoral people with their herds from a winter settlement to summer pasture') was practised.[24] The inhabitants of certain townships

will about the begenynge of aprell take the most parte of all there cattell and goo with them up unto suche highe lands & waste groundes towarde the border of Scotlande and theire builde theme lodges and sheales & remayne still with there said cattell in such hoopes and valyes wheare they can find any pasture for theme untill the monethe of auguste that they will repayre home agayne for gettynge yf there corne.

Tynedale men used Luseburn and Keilder 'to sheall & sommer with theyr goodes to pasture in the somer season'. Redesdale men 'do sheall & pasture with theyr cattales in somer' south of the river Coquet and in the south and west of Redesdale.[25] Many

'shielings' still survive.[26] Husbandmen might use wood for
building small houses; the headsmen of Tynedale had houses
made from great oak trees.[27] Stone tower houses and bastles were
more common on the coastal plains, and on the immediately
adjacent hills of Cumberland and Northumberland, pelehouses
in the central uplands. Most were built by landed men of considerable wealth. Many had been built before the early Tudor
period, which was probably marked by a lull: large scale
building and rebuilding of such tower houses took place in the
later sixteenth century as the crown acquired border lands and
allowed its customary tenants to pay lower rents.[28] There is no
evidence of industries or of substantial commerce: large villages
served as market centres.

Border society, especially in the higher areas, was composed of
closely-knit groups based on family connections—especially the
kinship of surnames, bonds of manrent (more particularly in
Scotland) and land tenure related to military service. Kinship
groups trace back to the fourteenth century, emerging from local
confederacies of men anxious to protect themselves from war in
the absence of greater magnates.[29] In 1550 Sir Robert Bowes
noted that 'of every surname theire be sundrye famylies or graves
as they call them of every of which there be certeyne headsmen
that leadeth and answereth for all the rest'.[30] Surnames stuck
together against outsiders who brought legal suits against
kinsmen for theft.[31]

If the theaff be of any great name or kyndred and be lawfully executed by order
of Justice the rest of his kynne or surname beare as much mallice which they call
deadly feade against such as followe the lawe against their cossen the theaf as
thoughe he had unlawfully kylled hym with a sword and will by all meanes they
can seeke revenge there vppon.

Feuding was constant.[32] There was often 'much theft' between
Tynedale and Redesdale: 'they will not seeke for their lawfull
remedyes according to justice but rather to revenge one wronge
by another'.[33] The blood feud was itself a form of social
regulation: a less primitive form was a code of border law based
on an elaborate system of monetary compensation for injuries,
reminiscent of the law codes of the Dark Ages.[34] More troublesome was plundering, especially among the upland surnames,

some of which made a living by battening on the agrarian production of the lowlands. 'There be very fewe hable men in all that countrey of North Tyndalle but they have used either to steale in England or Scotland.'[35] Thieving, of cattle and sheep, was a recognised way of earning one's living. Men from Tynedale and Redesdale plundered Englishmen and Scotsmen alike, even pillaging loyalists and rebels in Northumberland during the Pilgrimage of Grace.[36]

The turbulence of the borders had two causes. First, there had been a long history of warfare in the later middle ages. 'March society had had to live through so much war that it had come to live by it.'[37] The insecurity of war had fostered the cohesion of surname groups. Men were always expected to be on watch and to be ready to fight. During war raiding was officially encouraged, as in 1544–5; when peace returned, raiding had become a way of life. The Tynedalers 'determyne themselfes to contynue there in such sorte all their lyves rather than they wyll leave that countrey & serche to gett their lyvynge in other coun-treys & places by true labors or any other lawfull pollycies'.[38]

Secondly, adverse economic conditions played a part. The wars and plundering of the later middle ages improverished the borders.[39] Some land suitable for cultivation, such as Glendale, had been abandoned because of the lack of fortresses to shelter men and barmekins to shelter cattle during war. But by the mid-sixteenth century the underlying problem was rather the poverty and lack of employment resulting from local overpopulation.

Surely the great occasion of the disorder of both those contreys [wrote Bowes in 1550] is that there be moe inhabitants within either of them then the saide countreys maye susteyne to live truely ... they cannot uppon so smalle fermes without any other Craftes live truely but either be stealing in England or Scotland. [Tynedale] ys overcharched with so greatt a nomber of people mo then such profyttes as may be gotten & wonne out of the groundes within the said countrey are able to susteyne & kepe whereby the yonge and actyve people for lack of lyvyng be constrayned to steall or spoyle contynually ether in England or Scotland for the mayntenaunce of their lyvynge.

Tynedalers saw great numbers as a source of strength: moreover it is likely that partible inheritance was customary.[40]

The border was essentially a region not a line.[41] The borderers of one side had natural links with those on the other. 'Together they carried on an essentially agrarian existence and developed their own social organisation ignoring the more or less arbitrary political boundary which nominally separated them.'[42] In some places, it is true, there were specific disputes between Scots and English: over the site of the border itself, as at Carham, or in the Debateable Land; over Scots who daily brought their cattle into England and pastured them on English ground; over fishing in the Tweed, where it was alleged that Scots fishermen 'drew there netts over the whole river compassing soe that they alwayes land upon theire owne side'.[43] Nor did greater landowners such as the Percies share the borderers' disregard for nationality; and it was only when the Scottish state could not protect them against the English that some middling Scottish gentry were prepared to swear allegiance to the king of England.[44] But on the borders co-operation was common. Bowes and Ellerker noted 'Scottes there broughte & conducted into those partes for such evell purposes by the said Tyndalles & Ryddesdales', especially from Liddesdale. In 1550 Bowes described how Redesdalers and the laird of Ferniehirst and his tenants 'with theire cattell in common they doe pasture & eate the said ground in traverse in the somer tyme'. Cassop Bridge was a common passage for Tynedale and Liddesdale thieves 'with the stolen goodes from the one Realme to the other'. If crown officials rode against thieves, 'rather then they will be apprehended flye into Scotland and become outlawes and rebells'. Some Englishmen sold timber from Cheviot Forest to the Scots.[45]

Superimposed upon this feuding and thieving border society, and symbolised as it were by the border itself, were the national, political and dynastic quarrels between England and Scotland. These were not caused by the condition of the borders. 'Major conflicts between the two countries were affected only marginally by the ambiguities of the Tweed-Solway line', disputes over which were subsidiary to wider international issues, particularly the relationship of each country to France.[46] Borderers' activities in themselves rarely, if ever, provoked an outbreak of war between England and Scotland: raids were rather an instrument of policy or used as an excuse to justify further, and more forceful, military action.

From the fourteenth century English kings had appointed wardens in each of the three marches, with the dual responsibility of defending or attacking across the border when the kings of England and Scotland were at war, and of preserving a truce across the border and a semblance of law and order internally when they were at peace. A disadvantage of this arrangement was that only a powerful landowner would be able and have the personal interest to build up and to maintain the military forces required to police the border. Throughout the later middle ages wardens were selected from the leading border families and until 1483 they were in effect allowed to maintain private armies at the king's expense. But such wardens usually had their own interests to pursue, even to the detriment of royal service when an invasion was feared, and they might, in a period of weak or incompetent government, become dangerously overmighty subjects. A more common problem, however, was the lack of suitable men from the greatest families. If a Percy or a Neville was a minor or too old, or for various reasons of character or ability not thought capable of such responsibilities, then the crown had to rely for the rule of the northern borders on men with some local connections while nonetheless dependent upon the crown for their authority, men like Lord Dacre or Sir Thomas Wharton who were called upon to rule, not only in the west marches, where they had some influence, but also in the east and middle marches where they often faced difficulties.[47] In such a situation it would be useful to entrust overall military command when an invasion was feared or an aggressive forward strategy was being planned to a more powerful outsider.

Another factor in the erosion of the power of the warden was the increasing emphasis from the later fifteenth century on large numbers of footmen as opposed to a small corps of horse.[48] Although wardens had usually sent for assistance when more dangerous invasions were feared,[49] it was now more than ever expected that the military needs of the borders would not be met by the borders alone. Men had to be levied from the hinterland and they were placed under the command of a lieutenant-general. The lieutenant-general possessed the powers of a viceroy, acting on behalf of the king in his absence, holding authority over the wardens of the marches, and fulfilling, as will be shown, wide-ranging duties. Unlike the office of warden, the lieutenancy was a temporary appointment, held only when the need arose. Its temporary nature made it more of a public office

and its performance more of a tour of duty than any other
sixteenth-century post. The possible political dangers of a
powerful wardenry, the lack of suitable commanders among the
greatest border families and the military insufficiency of the
borders explain, in the long term, the summonses to the earls of
Shrewsbury in 1522, 1532, 1544–5, 1548 and 1557.

More particularly, the fourth earl was chosen in 1522 for three
reasons. First, the most experienced commander, the earl of
Surrey, was required for service in France. Shrewsbury was the
next most experienced; in Wolsey's opinion he was as 'active a
captain as can be chosen within your realme, mete, convenable
and necessary to be appointed for the ledinge of an armye ayeinst
Scotlande'.[50] Secondly, of the local families, the fifth earl of
Northumberland was not considered suitable while Lord Dacre
lacked authority in the east marches and was anyway fully
engaged on the west marches.[51] Yet Shrewsbury was connected
to the Dacres by marriage and this could strengthen both men.
That such relationships still carried weight is suggested by
Surrey's remark in September 1523 that if Shrewsbury were to
marry his daughter to Northumberland's son, then Percy 'shall
haue gret help and assistence of the lord Dacre [on the borders]
by reason of their alliance'.[52] Thirdly, Shrewsbury was himself
raising men from Shropshire, Staffordshire and Derbyshire.[53] In
the following year the more experienced Surrey was available for
northern service as Charles Brandon, duke of Suffolk, led the
campaign in France. In 1532 Shrewsbury was again appointed
lieutenant-general during a temporary fear of invasion. In
1544–45 his son, the fifth earl, was appointed lieutenant. He had
gained experience serving under the earl of Hertford in spring
1544 and when Hertford was sent to France, Shrewsbury was
chosen in his place. The further experience that he derived made
him an obvious choice in 1548 and again in 1557.

The earls' first task once appointed was to prepare themselves,
levy their forces and assemble at an appropriate place near the
borders (York in 1522, Darlington in 1544–5, Berwick in 1548,
York, then Newcastle, in 1557). The next step was to establish
their authority over other members of the council, resolving any
disputes, dispelling any ill-will and generally fostering good
relations. This was a problem in 1522. Although the fourth earl of
Shrewsbury assured Wolsey that 'it is not possible to have men of

better will and mynde to serve the king booth for his honor and surety of this his realme thenne my lordes her the noble men and commynnaltie of thes north partes be' and later Henry VIII that he 'neuer did see men more glad forwardes nor better willing men to serue', he also reported that since his arrival he had talked with several lords and honourable personages who 'conceiue they were not well enterteyned nor vsed at the laste busynes booth for want of money and vitelles', and that, Shrewsbury added, 'putteth all men in grete doute'.[54] This was an unpopular campaign. Lord Roos, warden of the east and middle marches, was quarrelling with Lord Ogle, Sir William Percy and Sir William Lisle.[55] Roos (Dacre reported from the west marches) wanted to be replaced 'remembring that he is not obeid in his office as vnto the same apperteyneth': on the most recent occasion 'he was not serued with the gentilmen of this Countrie as he shuld haue bene'.[56] In another letter Dacre wrote that 'those that com forwardes come with the worst will that ever did men, and some grete men there is that wold not com forwardes worthie punishment'.[57] Some of the bishop of Durham's force—including Lords Lumley and Hilton and many freeholders in Westmorland—refused to serve: one of the bishop's servants later suggested that fines should be levied on those who had been recalcitrant and the money raised to be distributed to reward those who had done service. The bad harvests of 1519-21 and the plague of 1520-2 (in which 3,000 were reported dead in the city of Durham and the parish of Darlington) severely hampered the mobilisation of the bishopric.[58]

In 1548 the fifth earl of Shrewsbury had to deal with Lord Grey of Wilton whom he replaced as lieutenant-general. A certain awkwardness in their relationship was to be expected and signs of strain appear in Grey's request in late August to be relieved of his remaining command.[59] A serious quarrel had taken place in June (before Shrewsbury's arrival on the borders) between Grey and John Uvedale, treasurer for the payment of the soldiers in the garrisons. Grey complained to Uvedale that his failure to issue money had caused 'a wonderful exclamacion' in Berwick. He endorsed his letter with the words 'hast' six times and 'for the life' three times and accompanied these exhortations with a pair of gallows. This letter reached Uvedale on his way to York, 'signed (as ye maye see)', he complained to the council, .

'with a payre of gallous'. Uvedale declared that he did not know
what Grey meant by that 'but surely it is a tokene mete for
murdrers, theves and others greate offendours, and not for soo
true a man and soo olde a servaunte as I haue bene at all tymes yn
my liff'. He refused to go on to Berwick in person and asked to be
excused from his post. No doubt the matter was smoothed over,
as he continued to serve, but the existence of such tensions
between military commanders and administrators shows further
why it was essential that in any important enterprise a powerful
magnate such as Shrewsbury should be employed on the
borders.[60]

In 1557 Shrewsbury was on good terms with all those under
him, with one significant exception. There was little love lost
between Shrewsbury and Thomas Percy, seventh earl of
Northumberland. It has already been noted that 'Shrewsbury
had no high opinion of Northumberland' and it is clear that he
was greatly concerned by Northumberland's lack of military
experience. On 26 August he ordered Sir James Croft (a veteran
who had earlier been sent to assist Shrewsbury) to go to
Northumberland as quickly as possible, 'for I am afeerd leste
there sholde be any rashe vnsett gyven upon thennyme'. Croft
was deliberately despatched by Shrewsbury to prevent
Northumberland making any costly blunders.[61] Northumberland showed his ignorance of military matters in September in
his request to Shrewsbury to know the rates of wages of soldiers
and captains, 'of which matter', observed Shrewsbury drily, 'I
thought your Lordship shulde haue bene long before this tyme
assertained'.[62] In early October Northumberland committed the
gross folly of summoning the captain of Wark Castle, which was
in imminent danger of attack, to confer with him at Alnwick:
'which yor doing I like not' was the blunt judgment of
Shrewsbury who ordered Northumberland in no uncertain
terms to cancel the summons, or if that were no longer possible, to
send back the captain at once.[63] But the poor relations between
Shrewsbury and Northumberland were not just the consequence
of the latter's military incompetence. It is likely that Shrewsbury
was displeased by the manner of Northumberland's restoration
in 1557 to the earldom that had been in abeyance since 1537. It is
as inadequate to argue that he 'owed his appointment to rank
rather than to any capacity to command' as it is to see his

restoration as the result of some deliberate policy of the Marian government to favour the ancient nobility.[64] He owed his restoration rather to the inability of the queen, Shrewsbury, and, in particular, Lord Wharton, warden of the east and middle marches, to dispense with the power of the Percies in Northumberland in a defensive campaign (the first since Northumberland had come of age). Northumberland's rise closely followed the growing Franco-Scottish threat. It was shortly after Stafford's abortive raid on Scarborough Castle that he was created Lord Percy and (a day later) Earl of Northumberland. As the Scottish threat increased, he was appointed high marshal. Finally on 2 August he was appointed joint-warden of the east and middle marches, the traditional Percy office, which Wharton now had to share with him.[65] A large grant of land followed in the middle of the month. There is no reason to suppose that Northumberland would have been restored but for the fear of invasion. There are hints that Northumberland, or his supporters, may have deliberately stirred up trouble, especially in July, to show that Wharton was incapable of defending the borders and that the return of a Percy to marcher office was therefore essential. Wharton had repeated difficulties with the gentlemen on the east marches.[66] The wording of the letter that the council sent to Shrewsbury, informing him of Northumberland's appointment, is highly suggestive. The council was sorry to hear 'of the vntowardnes of the Northumberlande men . . . whiche neverthelesse we haue sume hope will be partely reformed by the coming thether of our very good lorde the erle of Northumberlande' as joint warden 'which we suppose will be a good meane to bring these men to sume better conformitie'. Shrewsbury's anxiety is clearly revealed by the agitation in his letter to the council of 2 August, expressing understandable uncertainty about the precise nature of his authority on the borders.[67]

The victualling of soldiers was the next task for a lieutenant-general. Lack of victual was the perennial bane of northern warfare. It was the underlying failure of the English borders to produce sufficient food for the consumption of those who lived there that made it such a problem, the consequence of endemic raiding, periodic warfare, poor arable farming conditions and over-population. In peacetime grain had to be imported from Yorkshire, Lincolnshire and East Anglia. In war neither

garrisons nor large armies specially raised for a campaign could
be supported by the borders alone.[68] In 1544–5 Shrewsbury
found that lack of victual prevented the English from attempting
any decisive action. Hume Castle in Scotland might be captured
if two thousand men could be brought from Yorkshire but 'this
lacke and scarcitie of corn and victuall, which is through oute all
this countrey, seameth to be a speciall lett of this enterprise'.[69]
When Shrewsbury was asked to raise a large army in 1545 he
protested that it would be impossible to furnish it.[70] Lack of
victual made him reluctant to call up men from the Bishopric of
Durham to reinforce garrisons under pressure and also made the
likelihood of bishopric men giving prolonged service on the
borders remote.[71] Lack of victual affected him personally: 'I
cannot fynde in this countrey furnyture sufficient for myn owne
howsholde here.'[72] He repeatedly impressed upon the council
that there were no supplies available near the borders. If any
major new operation were to be planned, victual would have to
be obtained from south of the Trent. He supported the demands
of the merchants that in view of the bad harvests the ban on the
shipping northward of victual from Lincolnshire, Norfolk and
Holderness (reserved for the French campaign) should be lifted.[73]
Problems of victualling also affected Shrewsbury in the 1548
campaign. There were not enough carts to bring victual from
Berwick to the army camp in Scotland;[74] the victuallers in
Berwick had to be threatened with hanging before they would
run the risk of being attacked by the French and sail into the
Firth of Forth.[75] During the invasion scare of 1557 Shrewsbury
was again involved in the technical details of victualling. He was
in frequent correspondence with John Abingdon, based in
Berwick, the administrative centre of the defence of the east and
middle marches. Abingdon's letter to Shrewsbury of 29 August is
typical of the matters discussed. He informed Shrewsbury of the
quantities of wheat, meal, malt, hops, oxen, butter, cheese and
weyes that he had in stock. He had sent his purveyor along the
coast from Hartlepool to Hull to buy wheat and malt as cheaply
as he could. A week earlier he had sent victual to the key castles of
Wark, Norham and Ford. He would be able to bake 4,000
quarters of wheat and brew 100 tons of beer a week.[76] Victualling, then, was a daily and detailed preoccupation of a
lieutenant-general.

Victual had to be paid for; garrisons had to be paid their wages. Securing money was therefore another vital concern. It was lack of money that largely explained the disaffection of northerners in 1522. The fourth earl complained in September that the £10,000 which he had been promised would not be enough: if the army had to return without receiving wages great 'doute and dishonor' would follow.[77] When the fear of an invasion by the duke of Albany grew and Shrewsbury ordered the levying of 20,000 men to assist Lord Dacre, he was compelled to promise them their wages in writing, 'elles there setting forward wolde haue been doubtfull'.[78] In 1544–5 the fifth earl of Shrewsbury had to cope with the practical difficulties arising from the fact that the costs of war on two fronts were beyond the resources of the mid-Tudor monarchy. The recurring difficulty was the payment of the wages of the officers and soldiers on the borders. Wages were distributed monthly—the charge was some £2,600[79]— and as each pay day approached Shrewsbury would warn the council that it was imminent.[80] Neither Shrewsbury nor the government kept their own records and from time to time both would ask the treasurers for a full statement of moneys due and moneys in hand.[81] Non-payment of wages had two serious consequences. First, as Shrewsbury noted, 'the pour soudeours do not a litle grudge and compleyne for want of theyr wages'.[82] Secondly, since the cost of victuals was financed by a levy from wages just before they were disbursed, prolonged non-payment would diminish the ability of purveyors to provide victual.[83] Naturally Shrewsbury sought palliatives. Payment could simply be postponed. In August 1544 he suggested that the poorest soldiers in Berwick should be paid but that the 'better parte' should 'spare for a season'.[84] Much time was taken up in writing to the council asking for money. Now and again an officer of the government would be sent northwards with a sum of money towards the expenses of the campaign. A rough estimate would suggest that about 80–90 per cent of what was needed was eventually despatched, in arrears, and after much pleading.[85] In 1557 Shrewsbury complained on 17 August that 'wantyng money I can do nothyng to any effect be the necessite never so grett'.[86] Without money soldiers would give 'bad service':[87] without money 'I should therby dryve the people ... rather into muteny and gruge then otherwyse to retene them wyllyng to serue".[88] 'Gret mewteny ... for want of money' was reported from Berwick on 26 August.[89]

A further subject of detailed concern for a lieutenant-general was the provision of munitions, which had to be sent up to the borders from the south. In 1522 the fourth earl of Shrewsbury complained that ordnance from Nottingham which he had been promised had not arrived.[90] In 1544–5 the fifth earl received reports from the commanders on the borders that gunpowder, matches, bow strings were lacking and that there was no carriage for ordnance; he informed the council of the shortage, pointing out that no remedy could be found locally; the council asked for more information, ordered that meanwhile the marches should be furnished with as much munition as was necessary, and eventually (perhaps after further exchanges of letters) promised to send more.[91] In 1557 the fifth earl wrote to the council for greater supplies of munitions; to the surveyor of the ordnance to deal with unusable arquebuses; to those responsible for failing to unload a hoy carrying 1,000 bows.[92] Regular surveys had to be made of fortifications. During Shrewsbury's term of office in 1544–5 new work was considered or carried out at Berwick,[93] Holy Island,[94] Kelso,[95] Tynemouth[96] and Wark.[97] If the matter was simple, Shrewsbury took order himself: for example he set men to work on repairs to a bulwark on Holy Island that had partly collapsed in October.[98] More complex operations such as the erection of new fortifications at Kelso,[99] Tynemouth[100] and Wark[101] would require the advice of foreign experts sent by the king such as Gian Tommaso Scala and Archangelo Arcana.[102] The responsibilities of a lieutenant-general also included a range of miscellaneous problems: collecting and assessing intelligence of Scottish military plans and political developments:[103] seeing to the defence of coasts;[104] keeping Scottish prisoners safely;[105] dealing with administrative blunders (such as a letter addressed to Shrewsbury in July 1544 ordering him to come at once to the king, a letter that turned out to have been wrongly addressed and properly intended for the master mason of Berwick);[106] dealing with the consequences of a severe epidemic of influenza in 1557;[107] setting up an efficient service of posts;[108] curbing robberies committed by soldiers returning from the borders to their homes in Yorkshire.[109]

Service as lieutenant-general imposed considerable burdens

upon a nobleman. But administrative diligence was not the only necessary quality. Tactical judgment was vital as by far the most important duty of a lieutenant was the execution of the military aims of the government he served. In 1544–5 the fifth earl of Shrewsbury was sent to organise a holding campaign on the northern borders. In December 1543 the Scots had renegued on the marriage alliance (between Henry VIII's son and heir Edward and Mary, the daughter of the late Scottish King James V) that had been concluded by them (led by the earl of Arran) and the English in the treaty of Greenwich in July 1543, a treaty that had followed hard on the defeat of the Scots at Solway Moss in November 1542 and the death three weeks later of James V. Henry had then sent the earl of Hertford to punish and to frighten the Scots by a large-scale raid into Scotland, including the burning of Edinburgh in April-May 1544. Hertford was afterwards recalled to serve in France and Shrewsbury took over responsibility for border affairs.[110] At first Shrewsbury organised raids into Scotland: 'honest journeys', in which houses were burnt, prisoners, crops and livestock seized and large areas laid waste, would 'kepe the Scottes wakyng' and disrupt their harvest.[111] Then Shrewsbury attempted to consolidate an important part of Henry's Scottish policy, arrangements with individual Scots.[112] These 'assured Scots' would promise on oath to serve the English king, especially by advancing his affairs in Scotland, and would give hostages as an earnest (though not as a binding 'guarantee',[113] since they could not be executed or maltreated without adding yet another embittering source of feud among rival borders) of their good intentions. In return the English would refrain from mounting raids against any assured Scot and would assist him to attack (and to defend himself against) any Scots that remained enemies of the English king. Details of each contract were a matter for negotiation and Shrewsbury served as an intermediary between Henry and the council on the one hand and the Scottish lairds on the other.

In mid-July 1544 Andrew Kerr, laird of Ferniehirst, was captured.[114] Shrewsbury distrusted the initial offers made by him while he was a prisoner at Warkworth, intended, he feared, simply to buy time while the harvest was won,[115] but eventually an agreement was reached in October, including Ferniehirst and the laird of Cessford.[116] Shrewsbury had no illusions that the

Scots had come in out of any sympathy for the English cause: 'It is onelie the feare of the kynges majestes force and power that compellith the Scottes to com in after this sorte'.[117] The assured Scots were doing no more than recognising the superior might of the English and declaring in effect that the Scottish government that demanded their loyalty was unable to afford them the protection they required for their lives and their property against English raids. There was, however, no greater acceptance of English rule. Hopes that these Scots would attack their fellow countrymen, notably Walter Scott of Buccleuch and Branxholme, regarded by Shrewsbury as one of the king's greatest enemies, proved vain.[118] But it was not from any residual loyalty to the Scottish government or from any reluctance to become further involved with the English that the Scots refused to play a more positive part in advancing English interests within Scotland. It was rather that the English were not so overwhelmingly superior as to deter Scottish armies from threatening the assured Scots. This meant that the assured Scots could not dare to advance the English cause by pursuing their own rivalries (which coincided with English enmities). At times indeed the assured Scots felt so endangered that they called on English protection to counterbalance their own military weakness and geographical proximity to Scottish armies. This happened in late November 1544 when Scottish forces massed (but it turned out that their real target was the English-held strongpoint of Coldingham Abbey)[119] and again in early February 1545 when the earls of Arran, Angus, Bothwell and Glencairn and a great number of Scottish lords and gentlemen were gathering to attack them (and also Jedworth and Kelso).[120]

Shrewsbury called the Scottish advance 'sodayne' and ordered men from the bishopric of Durham to advance to the borders with all haste.[121] Sir Rafe Eure, warden of the east marches, refused to wait but set off for Jedworth with his own forces on 25 February: on hearing that the Scottish leaders were in Melrose, Sir Rafe advanced against them, drove them out and then burnt the abbey and town. But the Scots regrouped their forces, and as Sir Rafe returned to Jedworth on 27 February, they gave chase at Ancrum Moor, and 'pursued our men so fast that they were forced to light on fote and fight'. In the ensuing melee Sir Rafe Eure and Sir Brian Layton, the captain of Norham, were killed.[122]

At first Shrewsbury reported that[123]

> the chief cause of this ouerthrowe proceded of the treason of the assured Scottes
> of Tyvydale—whose aduise and chiefely the lardes of Bonjedworthe, it is sayed.
> that Sir Rafe Evres did onely folowe that day. And when the bataille was joyned
> they pretending to be our frendes, did kyll and take mo Englisshe men that day
> then any of thenemyes.

Earlier Shrewsbury claimed that he had often warned Sir Rafe
against 'the trust whiche he dyd put ouermoche in the reconciled
enemyes'.[124] But later Shrewsbury reported that it was 'at the
losse of the feelde'—and not, significantly, during the
fighting—that the Scots from Teviotdale had taken prisoners
and livestock.[125] It seems wholly characteristic that the assured
Scots should await the outcome of the battle before declaring
themselves and that they should show themselves effective at
gathering the spoils of a victory which they had not won. The
assured Scots were opportunists whose only loyalty was to
themselves and whose military and political support would go to
whomever could best protect them in the present. To suggest for
them a more decisive role in Ancrum Moor is to credit them with
a Scottish patriotism they did not possess and a wild disregard for
their own best interests. It was only in as far as they had to be
protected by the English that they were responsible for the defeat
at Ancrum Moor. Their disloyalty was an obvious scapegoat for
mistakes committed by the English: lack of good order, and Sir
Rafe Eure's recklessness in advancing so far and so fast and in
provoking the earl of Angus by desecrating the tombs of his
ancestors in Melrose Abbey. 'Having ever hithero had good
successe, [he] forgate by lyke that fortune is not alwayes one
woman.' Shrewsbury had done all he could beforehand to warn
him against rash adventures but there was no way of stopping
him.[126] It was not a disastrous defeat (some 180 were killed)[127]
and it is unconvincing to say that it 'drastically reversed the
balance of power and confidence in the north'[128] as the Scottish
regency proved quite unable to exploit its victory, and, above all,
to protect the assured Scots against Hertford's raid in late
summer 1545. It would be misleading to see the battle as of any
lasting significance: certainly it was no revenge for Flodden or

Solway Moss. Nor did his conduct of affairs reflect ill on
Shrewsbury. If he was asked to yield his place to Hertford in
April 1545, that was because his tour of duty had been done.[129]
He was then elected (after repeated failures in previous years) to
the order of the garter, a sign of Henry's satisfaction with the way
that he had in the face of considerable difficulties managed a by
no means unsuccessful holding campaign.[130]

    In 1548 Shrewsbury was called upon to lead a large army into
Scotland. By then English policy towards Scotland was directed
by Hertford, then duke of Somerset and Lord Protector, who,
aware of the futility, in the long run, of raids, both large-scale
such as that of spring 1544, and small-scale such as those that
Shrewsbury had organised in summer 1544, had advocated and
implemented the strategy of seizing and fortifying potential
strongpoints within Scotland. Several were won by sieges or
delivered to the English by sympathetic Scots in late 1547 and
early 1548 in the aftermath of Somerset's invasion of Scotland
with an army of some 20,000 in which he had crushed the Scots at
the battle of Pinkie. These strongpoints were garrisoned: from
this military presence it was thought that the political
domination of Scotland would surely flow.[131] The garrisons were
to shelter raiding parties, to command shipping on the Tay and
Forth, to watch Scottish troop movements and to protect the
assured Scots. Scots were also to be won over by the distribution
of bibles and printed propaganda, by the lavish granting of
pensions and by the dissolution of the monasteries.[132] The flaw in
this strategy was the constant danger that the French would
intervene (as they had briefly in June–July 1547) and attack the
strongpoints. Somerset had hoped that the establishment of
garrisons would obviate the need for huge armed invasions. But
the arrival of the French in June 1548 (and earlier fears of their
coming) led him to send a large army and a fleet of ships
northwards, with the aim of discouraging the French.
Shrewsbury was appointed lieutenant-general. After overseeing
the raising of forces in many northern counties (successfully,
judging from Lord Grey's comment when 200 men arrived on 15
June that Shrewsbury should be greatly thanked 'that so
dilligently and in so good ordre he hath sent forthe suche a bande
of tall personages wherein ... there is not one vnable man'),[133]
Shrewsbury arrived at Berwick by mid-July.[134] His most obvious

purpose was to relieve the garrison in the besieged town of Haddington. This was regarded by English, Scots and French alike as the most important of the potential strongpoints fortified by the English after Pinkie. Substantial fortifications had been erected in spring 1548, especially a four-bastioned thick curtain-wall of earth. Beaugué, a French captain, described Haddington as 'étant comme au coeur d'Ecosse', 'fit to insult over and annoy the whole kingdom'. Somerset told the French ambassador that Haddington enabled him to keep in subjection 'the best and most fertile country in Scotland'. Sir Thomas Palmer, a leading English captain, told Somerset that 'it is thoppinion of most men that kepyng Haddyngton ye wyne Skotland'; 'kepe that & ye shall do what ye wyll in Skotland; lyese that & ye put all the rest in hassard'. The French ambassador thought it was 'une des plus belles et fortes places après Thurin' and bigger than Calais; the French ambassador reconnoitred in late June and found the fortress stronger than he had expected.[135] The siege had begun on 30 June. It exposed the weakness of Haddington: its garrison could be succoured and victualled only by land, as the sea was too distant, and then only by a large army. A small army would soon be in great jeopardy: 'to aduenture any thing by lande, I thinke it not good except it were with a royall force', was one captain's warning.[136]

Shrewsbury faced considerable problems on arriving at Berwick. Relations between Englishmen serving on the borders were not always friendly. A recent attempt to exploit the departure of the Scots from the siege of Haddington had met with failure. This was an enterprise done 'all for glorie, whiche . . . God woll not alwayes suffre' rather than for any clear purpose. Overconfident after the success of an earlier venture to supply Haddington with powder, a group led by Sir Thomas Palmer and Sir Robert Bowes fell into an ambush: they and 120–80 men were captured and some sixty were killed. Initial reports made the defeat sound shattering. It cost Haddington a good deal of powder and a number of light horsemen.[137] Shrewsbury responded to this reverse, which happened just before he arrived on the borders, with great caution: that explains why there was no repetition of this fiasco. He was careful to wait until Lord Clinton, commanding the English fleet, was able to feign a landing at Leith and burn several towns on the opposite side of the Firth.[138] On 18 August Shrewsbury and Grey crossed the border leading 11,412 foot (including 2,000 German mercenaries) and 1,800 horsemen.[139] As the English army advanced, the French realised that they would be outnumbered and lifted the siege.[140] According to an Elizabethan account by Captain Dethick, the chronology of which is fanciful, the garrison of Haddington had been suffering so miserably from lack of supply 'that they were constraynde to eate horses, dogges, cattes and rattes'. Moving scenes took place when Shrewsbury relieved the town.[141]

The Earle let fall teares from his eyes, to see that suche valyant men shoulde suffer suche distresse, whose stowt hartes coulde not bee conquered with any afflictions. On the other syde, our wearied souldiers sent out the fountaynes of their eyes, for ioye, to see their deliuerance at hand. Thus with mournfull and ioyfull embrasinges they met.

Shrewsbury had persuaded the French to break off the siege and had successfully relieved and supplied the town: Haddington would now almost certainly be safe for the remainder of the season. But if this had been the most visible purpose of Shrewsbury's invasion, it was not the only objective. However moving the relief of the town in retrospect, Haddington had not been in any imminent danger. As Somerset told the French ambassador in early September, it could have been revictualled and supplied with powder, shot and tools by a much smaller force. There were in fact two further aims in this campaign. First, Shrewsbury and Grey were expected by Somerset to engage the French in battle, erasing the memory of the defeat in mid-July and reducing future threats. But while the English tried hard to do this, the French called on Scottish reinforcements, which forced the then outnumbered English to withdraw and wait until the Scottish forces had consumed their victuals and departed, by which time the English were facing growing difficulties of supply.[142] It is mistaken to suppose that Shrewsbury's army could have expelled the French from Scotland.[143] Somerset, who was very angry with Shrewsbury, probably wanted him to repeat what he himself had done in 1547 when he had led a successful raid into Scotland and crushed the Scots at Pinkie. But it would have been astonishing if Shrewsbury (or indeed Somerset, despite his boast to the French ambassador) could have done the same in 1548.[144] Somerset had been very fortunate to win the battle of Pinkie: only the tactical miscalculation of the Scottish commander in abandoning an almost impregnable position had given the English the chance to defeat the Scots.[145] It was unlikely that the Scots would repeat their error. Furthermore the reinforcement of the Scots by a contingent of some 5,000 Frenchmen under d'Essé had changed the balance of power. When Somerset railed against his commanders to the French ambassador, acusing them of doing 'tout le rebours de ce quy leur estoit ordonné', these criticisms appeared so misplaced to men in Shrewsbury's camp that it was rumoured that Somerset had given Shrewsbury this command to ruin him. After Shrewsbury had returned from Scotland, Somerset continued to complain, telling the French ambassador that Shrewsbury and Grey 'n'estoint vouluz aller rencontrer et combatre vos gentz comme il leur avoit ordonné'.[146]

The second further aim of the campaign of 1548 was the establishment of new fortified strongholds within Scotland. Shrewsbury was to fortify at Musselborough or at Aberlady (both nearer Edinburgh than Haddington was) 'if yt be possyble',[147] but because the French were not driven off that remained a dream. They were also to fortify in the Pease, a narrow funnel between the Lammermuir Hills and the coast, a mile from Cockburnspath and Dunglass, which would make it easier to supply Haddington by sea.[148] Shrewsbury was here hampered by his inability to take on the Scots and the French together; by the priority given to Clinton's naval enterprise in the mouth of the Tay; and by the consequent, and increasing, lack of victual and carts.[149] But Shrewsbury did manage to arrange the construction of 'a certeyne fortres vpon a hill besydes Dunglasse', supplying 176 pioneers and labourers from his army for that work between 9 September and 10 October.[150] The campaign then ended. Shrewsbury had failed to defeat the French and had failed to establish new fortifications near the heart of Scottish power. He had neither inflicted a decisive defeat on the French nor improved the English position. But he had broken the French siege of Haddington and refurbished that town; his attempt to lure the French into battle was foiled not by incompetence but by the arrival of the Scots and by his own lack of supplies; he avoided any defeats and mishaps; and, if his largest plans for new fortifications were thwarted, he was nonetheless able to fortify at Dunglass. Shrewsbury had done all that was possible in adverse circumstances. If the events of 1548 show the defects, even the bankruptcy, of Somerset's Scottish policy—the unsuitability of Haddington as a fortress, the re-emergence of French influence in Scotland, or indeed the betrothal of Mary to the French dauphin and her subsequent spiriting away to France—that cannot be blamed on Shrewsbury.

In 1557 the English feared that their involvement in war in north-east France alongside Philip II of Spain (to be marked by the victory of St Quentin in August 1557 and the loss of Calais in January 1558) would provoke Scottish attacks against England. Shrewsbury was called upon to direct the campaign on the northern borders, and to resist, if necessary, a Scottish–French invasion.[151] The key question that Shrewsbury had to answer in summer 1557 was just how serious that threat was and whether it justified the despatch of a main army to the borders. It was vital to avoid the premature expenditure of victual and money. Shrewsbury shrewdly described his strategy as being 'compelled to enforce the power by litle and by degrees lest by lyving together and comyng all at ons, we shuld for wante of vyctuelles be compellyd to retyre before thenyme'. He feared a war of attrition in which victory would go to the army that was the more skilful in husbanding its scarce resources of victual: 'the stryffe shalbe which of vs may contynue longest together for the tyme of yeare and wante of vyctuales'.[152] An even worse prospect was that the English army might be forced to fight at a disadvantage because of lack of victual, as had happened at Flodden. It was crucial to gather good intelligence and to interpret it accurately.

Shrewsbury judged matters rather well. In August he refused to send forward any of the men called up in North Yorkshire despite the alarmed tones in which Wharton (writing from Berwick) reported some raids that were no more than the daily stuff of life on the borders, and despite the requests of the earls of Westmorland and Northumberland.[153] He imposed his views upon them at a conference at Brancepeth on 2 September.[154] Throughout August and September he faced a relentless barrage of urgent information about the imminence of a Scottish invasion but he succeeded in calming the men on the borders and delayed sending up soldiers as long as he dared.[155] Not till 20 September did Shrewsbury, now convinced that an attack was likely, raise the greater part of the English forces. Possibly he too had lost his nerve, momentarily; perhaps he was misinformed; or perhaps, since the Scots did mass and briefly threaten Kelso, he was correct but simply could not have foreseen how shortlived the Scottish menace would prove. However this may be, there is a trace of annoyance with Northumberland and Westmorland in early October: 'here being nowe a good numbre of men assembled who do contynue and haue bene in this partes since the seconde of this monethe to the queenes majestyes no little charges', he wrote, underlining the whole sentence. He would not have called up as many men as he had if he had heard earlier from the council, but now any visible slackening would just encourage the Scots.[156] Suddenly news came that the Scots had disbanded. The invasion did not take place largely for reasons beyond Shrewsbury's control: namely the opposition of the Scottish nobility to their military involvement in what appeared to them increasingly as a purely French quarrel, and the delays caused by incessant bad weather.[157] But another reason why national peace between England and Scotland was preserved on the borders was the solidity of the preparations which he had supervised, as he quite properly pointed out to the council both before and after the Scots disbanded.[158] His success is best measured if it is remembered that the loss of Calais on the south front was not paralleled by the loss of Berwick on the north front. And his diligent service in a neglected campaign is further testimony to the continuing importance of the nobility in military affairs.

Notes

1 J.J. Scarisbrick, *Henry VIII*, (1968), p. 33; J.R. Hale, 'International relations in the west: diplomacy and war', in G.R. Potter, ed., *New Cambridge Modern History, vol. i. The Renaissance (c.1493–1520)* (Cambridge, 1957), pp. 261–2; C.S.L. Davies, 'The English people and war in the early sixteenth century', *Britain and the Netherlands, vol. vi. War and Society* (The Hague, 1978), pp. 1–18.

2. Davies, 'The English people and war', pp. 11–12.

3 *Historical Manuscripts Commission, Rutland, 12th report, appendix iv.* (4 vols in 3, 1888–1905), i. 35.

4 BL Add. MS 32657 fo. 12.
5 Lambeth Palace MS 707 fo. 110.
6 C.S.L. Davies, 'England and the French war, 1557-59', in J. Loach and R. Tittler, eds, *The Mid-Tudor Polity c.1450-1560* (1980), pp. 162-3.
7 A.R. Bridbury, 'The Hundred Years' War: costs and profits', in D.C. Coleman and A.H. John, eds, *Trade, Government and Economy in Pre-industrial England* (1976), p. 82.
8 Hall, *Chronicle*, p. 519.
9 As suggested by D.M. Loades, *Politics and the Nation 1450-1660* (1974), p. 125.
10 W. Busch, 'Englands Kriege im Jahre 1513: Guinegate und Flodden', *Historische Vierteljahrschrift, neue Folge*, xii (1910), p. 5; Scarisbrick, *Henry VIII*, ch. 2; Davies, 'The English people and war', p. 14. I hope to examine the motivations underlying Henry VIII's French wars further in a study of the Amicable Grant.
11 J.J. Goring, 'The military obligations of the English people 1511-1558', University of London Ph.D. thesis, 1955; *idem*, 'Social change and military decline in mid-Tudor England, *History*, lx (1975), pp. 185-97.
12 On the campaign see Scarisbrick, *Henry VIII*, ch. 2; C.G. Cruickshank, *Army Royal: Henry VIII's Invasion of France 1513* (Oxford, 1969); C.S.L. Davies, 'Supply services of English armed forces, 1509-50', University of Oxford D.Phil. thesis, 1963, pp. 209-11, 216-17, 220; R.B. Wernham, *Before the Armada: the Growth of English Foreign Policy 1485-1588* (1966), ch. 6.
13 *LP*, I ii 2051-3, 2392; Hall, *Chronicle*, p. 537.
14 *Cal. S.P., Venetian, 1509-19*, 185; Cruickshank, *Army Royal*, p. 5. On John Talbot see A.J. Pollard, *John Talbot and the War in France 1427-1453* (1983).
15 Hall, *Chronicle*, p. 650.
16. *Ibid.*, p. 551; *LP*, I ii 2227; the best accounts of the Battle of the Spurs are in Busch, art. cit., and C.W.C. Oman, *A History of the Art of War in the Sixteenth Century* (1937), pp. 291-5.
17 PRO SP1/4/fo. 92 (*LP*, I ii 2057); Davies, thesis cit., p. 211.
18 BL Harleian MS 6064 fo. 67 (*LP*, I ii 2027).
19 *LP*, I ii 2186, 2227.
20 Hall, *Chronicle*, p. 552; *LP*, I ii 2227, 2391.
21 Vergil, *Historia Anglica*, pp. 209, 223.
22 The reports by Sir Robert Bowes and Sir Rafe Ellerker in December 1542 and by Bowes in 1550 are full of information about border society. They are printed in J. Hodgson, *History of Northumberland* (3 parts in 6 vols, Newcastle, 1820-40), part iii vol ii. 171-246. All references are to this volume. Modern discussions are P.W. Dixon, 'Fortified houses in the Anglo-Scottish border: a study of the domestic architecture of the upland area in its social and economic context 1485-1625', University of Oxford D.Phil. thesis, 2 vols, 1976; R. Newton, 'The decay of the borders: Tudor Northumberland in transition', in C.W. Chalklin and M.A. Havinden, eds, *Rural Change and Urban Growth 1500-1800: Essays in English Regional History in Honour of W.G. Hoskins* (1974), pp. 1-31.
23 Hodgson, *Northumberland*, pp. 203-4, 220.

24 H.G. Ramm, R.W. McDowall and E. Mercer, *Shielings and Bastles* (Royal Commisson on Historical Monuments, England, 1970), p. 1.

25 Hodgson, *Northumberland*, pp. 220-1, 226, 230.

26 Ramm *et al*, *Shielings and Bastles*, pp. 1-43 and Dixon, thesis cit., i. 164-5 and ii. *passim.*

27 Hodgson, *Northumberland*, pp. 204, 232-3.

28 Dixon, thesis cit., i. 44, 130-59, 179; *idem*, 'Shielings and bastles: a reconsideration of some problems', *Archaeologia Aeliana*, 4th series, i (1972), pp. 254-56; *idem*, 'Towerhouses, pelehouses, and border society', *Archaeological Journal*, cxxxvi (1979), pp. 240-52; Ramm, *op. cit.*, pp. 61-104 esp. 71-2; R.W. Hoyle, 'Tenant right in the northern counties in the sixteenth century', paper read at History Faculty Library, Oxford, 1 June 1982.

29 J.A. Tuck, 'Northumbrian society in the fourteenth century', *Northern History*, vi (1971), pp. 27-8; A. Cardew, 'A study of society in the Anglo-Scottish borders 1455-1502', University of St Andrews Ph.D. thesis, 1974, pp. 3, 83; Dixon, thesis cit., i. 46-7; *idem*, 'Towerhouses, pelehouses', pp. 242-6.

30 Hodgson, *Northumberland*, pp. 229-30; cf. Dixon, thesis cit., i. 53.

31 Hodgson, *Northumberland*, pp. 233-4.

32 Cf. T.I. Rae, *The Administration of the Scottish Frontier 1513-1603* (Edinburgh, 1966).

33 Hodgson, *Northumberland*, p. 224.

34 T. Hodgkin, *The Wardens of the Northern Marches* (1908), p. 15; D.L.W. Tough, *The Last Years of a Frontier* (Oxford, 1928), pp. 100-11. Cf. J. Wormald, 'Bloodfeud, kindred and government in early modern Scotland', *Past and Present*, lxxxvii (1980), pp. 54-97.

35 Hodgson, *Northumberland*, p. 232.

36 Dixon, thesis cit., i. 59; M.E. James, 'Change and continuity in the Tudor north', *Borthwick Papers*, xxvii (1965), p. 6; Rae, *Scottish Frontier*, p. 4; Hodgkin, *Wardens*, p. 5; Tough, *Last years*, p. 47; D. Hay, 'England, Scotland and Europe: the problem of the frontier', *Transactions of the Royal Historical Society*, 5th series, xxv (1975), pp. 80-1; *idem*, 'Booty in border warfare', *Transactions of the Dumfriesshire and Galloway Natural History and Antiquarian Society*, 3rd series, xxxi (1954 for 1952-3), pp. 145-66.

37 J. Campbell, 'England, Scotland and the Hundred Years' War in the fourteenth century', in J.R. Hale, J.R.L. Highfield and B. Smalley, eds, *Europe in the late middle ages* (1965), p. 214.

38 Hodgson, *Northumberland*, p. 233; cf. p. 243.

39 E. Miller, 'War in the north: the Anglo-Scottish wars of the middle ages', - St John's College, Cambridge lecture 1959-60 in the University of Hull, 1960, esp. pp. 5-8, 10.

40 Hodgson, *Northumberland*, pp. 187-8 (cf. 207), 217, 224-5, 233-4, 237; Dixon, thesis cit., i. 109-15 (on partible inheritance).

41 James, 'Change and continuity', p. 3; Dixon, thesis cit., i. 10; Cardew, thesis cit., p. 1; cf. O. Lattimore, 'The frontier in history', *Relazioni of the International Congress of Historical Sciences*, Rome, 1955 (Florence, 1956), i. 106. For international comparisons see Hay, 'England, Scotland and Europe', pp. 83, 88-9.

42 Rae, *Scottish Frontier*, p. 4.
43 Hodgson, *Northumberland*, pp. 173, 186-90, 177-8, 219, 197.
44 Cardew, thesis cit., p. 59 and *see below* pp. 121-3.
45 Hodgson, *Northumberland*, pp. 228-9, 238, 213, 239, 205.
46 Hay, 'England, Scotland and Europe', p. 79.
47 R.R. Reid, 'The office of warden of the marches: its origin and early history', *English Historical Review*, xxxii (1917), pp. 479-96; R.L. Storey, 'The wardens of the marches of England towards Scotland, 1377-1489', *English Historical Review*, lxxii (1957), pp. 593-615; James, 'Change and continuity', pp. 5-6; Cardew, thesis cit., pp. 286, 301-2; M.L. Bush, 'The problem of the far north', *Northern History*, vi (1971), pp. 40-63; P.J. Gwyn, 'Wolsey and the north', unpublished paper.
48 Rae, *Scottish Frontier*, p. 45. On this large subject of the 'military reformation' (the phrase is J.R. Hale's) see J.R. Hale, *Renaissance Europe, 1480-1520* (1971), pp. 25, 91, 191-2; G. Parker, *The Army of Flanders and the Spanish Road* (Cambridge, 1972), pp. 5-6; M. Roberts, *Gustavus Adolphus* (2 vols, 1953-8), ii. 169-89; *idem*, 'The military revolution 1560-1660' in his *Essays in Swedish History* (1967), pp. 195-225; G. Parker, 'The "military revolution", 1560-1660—a myth?', *Journal of Modern History*, xlviii (1976), pp. 195-214.
49 Campbell, 'England, Scotland', pp. 192-3.
50 *State Papers*, i. xxi p. 30 (*LP*, III ii 1462 (2)).
51 *LP*, III ii 2536.
52 *LP*, III ii 3321.
53 *LP*, III ii 2164.
54 BL Cotton MS Caligula B ii fo. 99 (*LP*, III ii 2503); B iii fo. 155 (*LP*, III ii 2523).
55 *LP*, III ii 2402.
56 BL Cotton MS Caligula B i fo. 21 (*LP*, III ii 2598).
57 *Ibid.*, B ii fo. 310.
58 *Ibid.*, B iii fo. 301 (*LP*, III ii 2546); *LP*, III ii 2531; M.E. James, *Family, Lineage and Civil Society: a Study of Society, Politics and Mentality in the Durham Region 1500-1640* (Oxford, 1974), p. 8.
59 PRO SP50/4/fos. 103, 103 (1), 105.
60 PRO SP15/2/fos. 64, 64 (1).
61 C.A. Mackwell, 'The early career of Sir James Croft 1518-70', University of Oxford B.Litt. thesis, 1970, p. 72; Talbot Papers D 124; R.E. Ham, 'The autobiography of Sir James Croft', *Bulletin of the Institute of Historical Research*, 1 (1977), p. 54.
62 Talbot Papers D 173.
63. Talbot Papers D 226.
64 Mackwell, thesis cit., p. 72.
65 Rymer, *Foedera*, xv. 461-3, 468-77; *APC*, vi. 92-3; *Historical Manuscripts Commission, Pepys MSS, Magdalene College, Cambridge* (1911), p. 2.
66 Talbot Papers C 296, 328, D 24; *APC*, vi. 132-3.
67 Talbot Papers D 70.
68 Tough, *Last years*, p. 45.
69 BL Add. MS 32656 fo. 95 (*LP*, XIX ii 760).

70 PRO SP1/200/fo. 44.
71 BL Add. MS 32656 fo. 162 (*LP*, XX i 253), cf. fo. 178 (*LP*, XX i 295) and Talbot Papers A 313.
72 PRO SP1/200/fo. 13.
73 BL Add. MS 32655 fo. 95 (*LP*, XIX i 906); fo. 134 (*LP*, XIX ii 17), fo. 170 (*LP*, XIX ii 183); fo. 178 (*LP*, XIX ii 211); fo. 182 (*LP*, XIX ii 217 (2)); fo. 184 (*LP*, XIX ii 226); fo. 195 (*LP*, XIX ii 254); PRO SP1/200/fos. 13, 44.
74 Davies, thesis cit., pp. 174, 261; Talbot Papers B 15, 17, 27; PRO SP50/4/fo. 104.
75 PRO SP50/4/fo. 104; Talbot Papers B 15.
76 Talbot Papers D 141.
77 BL Cotton MS Caligula B ii fo. 99 (*LP*, III ii 2503).
78 *Ibid.* B ii fo. 310 (*LP*, III ii 2536); iii fo. 155 (*LP*, III ii 2523); *LP*, III ii 2524.
79 BL Add. MS 23655 fo. 234 (*LP*, XIX ii 439).
80 BL Add. MS 32655 fo. 156 (*LP*, XIX ii 128) (August); fo. 166 (*LP*, XIX ii 173) (September); fo. 243 (*LP*, XIX ii 478); fo. 245 (*LP*, XIX ii 486), fo. 252 (*LP*, XIX ii 521) (October); 32656 fo. 8 (*LP*, XIX ii 540) (November); fo. 104 (*LP*, XIX ii 779) (December); fo. 134 (*LP*, XX i 190) (February); fo. 166 (*LP*, XX i 276); fo 178 (*LP*, XX i 295); fo. 182 (*LP*, XX i 312) (March); PRO SP1/200/fo. 44 (April).
81 BL Add. MS 32655 fo. 132 (*LP*, XIX ii 7), fo. 234 (*LP*, XIX ii 448); 32656 fo. 137 (*LP*, XX i 175 (2)).
82 BL Add. MS 32655 fo. 169 (*LP*, XIX ii 183). Cf. also fo. 234 (*LP*, XIX ii 448); fo. 243 (*LP*, XIX ii 478) and 32656 fo. 8 (*LP*, XX i 541).
83 BL Add. MS 32655 fo. 148 (*LP*, XIX ii 59). Cf. also fo. 134 (*LP*, XIX ii 17).
84 BL Add. MS 32655 fo. 148 (*LP*, XIX ii 59).
85 *Ibid.* fo. 93 (*LP*, XIX i 904); fo. 173 (*LP*, XIX ii 197); fo. 184 (*LP*, XIX ii 226); fo. 190 (*LP*, XIX ii 247); Lambeth Palace MS 695 fo. 86; BL Add. MS 32656 fo. 4 (*LP*, XIX ii 533), fo. 24 (LP, XIX ii 567), fo. 69 (*LP*, XIX ii 684), fo. 87 (*LP*, XIX ii 708), fo. 136 (*LP*, XX i 175); Talbot Papers A 289, 291; BL Add. MS 32656 fo. 166 (*LP*, XX i 276); PRO SP1/198/fo. 205.
86 Talbot Papers D 93.
87 *Cal. S.P. Dom., Addenda*, p. 458.
88 Talbot Papers D 93.
89 Talbot Papers D 128. Cf. on mutinies in general Parker, *Army of Flanders*, p. 205.
90 BL Cotton MS Caligula B i fo. 303 (*LP*, III ii 2544); iii fo. 155 (*LP*, III ii 2523).
91 BL Add. MS 32655 fo. 129 (*LP*, XIX ii 2), fo. 134 (*LP*, XIX ii 17), fo. 150 (*LP*, XIX ii 78); Talbot Papers P 275. Cf. Talbot Papers A 137; BL Add MS 32656 fo. 203 (*LP*, XIX i 359), fo. 226 (*LP*, XX i 420) and Talbot Papers A 335; PRO SP1/199/fo. 192; SP1/200/fos. 13, 15, 18, 53.
92 *APC*, vi. 121; *Cal. S.P. Dom. Addenda*, p. 455; Talbot Papers D 154, 232.
93 BL Add. MS 32655 fo. 138 (*LP*, XIX ii 25); fo. 140 (*LP*, XIX ii 34); 32656 fo. 15 (*LP*, XIX ii 553); fo. 136 (*LP*, XX i 175), fo. 203 (*LP*, XX i 359), fo. 220-2 (*LP*, XX i 395).
94 BL Add. MS 32655 fo. 209 (*LP*, XIX ii 345). Cf. M.H. Merriman, 'Holy Island', in H.M. Colvin, ed., *The History of the King's Works iv (part ii)*

(1982), pp. 675-6.

95 BL Add. MS 32656 fo. 128 (*LP*, XX i 142).

96 *Ibid.* fos 152-4 (*LP*, XX i 205-6); fo. 193 (*LP*, XX i 309); Talbot Papers A 247; PRO SP1/200/fo. 123.

97 BL Add. MS 32656 fo. 113 (*LP*, XIX ii 792), fos. 119-20 (*LP*, XX i 53 (i) and (ii); fo. 134 (*LP*, XX i 190), fo. 136 (*LP*, XX i 175), fo. 139 (*LP*, XX i 166); Talbot Papers A 235.

98 BL Add. MS 32655 fo. 209 (*LP*, XIX ii 345). Cf. 32656 fo. 113 (*LP*, XIX ii 792).

99 BL Add. MS 32656 fo. 128 (*LP*, XX i 142).

100 Talbot Papers A 247; M.H. Merriman, 'Tynemouth', *History of the King's Works iv. (part ii)*, pp. 683-86.

101 BL Add. MS 32656 fo. 139 (*LP*, XX i 166).

102 Talbot Papers A 247; BL Add. MS 32656 fo. 128 (*LP*, XX i 142); cf. J.R. Hale, 'The defence of the realm 1485-1558', *History of the King's Works iv. (part ii)*, p. 392.

103 e.g. in 1557: Talbot Papers D 150, 220.

104 e.g. in 1544-5: BL Add. MS 32655 fos. 192, 194, 207, 209, 212, 214, 216, 224, 243, 248, 251; 32656 fos. 2, 5b, 7, 8, 16, 20, 21, 37, 39, 52, 54, 56 (*LP*, XIX ii 255, 256, 262, 321, 345, 348, 362, 478, 513, 514, 529, 530, 539, 540, 541, 554, 560, 599, 602, 620, 621, 634; XX i 189): PRO SP1/198/fo. 192; Talbot Papers A 309.

105 e.g. in 1544-5 BL Add. MS 32656 fo. 100 (*LP*, XIX i 931); Talbot Papers A fos. 161, 235, 363; PRO SP1/200/fo. 169.

106 BL Add. MS 32655 fo. 91 (*LP*, XIX i 881).

107 F. J. Fisher, 'Influenza and inflation in Tudor England', *Economic History Review*, 2nd series, xviii (1965), pp. 125-8; Strype, *Ecclesiastical Memorials*, iii. 156-7; Talbot Papers D 182, 194, 209.

108 *APC*, vi. 136, 138.

109 Talbot Papers D 282.

110 On the background to the 1544-5 campaign see especially M.H. Merriman, 'The struggle for the marriage of Mary Queen of Scots: English and French intervention in Scotland 1545-50', University of London Ph.D. thesis, 1975, esp. chs. i and ii; Scarisbrick, *Henry VIII*, pp. 433-5; Wernham, *Before the Armada*, ch. xii; A.J. Slavin, *Politics and Profit: a study of Sir Ralph Sadler 1507-1547* (Cambridge, 1966), pp. 100-31; Davies, thesis cit., pp. 249-57; D.M. Head, 'Henry VIII's Scottish policy: a reassessment', *Scottish Historical Review*, lxi (1982), esp. 16-23.

111 BL Add. MS 32655 fos. 154, 156, 168, 201 (*LP*, XIX ii 172, 284 for last two).

112 For a detailed examination of this throughout the 1540s see M.H. Merriman, 'The assured Scots', *Scottish Historical Review*, xlvii (1968), pp. 10-34.

113 *Ibid.*, p. 12.

114 BL Add. MS 32655 fo. 104 (*LP*, XIX i 945).

115 *Ibid.*, fos. 154, 156, 197 (*LP*, XIX ii 99, 128, 274).

116 *Ibid.*, fos. 238, 241; 32656 fo. 5b, 24 (*LP*, XIX ii 448, 468, 540, 567); Talbot Papers A 149.

117 BL Add. MS 32656 fo. 32 (*LP*, XIX ii 598).
118 *Ibid.*, fo. 5b (*LP*, XIX ii 540), fo. 160 (*LP*, XIX ii 133), fo. 199 (*LP*, XIX ii 274); Talbot Papers A 149. In his article M.H. Merriman implies, and in his thesis he asserts, that it was immediately after making their assurance that they spoiled Scots but his evidence refers either to other matters or to raids that took place in the wholly different situation of 1547.
119 BL Add. MS 32656 fos. 62, 65, 71, 73, 75, 85-7 (*LP*, XIX ii 668, 676, 691, 693, 694, 707-8); Talbot Papers A 183.
120 J. Bain, *Hamilton Papers*, (Edinburgh, 2 vols, 1890-2), ii. 409.
121 BL Add. MS 32656 fo. 158 (*LP*, XX i 248).
122 *Ibid.*, 32656 fo. 185 (LP, XX i 311); Talbot Papers A 273, 279; PRO SP1/198/fo. 82.
123 *Ibid.*, fo. 180 (*LP*, XX i 301).
124 *Ibid.*, fo. 170 (*LP*, XX i 285).
125 *Ibid.*, fo. 182 (*LP*, XX i 312).
126 *Ibid.*, fos. 108 (*LP*, XIX ii 790), 170, 180, 182 (*LP*, XX i 285, 301, 312); Talbot Papers A 239; Scarisbrick *Henry VIII*, p. 452; *State Papers*, v. 419.
127 *Ibid.*, fos. 198, 195 (*LP*, XX i 328, 339); Talbot Papers A 343. The figure of 1,400 killed (L.B. Smith, *Henry VIII: the Mask of Royalty* (1973), p. 246) is a vast exaggeration.
128 Hale, *History of the King's Works vol. iv (part ii)*, p. 384.
129 *LP*, XX i 513.
130 *LP*, XX i 566-7.
131 M.L. Bush, *The Government Policy of Protector Somerset* (1975), pp. 5, 11-13; Merriman, thesis cit., pp. 203-12; Hale, *History of the King's Works vol. iv (part ii)*, p. 397; M.H. Merriman, "The fortresses in Scotland 1547-50", in *History of the King's Works vol. iv (part ii)*, pp. 694-726; G. Donaldson, *Scotland: James V to James VII* (Edinburgh, 1965), pp. 76-78; Davies, thesis cit., p. 244.
132 Bush, *Government Policy*, p. 18; Merriman, thesis cit., pp. 241-57; Wernham, *Before the Armada*, p. 171; M.H. Merriman, 'War and propaganda during the "rough wooing"', *Scottish Tradition*, ix/x (1980), pp. 20-30.
133 PRO SP50/4/fos. 27, 30.
134 PRO SP15/3/fo. 6.
135 Bush, *Government Policy*, pp. 15, 18; Jean de Beaugué, *Histoire de la guerre d'Escosse*, ed. le comte de Montalembert (Bordeaux, 1862), p. 44; Odet, p. 383, 387; Teulet, i. 173, 182; BL Add. MS 32657 fo. 7; PRO SP50/4/fos. 47, 51.
136 PRO SP50/4/fo. 76; cf. Beaugué, *Histoire*, pp. 42-4; Bush, *Government Policy*, p. 24.
137 PRO SP50/4/fos. 76, 86, SP10/4/fo. 38, SP15/3/fo. 12; BL Add. MS 32657 fo. 37; Odet, pp. 440, 443; *Cal. S.P. Spanish*, ix. 289; Beaugué, *Histoire*, pp. 44, 83-5, 90, 92; Teulet, p. 184; Bush, *Government Policy*, p. 24.
138 PRO SP50/4/fo. 102.
139 Odet, pp. 469, 479; PRO SP50/4/fo. 99.
140 Beaugué, *Histoire*, pp. 115-16; *Cal. S.P., Spanish*, ix. 308-9; Teulet, p. 185; Holinshed, *Chronicle*, iii. 893; PRO SP15/3/fo. 17 (1).

141 Ulpian Fulwell, *The Flower of Fame: whereunto is annexed . . . a discourse of the worthie seruice that was done at Haddington in Scotlande, the seconde yere of the raigne of king Edward the sixt* (1575), fos. 51–2; cf. Hollinshed, *Chronicle*, iii. 894.

142 Holinshed, *Chronicle*, iii. 894–95; Beaugué, *Histoire*, pp. 117–18, 123–4.

143 As suggested by Jordan, *Edward VI*, i. 288.

144 Odet, p. 469, 483; *Cal. S.P., Spanish*, ix. 286; PRO SP10/4/fo. 43; SP50/4/fo. 95.

145 Davies, thesis cit., pp. 258–9.

146 Odet, pp. 465, 469, 483.

147 PRO SP10/4/fo. 44; SP50/4/fo. 104; Talbot Papers B 15.

148 PRO SP50/4/fos. 44, 92; Merriman, *History of the King's Works*, p. 694.

149 Talbot Papers B 27.

150 PRO E351/3540; Merriman, *History of the King's Works*, pp. 722–3; Bodleian MS Top. Yorks c. 45 fos. 45ᵥ; 59.

151 See in general M.H. Merriman, 'Berwick', in *History of the King's Works iv (part ii)*, pp. 646–8; C.S.L. Davies, 'England and the French war 1557–59', in J. Loach and R. Tittler, eds, *The Mid-Tudor Polity c.1540–1560* (1980), esp. pp. 167–8; Wernham, *Before the Armada*, pp. 230–1; Mackwell, thesis cit., pp. 70–1; *Cal. S.P., Spanish, 1554–58*, pp. xix–xxi; Harbison, *Rival Ambassadors*, esp. chs x, xii.

152 Talbot Papers D 238, 288.

153 Talbot Papers D 66, 72, 74, 77, 81.

154 Talbot Papers D 147, 163, 167, 169, 174, 179.

155 Talbot Papers D 80, 89, 128, 151, 153, 162, 177, 197, 210x, 211, 228, 232.

156 Talbot Papers D 182, 228, 238.

157 Talbot Papers D 228, 230d.

158 Talbot Papers D 238, 251.

PART THREE : ECONOMY

5 The wealth, connections and influence of the earls of Shrewsbury

In the early Tudor period the earls of Shrewsbury were a northern Midlands landed family with concentrations of manors in Shropshire, Derbyshire and in the area around Sheffield known as Hallamshire. Their ancestors of the twelfth and thirteenth centuries had been lesser landed knights in southern Herefordshire: between 1387 and 1422 shrewd marriages and premature deaths led to the fusion of the inheritances of the Talbots in Herefordshire, the le Stranges in Shropshire and the Furnivalls in Yorkshire. In the early fifteenth century the centre of gravity of their patrimony shifted northwards from Hereford-shire to Shropshire; in the later fifteenth century it shifted again, eastwards to Derbyshire and south Yorkshire.[1] The most important early Tudor estates of the Talbots were those around Sheffield, described by the fourth earl in 1534 as 'certen of my best landes'.[2] Some mid-fifteenth century accounts suggest that the first earl had a tiny demesne of no more than a garden and two or three closes, with the rest of his estate let out on lease to small farmers at apparently moderate rents: it is likely that this changed little.[3] Hallamshire was a region of cattle and sheep-rearing, sometimes with dairying on fells and moorland, and with corn and stock-raising variously combined in clay vales.[4] Sheffield was just a small market town: the bulk of the land was held by free burgage tenure, charged with a contribution to the yearly fee-farm payable to the earls. The inhabitants dealt with their lord as a community through their elected bailiff. In the mid-sixteenth century a dispute over the revenues of certain lands was resolved by the incorporation of the town. At this time it was described as 24 miles in circuit with 2,000 people: 'verey grett and populus haveynge within the same xiiii hamlets whiche for the moste part are never woyd of plags of poore and impotent persons inhabytynge within the same'.[5]

139

The Talbots also possessed many manors in Derbyshire acquired through inheritance and by purchase.[6] The core of the fifteenth-century patrimony had been based on Shrewsbury's town (as it was described in 1555) of Whitchurch, Shopshire, a town firmly under seigneurial authority with its bakehouse, mills, weekly market and annual fair all controlled by the lord. This estate of 32,000 acres of mixed farming land— oats, hay and cattle—straddled the Midland gap where lowland and higher farming zones met. Only one sixth was demesne land: fixed and assessed rents were the largest source of income on this rentier estate.[7] In Herefordshire the Talbots continued to hold the lordship of Archenfield, between Monmouth and Hereford.[8] They also possessed manors in several other counties and Furnivall's Inn in London.[9] They were absentee landowners in Ireland, owning five manors in county Wexford, acquired by the first earl, but often in disorder, not least because of the absence of the earls. In the early sixteenth century the fourth earl was issued a warrant to arm forty of his retainers for quelling the rebels in Ireland who were denying him his revenues. Explaining at length his conduct towards the earl's tenants in Wexford, the bishop of Ossory wrote that he had gone only to reform 'such ennormytes and variaunces' between Shrewsbury's tenants and the Irish, calling Shrewsbury's tenants the most inordinate and sensual people that he knew in all the country. The Talbots' Irish possessions were confiscated by the crown in 1536. In 1591 the burgesses of Wexford appealed to the then earl of Shrewsbury recalling 'the quiete happie and peaceable government of your lordships wourthie progenitore ... imprented in the hartes of all this countrie people, as well by relacion of some ealders which yet livinge have tasted the fruites of the same, as by aunicent records and presidentes yet remaneinge'.[10]

Sheffield Castle was the principal seat of the Talbots, judging from the inventory drawn up after the death of the fourth earl and from the address of many letters. It was described in 1637 as 'very spacious, built around an inward court. On the south side an outward courtyard or fould, builded round with divers howses of officers, as an armoury, barns, stables, and divers lodgings'. The castle included a chapel served by the canons of Worksop. It was destroyed in the civil war and nothing is visible now.[11] It was perhaps displaced in the affections of the Talbots by a 'stately pile' called Sheffield Lodge or Manor, most probably greatly enlarged if not entirely built by the fourth earl and extended by his son. Leland reckoned it 'a goodly lodge or manor place on a hil top' in the midst of a deer park. It had an inner and an outer court. It was certainly more than a hunting lodge: Wolsey was housed there in 1530, and the body of the fifth earl was placed in the chapel there before his funeral.[12] The fourth earl was especially fond of South Wingfield—'but a maner place, but yt far passith Sheffild Castel' according to Leland—purchased from its builder, Ralph, lord Cromwell, by the second earl by 1459.[13] The fourth earl was also building a 'fair lodge' in Worksop park which he rented for 13s 4d yearly from Worksop Priory: Leland noted that he had been on the point of finishing it before his death 'as apperith by much hewyd stone lying there'.[14] 'A very fair place or lodge' at Blackmere, near Whitchurch, had been the principal dwelling of the fifteenth-century Talbots. In the 1550s, however, the fifth earl was informed that his lodge needed a new covering with shingles, as did the kitchen and gallery. Presumably it was the same building that was described in 1561 as 'the late castle of Blackmeare decayed of longe tyme and polled down and some money therof maid by Fraunces the late earle of Shrewisburie ... the gate house thereof is stonding and well covered with lead and drye'.[15] The Talbots also possessed Goodrich Castle, Herefordshire, Hardwick, then 'a parke and a maner place or lodge', a house at Handsworth offered to the future fifth earl in the 1520s, 'a very goodly place like a castle' at Bramscroft near Ludlow, 'a maner place of tymbar' where the fourth earl was born at Shifnal, and two London residences, a house in Chelsea and a mansion, Coldharbour, in the city.[16]

Between 1537 and 1553 the Talbots added considerably to their patrimony. On 6 October 1537 the fourth earl was granted Rufford Abbey and virtually all of its estates (including the manor of Worksop and the lordship of Rotherham) in recognition of the confiscation in the previous year of Shrewsbury's Irish properties. It was a generous exchange.[17] In 1541 the fifth earl exchanged Farnham Royal, Buckinghamshire, for Worksop Priory and £485 8s 6d (possibly a sum related more to Shrewsbury's debts to the crown than to the intrinsic values of the properties).[18] The earls did not wholly neglect their Herefordshire and Shropshire interests: in June 1548 the fourth

earl was granted Flanesford Priory, the dissolution of which he
had earlier tried to prevent because some of his ancestors were
buried there;[19] in 1545 the fifth earl bought lands formerly part of
Wombridge Priory, consolidating his holdings around Shifnal.[20]

The fifth earl took a great interest in the sales of college and
chantry lands in the late 1540s. Not the least of the problems
facing a buyer was to ensure that he was buying properties of
value. Robert Swyft informed Shrewsbury how he had spoken
with John Beaumont, one of the commissioners of gilds and
chantries in Derbyshire, who had offered to help in determining
the true value of lands lately belonging to the chantries. There
were two chantries at Crich, Derbyshire: one that Swyft
supposed that Shrewsbury did not want, and one that had been
valued at £10 17s 4d. Swyft advised his master to send a trusty
fellow to Crich to secure a true rental.[21] A further problem for the
would-be buyer was the reluctance of the commissioners to make
a firm contract while they were still hoping for a higher offer. 'I
can be at no full poynte for your chauntres by reason they hold
everye thinge so dere and besydes that as yet they wold go throwe
with no man but see the vttermost what men wyll offer', wrote
Swyft.[22] On 11 April 1549 Shrewsbury paid £702 4s 2½d for
properties worth £34 15s 3d, including chantry lands in Crich,
Dronfield and Rotherham. This purchase further consolidated
the Talbot patrimony around Hallamshire and northern
Derbyshire. An unusual feature of this transaction was that
Shrewsbury was allowed to buy the lead on the principal
building of the college of Jesus in Rotherham. It is also significant
that these lands were to be held not in chief, but of the king as of
his manor of Pentriche, Derbyshire, that is to say, by a favourable
tenure.[23] In May 1549 Mary Talbot, countess of Northumberland, sister of the fifth earl, was granted a package of rectories,
including those of Sheffield, Ecclesfield and Bradfield, worth
£200 a year, rent free for life. On 10 July 1552 Shrewsbury was 'in
consideracion of seruice' granted the reversion of these rectories
and in addition gained a further package of rectories and
advowsons as well as the lordship, manor, park, and yearly fair of
Kimberworth, Yorkshire, which included a water mill, two
fulling mills, two closes of meadows and a mine of coals. He paid
nothing for Kimberworth (for which he would pay an annual
rent of £57 8s 10½d) and just £200 (or one year's purchase) to the

court of augmentations after Mary Talbot's death for the reversion of her properties. He was to hold Kimberworth in chief, but the fraction of a knight's service that he was to owe would be only one twentieth, a reduction from the usual one tenth.[24] His heir George, Lord Talbot, made a joint purchase with Richard Swift of Pullam, Lincolnshire, of a package of monastic lands worth £55 5s 2d a year for £1,334 19s 6d. Part was to be held in chief, but by the service of only one fortieth of a knight's fee; the rest was to be held of the king as of his manor of East Greenwich by fealty only in free socage, that is by an unusually favourable tenure.[25] He also received Bolsover Castle worth £118 a year.[26]

The fifth earl received a further grant of lands 'in consideracion of seruice' on 30 June 1553: he obtained several London properties formerly belonging to the bishopric of Durham together with some lands from Pontefract Priory and St Robert, Knaresborough, worth £66 16s 1½d a year. He paid just £11 19s 4½d a year (for one of the granges). Again the tenures were extremely favourable, some for service of as little as one fiftieth of a knight's fee.[27] The benefits that the Talbots obtained from these exchanges, grants and purchases are obvious: the greatest was the opportunity to consolidate their holdings. Some new acquisitions were sold (and had perhaps been bought with resale in mind). These dealings were the most important transactions of the earls, marriage settlements apart. Only in 1516 are there plentiful references to other sales or purchases: then the fourth earl was buying lands for £240 from Lord Conyers.[28]

It is not possible conclusively to show the value of the estates of the Talbots: what evidence there is suggests that this was a period of stagnation, if not decline. The total income from the lands that the fifth earl inherited was put at £1,735 in 1538–9.[29] A *valor* of the lands of the fifth earl c.1558–60 gives clear values of the Talbot estates grouped by counties. The total value was £1,518 9s 6½d. This was made up of £503 11s 1½d from Hallamshire, £201 1s 8½d and £189 13s from two receiverships in Shropshire, £276 17s 8d from Nottinghamshire and Yorkshire combined, £153 7s 8d from Derbyshire and Staffordshire, £78 8s 3d from Gloucestershire and £115 10s 7½d from Herefordshire.[30] There are no other complete listings. There is a *valor* of the Shropshire estates for 1521–2 which valued them at £505 15s 6¾d;[31] the later *valor* valued them at £390 14s 8½d or 20 per cent less. Rents from the Shropshire estates had been some 10–15 per cent lower in the period 1473–1522 than in the 1430s: there is no sign of any increase after 1521–2 when some reforms (of which the *valor* was itself probably part) were essayed. 'In the hands of an earl of Shrewsbury more concerned with his lands elsewhere, a certain laxity crept in.'[32] In 1556, for example, Shrewsbury was informed that his red deer was decayed at Blackmere.[33] Some Hallamshire evidence points to stagnating revenues. These estates yielded from £412 11s 9d to £515 2s 7d between 1478 and 1484, £340 8s 4½d in 1538–9, £503 11s 1½d in the later *valor*. Some less reliable values (based on Nathaniel Johnston's manuscript jottings) suggest yields of £375 in 1486, £323 in 1514 and £328 in 1560.[34] Certainly there was no sustained increase in the yields of the Talbot estates: at best there was stagnation with some sharp fluctuations, at worst, as in Shropshire, there may have been decline.

The Talbot patrimony was administered in a conventional fashion. A manorial court met regularly at Sheffield during the lives of the fourth and fifth earls. The transactions most commonly recorded were simple ones: a son was granted a licence to succeed his father in the tenure of certain lands and paid an entry fine; lands were surrendered, new lands taken out; disputes over partitions of land or provisions of dower. An impressionistic survey of the total revenues collected by fines does suggest that from the mid-1540s larger sums were being raised but this may simply reflect a greater turnover of holdings: there is no evidence of any significant changes in the average levels of fines. A sample of family holdings suggests that when titles were renewed the entry fines were almost always the same. Moreover entry fines were not a very large source of revenue: only in 1498–9 was the total revenue raised by fines greater than £3.[35]

There is little sign that the fourth and fifth earls had serious disputes with their tenants. There is no early Tudor equivalent of the Glossopdale dispute of the late 1570s in which the sixth earl's tenants successfully complained to the council against the massive increases he was attempting to impose.[36] This may reflect a paternalistic nirvana, the sheer weight of the power of the earls, or, more prosaically, the absence of evidence. There are a few hints that the earls were enclosing a little land but no riotous attacks against any of their enclosures.[37] Some poaching at Blackmere park ended in violence and arrests in 1555.[38] There were a number of disputes between the earls and their tenants on the one hand and neighbouring landowners and their tenants on the other: few led to any protracted contention.[39]

The fourth and fifth earls derived some income from the profits of mining and iron-working, especially from the manufacture of cutlery. 'In the fifteenth and early sixteenth centuries the earl of Shrewsbury seems to have been the premier entrepreneur.'[40] There are many references to lead in the Alen correspondence in 1516. One Rafe Dodnor had sold twenty fothers (2184 lbs) of the lead he had bought from Alen: he had received £4 6s a fother but he would now be happy to accept no more than he had paid Alen for them, namely £4 4s, for the rest. 'The waynes that com up dayly looses the price of lead; howbeit I her not the contrary but thei sell above £4 the foder.' A few weeks later the price had dropped. Alen had arranged a bargain with Sir John Cut that Sir John would accept 30 fothers of lead at £4 2s 8d a fother as payment for a debt Shrewsbury owed him and would pay what was over when he received the lead.[41] In the course of a dispute over the manor of Ecclesall in 1587 witnesses testified how men had caved there for lead and burnt lead in boles (simple, small stone furnaces) in the time of the fourth and fifth earls.[42] Iron-making was also taking place in Hallamshire and Derbyshire:[43] the earls of Shrewsbury were notably involved in iron-smelting and iron-working. Edward Eyre, a servant of the fourth earl by 1533, held smithies, and John Parker, who died in 1552, held lands of the earls including a water wheel and water course and smithies at Wadsley and Treeton.[44] 'Ther be many smithes and cuttelars in Halamshire', noted Leland.[45] In 1547 Richard King of Sheffield gave his daughter Anne his 'greteste panne, the counter, the best stithie, bellowes, hammeres and tonges, with all things belonging to the same harthe'; to George, his son, 'an axiltre of yron'; and to his servant, 'the litle stithie, the bellowes, a pair of tonges, a stovente, a harthe staffe'.[46] Cutlery was an old-established craft.[47] Cutlery manufacture was firmly under the control of the earls exercised through the manorial court. Cutlers came to the court to take distinctive marks. On 2 October 1554 'to that court came William Elles and took of the lord a private mark by himself for making iron knives' of which he should have exclusive use: anyone convicted of using his mark should pay £1 to the lord of the manor and make amends to Elles.[48]

The influence of the earls was not confined to those lands which they inherited or acquired. They were also appointed by the crown to a number of stewardships of crown lands which gave them opportunities to further their influence. Here their offices on the Derbyshire estates of the duchy of Lancaster are of special significance. On 21 May 1509 the fourth earl was appointed steward of Tutbury, Newcastle-under-Lyme, Ashbourne, Wirksworth and other manors including High Peak: on 18 November 1529 the later fifth earl was appointed to succeed for life after his father's death. A further grant of duchy office followed on 27 November 1549 when the fifth earl's son and Sir Henry Savile were granted the constabulary of Pontefract Castle and the stewardship of the honour of Pontefract for life.[49] These offices were remunerated: a partial list suggests total annual fees of about £51.[50] More important still was the patronage that these offices (which embraced much of Derbyshire) gave the Talbots: most of their deputies were minor Derbyshire gentry.[51] Of course some of these may have virtually appointed themselves and there is the occasional sign that the earls were not fully in control. The courts were not kept at Tutbury one year. In 1559 Adam Cave, an officer on the Duchy lands, apologised to Shrewsbury for not dealing with certain troubles. The spoil of deer and wood in Needwood Chase was very great. Cave was very sorry that he had not been able to meet Shrewsbury 'for that I can not as I wolde see the faultes of your Deputies officers reformed'.[52] On 11 July 1525 the fourth earl and his son Francis were granted for life in survivorship the stewardship of the lordships of Radnor, Maelienydd, Wigmore and associated offices: combined with their possession of Goodrich, this made them marcher lords, but there is little evidence that they attempted to exploit this position.[53] The earls also held other regional offices on behalf of the crown. In May 1548 the fifth earl was appointed justice in eyre of the forests beyond Trent, with an annuity of £100, an office carrying with it much patronage.[54] He also served as lord president of the council in the north from 1549 to his death in 1560. His fees were £800 a year in 1549, £1,000 a year by 1554–5. It is impossible to say whether Shrewsbury suffered like the third earl of Huntingdon who in 1587 claimed to have spent more than

£20,000 over his allowance since he went north: in the absence of any complaints, it seems unlikely that Shrewsbury lost much through this service.[55]

The Talbots also held posts in the central administration. The fourth earl was appointed a chamberlain of the exchequer in 1509, possibly as part of the reaction against the severity of Henry VII in his later years.[56] In October 1509 and February 1511 Shrewsbury signed warrants of £10 for wheels for fawcons and serpentines.[57] But generally the office was a sinecure. Neither the fourth nor the fifth earl of Shrewsbury was a reforming chamberlain of the exchequer, unlike Henry, lord Stafford, who zealously studied the *Dialogus de Scaccario* to discover his responsibilities and rights, sought to revive the old arrangements, attempted to reduce the powers of under-officials such as the writer of the tallies who now controlled the tellers, accused the tellers of theft and embezzlement and tried to institute an audit based on the comparison of counterpells made by chamberlains. Early in Elizabeth's reign Stafford presented articles of information to Queen and council. He complained that the Lord Treasurer's clerks and underclerks had for many years omitted to cause Shrewsbury's deputies and Stafford's predecessors to keep counterpells in order to check the treasurer's pells. 'Seynce this ordre hathe bene leste and omytted and the chamberleynes suffered to take theire fees and not to traveile to exercyse there office accordinge to theire othes but have lefte deputies which have bene lytle regarded in their absence' matters had gone badly awry. Records were neglected, in several places 'so evell loked after that they have bene vtterlie perished with pigeons donge'. One usher had gone so far as to sell records in St Paul's Churchyard. Tellers embezzled, dying owing as much as £2,000 to the crown. In short, 'notable polytyque ordre was broken'. In response to Stafford's charges, a commission was set up, including the fifth earl, but it faced much obstruction in its efforts to take better order. Even if some of his complaints were extravagant, clearly neither the fourth nor the fifth earl of Shrewsbury had done much to prevent these evils.[58] For them the office was above all a source of revenue. Each chamberlain received an annual fee of £52 3s 4d from the crown, payable in two instalments and collected by deputies. It was sufficiently important for there to be several references in the Talbot correspondence to it. For example in c.1550 Humfrey Bentley wrote that he had received £100 for Shrewsbury's fee and hoped to get the rest within a week: he was working hard for it.[59] The fourth earl was also appointed Lord Steward of the royal household in 1502 on the death of Lord Willoughby de Broke. That the earl was almost always referred to and addressed as Lord Steward suggests that the office carried a certain status, although the duties attached were nominal.[60]

The Talbots possessed considerable ecclesiastical interests. Before the dissolution, the fourth earl was steward of eleven monasteries, more than any other nobleman.[61] What influence stewardship might bring was indicated by the abbot of Lilleshull, Yorkshire. He informed a supplicant that Shrewsbury 'is our very good lord, and tender lord in all our rightfull causes'. 'Considering how good lord he hath bene, and yet allwayes unto us ys ... we may in no wyse abyd the displeasur of the sayd lord'.[62] Shrewsbury was consulted over the election of the prior of Worksop in 1529; argued for the election of one of the brethren rather than a stranger as prior of Tutbury in 1535; persuaded the abbot of Combermere who was then staying with him to grant a lease to one of Shrewsbury's tenants.[63] The distribution of monastic and chantry lands greatly increased the numbers of advowsons that the Talbots held but from limited evidence there is little sign of any consistent policy of patronage in the 1540s and 1550s.

The earls enjoyed some urban influence outside their patrimony, notably in York. In 1545 the mayor and aldermen petitioned 'ther especiall good lorde, the Erle of Shrewsbury' that he would urge that the mint at York should go forward. In December 1549 they agreed 'that ther shalbe an honourable present preparyd to be gevyn to the right honourable Erle of Shrewsbury at his commyng to this Citie' on his appointment as lord president in the council in the north. The streets of York were to be cleaned of dunghills and the common brewers were 'to brewe reasonable ale' for Shrewsbury's arrival. On 22 February 1550 it was agreed to give a present to Shrewsbury's countess. In 1552 Shrewsbury threatened the city that if proper measures were not taken to deal with an outbreak of plague he would hold the next sitting of the council in the north away from York. But soon after, he and other members of the council offered a sum towards 'the bryngyng in of a conduct with water unto this citie', a gesture which evoked profuse thanks from the council of York. In the same year a memorandum presented to the mayor and aldermen arguing that the next parliament would be a suitable occasion to have clothmaking better supervised referred to the goodwill that Shrewsbury bore to the town. In 1553–4 Shrewsbury assisted the city in its battle to secure remission of taxation. In August 1553 he was thanked 'specially for your paynes in gyttyng parte of our lait tax released'; in March 1554 the burgesses of the city were told to discuss their plans with Shrewsbury 'whoo hath done most for the Cite therein and knoweth the sayd sewte from the begynyng to the endyng'. In August 1557 the council agreed to present Shrewsbury 'two hoggusheads of wyne, thone of redd and thother white, and one ponchon of frenche wyne in consideration he is speciall good lord to this poore citie'.[64]

The Talbots then enjoyed influence and income from a number of sources. But what was their general economic position? Debt is often used as a litmus. The Talbots were often recorded as in debt to the crown. But such debts were not always as crippling as they might seem: the term covered arrears of taxation, payments due for wardships purchased, moneys lent by the crown, and fines and recognisances imposed as instruments of political control. Such debts might be paid off over many years, or even waived; but occasionally stricter pressure was applied. The fourth earl borrowed £1,000 from the crown in August 1509 and a further £1,000 on 27 May 1513 (the latter, perhaps, to support him during the French campaign): recognisances taken out to ensure repayment were cancelled in 1519 'forasmoche as the said erle haithe made vnto vs such sufficient surety of landes and tenamentes for payment'.[65] He obviously incurred further debts. In February 1521 he was named for £3,280 9s 5d in a list of money owed to the king and recovered: only one peer was named for a higher sum. In 1523 Shrewsbury and others unspecified were listed as owing £133 6s 8d: lands had been recovered for £1,800.[66] In June 1527 Shrewsbury made an indenture (which does not survive) with Wolsey and Sir Henry Wyatt to pay off a debt to the crown of £3,195 9s 5½d at £133 6s 8d a year. According to this agreement, described by Shrewsbury some years later, 'certen of my best

landes to the value of fyve hundrethe markes [were] recouered for
the sure payment thereof.' In 1534 Shrewsbury was selling a
wood to the king. But when his chaplain John Moreton went to
collect the money due, Sir Brian Tuke wanted to keep it because
Shrewsbury 'shulde be in debted vnto the kinges grace in sex
hundrethe markes' upon indentures that he had made with
Wolsey and Wyatt. Shrewsbury complained that he had made
arrangements for the payment of his debts: 'I trust good
substaunce of the same I have payd accordyng to the said
indentures so as I thynke there woll not so gret some be founde
vpon a due reconyng as is surmysed.' He impressed upon
Cromwell that 'yf it be not the kinges plesor to be so good lord
vnto me that I may have the said money I shalbe compelled to
make further shyfte whiche wolbe to my gret losse' and promised
to pay his debts according to the indentures during the next
term.[67] An indenture of October 1535 records the granting of the
earl's Hallamshire manors to trustees to secure the payment of
200 marks (£133 6s 8d) a year to the king in respect of his debts. It
is not clear why it was made then, or how it differs from that of
1527, but the earl was manifestly under pressure to make regular
repayments.[68] When he made his will in August 1537 he
allocated the revenues of specified lands (interestingly not his
Hallamshire manors but Whitchurch, Shropshire, Worksop,
Tylney and Stirrop, Nottinghamshire, and
Donnington,Yorkshire) to pay off his debts to the king.[69] The
facts are clearer than their exact significance. The fifth earl was
bound to pay £1,500 at the rate of 100 marks each Michaelmas
for livery of his lands; he later got into debt for the wardship of
John, lord Bray, which he purchased in 1540. On 13 November
1549, at a crucial moment in the power struggles following the
fall of Protector Somerset, Shrewsbury was excused all his debts.
There was still £795 9s 5½d owing from the fourth earl's
indenture of 1527, there was £433 6s 8d unpaid for Earl Francis'
livery of lands and there was £133 6s 8d due for the wardship of
Lord Bray.[70]

The Talbots also had private debts. Some of these were
obviously loans, others were arrears on sums contracted to be
paid, for example, for a marriage, others still may have been for
goods purchased on credit from tradesmen. Shortage of ready
cash was a common noble problem, as is shown by the many

references in the Alen letters in 1516. In one letter Alen informed the fourth earl that he would use the money that Shrewsbury had sent up to London to pay Lord Conyers from whom Shrewsbury had bought lands and 'deferr them that shulde have the sayd said money unto suche tyme as I can fynde better remedye'. On 6 May he wrote that he had borrowed two hundred marks to pay the abbot of Westminster, promising to repay his new creditor in fourteen days: 'I beseche your lordeship I maye kepe promes.' Creditors might be won over by favours: on 8 June Alen wrote 'yf hit please yor Lordship to send to Coventre, to my lord Abbot of Westmynstr (at the generall chaptre agaynst Saynt Peters day, wich shalbe the xxixth day of this monethe) some veneson, your Lordship dose him gret comfort'. On 17 July he was anxious: 'her is dyverse men cometh to have money; I beseche your Lordship I may know your pleasure what answer I shall make unto them'.[71]

It might be possible to argue that the fourth earl was living beyond his means, improverished by his building and by the marriages of his three daughters, and that the finances of the Talbots remained shaky until bolstered up by the cancellation of debt in 1549 and the grants of church lands in mid-century. But it would be mistaken to make much of the day-to-day difficulties of the earls' servants. There is nothing here to compare, say, with the substantial debts of the first earl of Huntingdon, amounting to £9,466 4s 2d in March 1538.[72] Apart from the alienations of 1527 and 1535 there is no sign of any large-scale mortgaging or sales of land, and sporadic references to sales of woods after 1534 amount to little.[73] Moreover the Talbots were lenders as well as borrowers: the duke of Suffolk owed £200 in 1516–17, Sir Weston Browne £66 13s 4d.[74] Did the Talbots feel rich enough to take money for granted as something that would always be ultimately available, whatever the short-term difficulties? Did they always know just where they stood?[75]

Whatever the state of their finances, the earls of Shrewsbury certainly lived well. An account for the period 1–14 October 1559 records household expenditure of £26 12s 4d of which £13 17s 2d was for wheat and malt. Does this imply an annual expenditure of some £700?[76] Most other references are not to bread or ale but to exotic commodities such as quails, lings, capons and congars. In May 1516 Thomas Alen sent Shrewsbury by the carrier of Rotherham ten pasties of congars 'wiche was the grettest and the fattyst that ever I sawe', acknowledged by Shrewsbury as 'verray good and swete'.[77] Both earls were buyers of important wines.[78] Both spent substantial sums on clothing and material. In 1516 Alen was buying shoes and a hat for the fourth earl. An inventory of the effects of the fourth earl lists robes of estate, parliament and garter robes, a suite of rich cloth of gold, gowns of many kinds including tawny velvet furred with sables, black satin furred with sables and black damask furred with black cony, coats, jewels, rings, chains, brooches, girdles, pearls.[79] They bought many hangings for their residences. In 1516 the fourth earl was buying from Tournai; in 1555 the fifth earl was buying from Norwich. The inventory of the fourth earl listed among many others eleven pieces of Alexander, forty of vice and virtue, fifty-seven of tapestry work. He had carpets, including carpets for tables, and large numbers of beds, sheets and mattresses. There was plenty of kitchen stuff and general houseware, including pots with standing or flat talbots on the cover, goblets, cups, spoons, salts, ale cruses, candlesticks, basins, shaving pots and so on. The fourth earl purchased seeds for his garden, and on another occasion, a ream of paper and a pound of red wax. At Sheffield the fourth earl also left coin of all sorts worth nearly £1,500.[80]

The earls' favourite pastime was hunting. When Wolsey was at Sheffield Manor 'therle would often requyer hyme to kyll a doo or ij ther in the parke'. In September 1549 the fifth earl invited the earl of Huntingdon to join him 'to kyll a stagg or too'.[81] The fourth earl kept minstrels. The fifth earl played cards with the earl of Rutland, winning 19s on one occasion in October 1539.[82] Of literary and cultural interests there is little sign. Both earls could read and write; the fourth earl knew Christopher Urswick, dean of Windsor, and was once described as a friend of Erasmus.[83] In September 1512 the fourth earl endowed the prior and convent of St Cuthbert, Worksop, to build a school within the priory.[84] Possibly he had some connection with two Sheffield men who went on to Cambridge, one a Fellow of King's from 1515 to his death in 1517, the other the first Regius Professor of Physic at Cambridge from 1540 to 1554.[85] There are no references at all to books in his will or in the inventory of his effects. In 1550 one of the fifth earl's servants was buying statutes and four parts of the Bible for him.[86] Two books were dedicated to him but that reflected the political purposes of the authors rather than any literary patronage by the earl.[87] There is nothing here to compare with the impressive collection of books by Henry, lord Stafford.[88]

Quite possibly the principal concern of the Talbots was the arrangement of marriages for their children. Marriages were contracted by the earls for their children into other leading noble families in order to continue their line and to cement alliances between families. Thus the fourth earl married his daughters to the men who were to become earl of Cumberland, earl of Northumberland and Lord Dacre, for good measure marrying his son and heir to Dacre's sister. Thus the fifth earl of Shrewsbury married his son to a daughter of the Manners earls of Rutland and his widowed step-sister to the earl of Pembroke. Arrangements, especially of property, were complex and often caused difficulties. The fourth earl was on the point of suing Lord Clifford for not performing agreements about the feoffment of his daughter.[89] The marriage between the fourth earl's daughter Mary and Henry Percy, later sixth earl of Northumberland, went spectacularly awry. The marriage took place in 1524: by 1529 Northumberland was telling Shrewsbury's servant that 'I woll neuer come in her company as longe as I lyued.' Refusing to let him see her, he said he would not suffer 'hir speek with none to contrive no malicious notes agaynst me'; her 'werdes anenst me might haue ben verey wele amendyt'. Mary was 'in fere of posonyng'. Northumberland offered to send her back to her father 'with a reasonable fyndyng'. As Mary at this time gave birth to a stillborn child, the marriage may only just have broken down.[90] But Mary then left her husband and lived with her father and brother. A long wrangle ensued as the Talbots tried to get that 'reasonable fyndyng' promised by her husband. The fourth earl wrote to Henry VIII and Cromwell in 1536; sent a messenger to Northumberland in the middle of the Pilgrimage of Grace on hearing that he was dangerously ill; negotiated with Cromwell and the king in late 1537 and early 1538, involving the Lord Chancellor as well. By this time Northumberland had died, leaving his lands to the crown, which he had possibly done to thwart his wife. The fifth earl continued the battle. In May 1542 Mary Talbot exhibited a petition to the king at his coming to Greenwich. But the original marriage had evidently been unusual in that the fourth earl had given no money to the Percies which raised doubts about her rights. Not until 1549 was she made a grant—of rectories worth £200 a year—but still there were negotiations and petitions, Mary receiving a good and comfortable answer after delivering a petition to Queen Mary in her privy closet at St James's.[91]

Marriages of daughters were costly. The fourth earl should have paid 2,500 marks to the fifth earl of Northumberland for Mary Talbot.[92] He paid Lord Dacre £1,000 for Elizabeth Talbot's marriage to Dacre's son.[93] When the third duke of Buckingham offered the fourth earl marriage alliances which Shrewsbury rejected as too expensive, he was apparently demanding at least 3,000 marks for his son.[94] Clearly an earl of Shrewsbury could also demand a high price when marrying his son: the earl of Rutland paid the fifth earl 3,000 marks for the marriage of his daughter Gertrude to George, the later sixth earl.[95] The purchase of a wardship was an alternative, and possibly a cheaper, method of providing for the marriage of a daughter, but it was not free from problems. The fifth earl purchased the wardship of John, lord Bray in June 1542 for 1,200 marks and married his daughter Anne to him. By 1550 Bray was on bad terms with his father-in-law. He wrote to him that since he had come to court 'ytt ys shewed me that your lordshyppe shulde be dyspleasyd with me for that I cam nott vnto yow, and your lordshyppe shuld say yey wold send home my wyffe yff in case I make not the more speyd vnto yow'. Bray implied he would behave better 'yff i hadde a home or howse to receve her vnto' and asked Shrewsbury to bear with him while he sorted out his financial matters. A little later he wrote that although he remained at court he had not forgotten Shrewsbury but would be ready at all times at Shrewsbury's command to do the best service in his power, 'deseringe your Lordshipp to thinke no vnkyndnes that I have not or this tyme wrytten vnto you according to my promes made vnto your seruante'. In 1556 Bray was involved in Dudley's conspiracy and was imprisoned. Both the earl of Shrewsbury and his wife made suits in his favour. Lady Bray was allowed an audience with the Queen who 'gave her great praysse and ernestlye said that God sent oft tymes to good women evell husbands'. Bray was eventually released in May 1557, redeeming his reputation with his life in the French war that year.[96]

In their own later marriages the earls took ladies of lower social rank: genuine affection was present. The fifth earl's first wife Mary Dacre died in 1538: his second wife was Grace, daughter of a Derbyshire gentleman and widow of Francis Carless. On her death in 1558 the earl of Westmorland (to whom she had sent a token the previous year) wrote to Shrewsbury to express his sadness on hearing the news.

God geveth man in all things for his comforthe so in his deue tyme and at his pleasure he woll take againe this worldlie thinges, vnto whose will and determynacion, your Lordship and all men must conforme theymselfes and be willingly content to depart with those thinges whiche we love best, yea and our owne life at last.

Sir William Cordell, master of the rolls, was 'very sorye for the cause of your Lordshipes hevynes: yf yt had pleased god otherwise whose will and determynacion must pacyently be suffered'. Shrewsbury asked for his son George, then serving on the northern borders, to be licensed to come to him: clearly Shrewsbury's grief was deep.[97] A year later he was seeking the hand of Elizabeth, widow of Sir Thomas Pope, the founder of Trinity College, Oxford. In September 1559 she had sent Shrewsbury a token that he thought worthy of a prince—'no erthle tyng could haue donn more'—and he had visited her at her house at Tittenhanger. But in December she complained that rumours were being spread at court and in the city by some who thought themselves Shrewsbury's close friends that Shrewsbury was coming to London to conclude a marriage from which she could not draw back as she had made so many promises and accepted so many tokens. But Lady Pope insisted that she had made no promises, neither in writing nor in spoken words. She sent back a ring Shrewsbury had sent her. 'And ffurther wyche was most to my greffe', wrote Shrewsbury, he had learned 'that your pleasure and desyer is that I shuld be no more a suter to yow' and should neither visit her nor send her anything. If she really meant it, he must take it 'as a punysment sent vnto me ffrome God.'

By April 1560, however, matters were moving more smoothly. Lady Pope was 'moste hartlye sorey' to hear of Shrewsbury's ill-health, 'no lesse grewous for me to here of then yf the lyke had happende vnto my selfe'. Shrewsbury was prepared, reluctantly, to accept the stiff terms that she was demanding, bonds in recognisance for 10,000 marks, which he thought very great 'for the doing of that which myne owne good will more than any bonde canne shuld move me vnto'. He would allow Lady Pope her way over furniture, jewels and household stuff. He neverthe-less saw himself as 'a faithless man altogethers constrayned by bonde—whome I trust the worlde cannot chardge with juste cause of mystreating in any degre with any creature'. Much less was such mistreatment to be feared 'betwene vs whose hartes I thinke God hathe disposed in loving good will one to another betweene whom also my truste is bothe truste and love shall daily encreace'. He was prepared to be bound, he continued, but again his indignation surfaced as he complained 'all which thinges well wayed, me thinkith there is no suche earneste cause to haue me so stronghtley bounde'. He was content to wait till Midsummer, in which case Lady Pope would no longer demand any bonds, or to be bound if the marriage were to take place the next day. The cause of Lady Pope's mistrustfulness was her desire fully to implement the will of her late husband, a matter complicated by his debts. The marriage never took place: Shrewsbury did not recover from his illness, dying later that year.[98]

The earls were concerned by the upbringing of their heirs. There are signs of a quarrel between the fourth earl and the newly married Francis and his wife in late 1523. Francis wrote to his father-in-law that he was being required to live at court and not in his father's house.[99] Francis in turn kept a firm hand on his son George, judging from George's later comments (in complaining of his son's debts and deception) that 'for myne owne parte I never durste deale in lyke tearmes with my father, nor make any meanes by motion or otherwise for the sale of anie landes in hys lyfetyme'.[100] In October 1557 George had set his hand to a letter from the earl of Northumberland, earning himself a stern paternal rebuke. "Tak heed for doing that you may repent another daye ... I wold wish that you shuld be as forwarde in the king and quenes seruys as any man but in no wise to meddle in another mans offyce'.[101]

A large number of men served the fourth and fifth earls of Shrewsbury. Most is known about those who wrote to the earls from London. Outstanding among these was Robert Swyft the younger, member of a family which had long been in service with the earls. His earliest letter dates from before the fall of Wolsey; in the early 1530s he was attending to the building of the fourth earl's chantry; in 1541 he was negotiating the exchange of Farnham Royal and Worksop; in 1542 he was assisting Lady Northumberland; in 1546 he was writing about Lord Bray and Shrewsbury's debts; in 1548 he was collecting money due from the earl of Rutland and discussing chantry lands in Derbyshire. In 1554 he enrolled Shrewsbury's letters patent for the site of the priory of Knaresborough. He was also hoping to collect Shrewsbury's exchequer fees: no one, he reported, had received any yet, 'but I intende to practisse my olde experience'. Between 1554 and his death in 1558 he wrote several letters of general news from court.[102] It is not clear exactly what post Swyft held nor is it possible to point precisely to rewards received from the earls. In 1549 the fifth earl granted him lands in Staley lately belonging to the college of Jesus, Rotherham. Possibly the earls assisted his marriage to the heiress of Nicholas Wickersley, Yorkshire. Possibly his Talbot connections provided the money for him to buy abbey and chantry lands in the 1540s and 1550s. He was named the first burgess of Sheffield after the town was incorporated in 1554.[103]

Another important servant of the fifth earl was Thomas Gargrave who made a career as a lawyer in the 1530s and 1540s. In 1545 he was appointed to the council in the north on the death of Sir Thomas Tempest. Tempest had received an annual fee of 100 marks but it was agreed that Gargrave should receive just £50 as he was not a knight. While Gargrave was in Shrewsbury's service he was knighted: in 1549 he wrote to him asking him to move Somerset to increase his fee 'seyng yt hayth pleasyd you to preferre me to that degre' of knight. Gargrave fulsomely offered Shrewsbury 'my contynuall prayer, and faythefull syrvyce, as of my bounden deuty apperteynyth', 'desyring your lordship that if ther be any thing wheryn I may do your Lordship syryce that I may have knowledge thereof, and, to my power, I shall be as ready therunto as any yor Lordships servant', and apologised profusely to him for having missed him at court. He continued to serve Shrewsbury, writing letters of news from court and during the Scottish campaign of 1557.[104] It is difficult to judge just how much of his promotion he owed to Shrewsbury: he was burgess

for the city of York in 1547, knight for the county in 1555 and
1559, speaker in 1559, vice-president of the council in the north
from 1556. Early in 1556 Shrewsbury rebuked him for his
behaviour in parliament: Gargrave apologised, but rather less
than obsequiously:[105]

And ryght sory I am that my only syttynge styll in the passynge of one byll [the
exiles' bill?] in the parlyament without any obstynacy or other doynge or
spekynge shuld be so takyn and that also I shuld be so reportyd in relygeon. My
doynges & sayinges wheryn I referre to the iudgment of al that hath herd me or
sene my conversacion. But howsoever I be takyn or reportyd I shall god
wyllynge to my power be redy wyth my seruyce to the god [kyng &] quenes
majestie as I shall at al tymes be appoynted or comanded & to the best of my
knowlege at al tymes shewe my self a true & obedyent subiett to thayr
majesties'.

Here it is interesting to note that Gargrave was one of the
executors of the protestant archbishop of York, Robert Holgate,
on 8 December 1556.[106] Many of the servants of the earls were
priests: Thomas Alen, whose letters from London throw so much
light on the politics of 1516–17; Edward Hatfield, presented to
Treeton by the fifth earl in 1540 and by 1542 also vicar of
Ecclesfield, whose responsibilities included Lady Northumberland, the marriage alliance with the earl of Rutland,
Shrewsbury's exchequer fees, the wardship of Lord Bray and
matters in Shrewsbury's Herefordshire lordship;[107] John
Moreton, presented by the fourth earl to Hansworth in 1532,
concerned with marriages.[108] Other servants are clearly
recognisable as estate officials. Thurstan Woodcock, a witness of
the fourth earl's will in 1538, was the earls' agent in Staffordshire
and Shropshire.[109] John Scudamore was the fifth earl's principal
officer in Herefordshire.[110] Minor servants included Robert
Adlington who informed the fifth earl in 1559 that he was very ill
and dying. He had 'of longe season' given the earl good service
'wherein throughe muche watchinge cold and travayle I haue
gotten (as I thynke) a greate parte of mye dysease and (as I feare)
the shorteninge of mye tyme'. He asked Shrewsbury to aid his
wife and children—and for his office to be given to his son.[111]

It is interesting to note continuity of service, especially among
receivers and bailiffs, for example that of the Greve family.
Thomas Greve rendered account for Bradfield Forest in 1470

and 1477, Richard Greve in 1486 and 1514, and John Greve in 1560. Thomas Greve also rendered account for Bolderstone Forest 1470 and 1477 and was succeeded by William Greve in 1486 and 1514 and by Thomas Greve in 1560. A Nicholas Greve rendered account for Riveling Forest in 1486 and 1514, a Robert Greve in 1560.[112] The Talbots do not seem to have had an official charged with overall responsibility for the collection of their landed revenues: there are no references to anyone like Edmund Turner or Richard Sacheverell, receivers-general to the earl of Worcester and Lord Hastings.[113] Possibly the administration of the estates was divided between Hallamshire and Derbyshire on the one hand and Shropshire on the other. Certainly the Talbots had a council responsible for estate and legal matters and they employed a number of men, of whom Robert Swyft was the most striking example, as their trusted assistants, supervising and reporting on all aspects of their business. Below these were stewards and receivers such as Thurstan Woodcock and Thomas Sutton, men of some landed substance. The Talbots also employed a large number of bailiffs and reeves, responsible for the revenues of a single manor or for some minor office, who accounted for small sums. It is not known how such men were chosen but the same men often held office for long periods and were succeeded by men of the same surname. Little additional information is available here, save to say that there is no evidence that the earls were, or suspected that they were, victims of fraud. Not much is known about the size and staff of the earls' households. A list of 1558 records 12 gentlemen, 13 yeomen and grooms, 3 horsekeepers, 3 children of the kitchen, 5 gentle-women, a number of gentlemen's servants and seven or eight of lord Talbot's men.[114]

The Talbots had close connections with a number of families of local or regional importance. Some men were brought up in the Talbot household and remained attached to the earls. Sir Thomas Cockayne (1521–92) of Ashbourne, Derbyshire, referred in the dedication to the seventh earl of his *Short Treatise of Hunting* (1591) to 'my said experience vnder your most noble grandfather [that is the fifth earl] whose seruant I was in my younger yeares, and brought vp in his house' and from whom he had received many favours. In 1548 he had served under the fifth earl in the relief of Haddington. In December that year he wrote apologising to Shrewsbury that he had not met him when the earl had travelled through the country and adding his hopes of seeing him before Christmas. He was the bearer of the banner of arms at Shrewsbury's funeral.[115] Sir Henry Savile, reckoned among the seven most important laymen in the West Riding of Yorkshire, was a close connection of the Talbots. He assisted the fourth earl during the Pilgrimage of Grace and attended his funeral; he welcomed Lord Talbot who 'killed two stags in Wharncliff walks', to his house in 1546. Talbot later took care of Sir Henry's heir, Edward, who was mentally retarded.[116] The Talbots had close contacts with the Hastings family. The fourth earl had been a ward of William, lord Hastings (d. 1483), and had been married to Hastings' daughter Anne. Hastings' widow bequeathed 'to myn especiall good lorde' Shrewsbury vestments and hangings. William's son Edward (1466–1506) wrote to Shrewsbury 'to besech yor lordshyppe to hel[p] . . . me to bestowe George [his son] to a maryage'. He remitted his burial, should he not die within twenty miles of London, to his executors 'by the oversight of the erle of Shrewsbury'. Edward's son George (?1488–1544), earl of Huntingdon from 1529, was joined with Shrewsbury in a number of recognisances in the later years of Henry VII's reign and served under Shrewsbury in the army royal of 1513. Francis Talbot, the future fifth earl, was one of his feoffees in 1517 and 'dyned and souped' with him three of four times during his illness in November 1528. George's son and heir, Francis, second earl, was invited to join the fifth earl hunting in 1549.[117] But Huntingdon's brother was not on good terms with Shrewsbury. He was asked by the earl of Derby to use his influence with Queen Mary to deny Shrewsbury the lieutenancy of Lancashire and Cheshire. In 1557 he complained that Shrewsbury's bailiff in the Peak Forest had imprisoned his servants and impounded his cattle.[118]

A number of men, about whom not a great deal is known, expressed their dependence on or gratitude to the earls in effusive terms. William Bassett, MP, acknowledged Shrewsbury as his 'singular good lord'. Charles Moreton was ready in 1545 'rather to serve your lordeshyp then any man in the realme next unto the kynges maiestie' (but he claimed to be unable to raise ten soldiers). Sir Thomas Holcroft referred to the kindness and gentleness that he had always found at Shrewsbury's hands, offering to wait on him and to do him any service.[119] In their 'country' the Talbots could arouse considerable awe. Thomas Babington, important enough to claim the office of the bailiwick and pardon of the palace of Westminster during the coronation of Queen Mary, and bold enough to consider refusing the forced loan of August 1556, did not dare offend Shrewsbury locally. In April 1551 Babington wrote to Shrewsbury that he had learned that three of his servants had trespassed into the earl's park at Wingfield. Babington assured Shrewsbury that he had not known of it in advance, that he would have stopped it if he had, that he had many times warned his household against it and that he was sending the three trespassers to Shrewsbury for exemplary punishment.[120] Against that there was Sir John Byron, who once complained that the fifth earl and his officers had denied Byron justice in the High Peak. This, wrote Shrewsbury, 'is vntruely wrytten and with out any cause gyven of me on my parte'. When Byron's servant had been with Shrewsbury, ' I had suche busynes by the kynges comandement whiche wylle I lyve shall be obeyede afor any lettr that shall come fro Sir John Byron'.[121] Some men were connected with the Talbots because they were tenants or deputies of the earls, especially on the duchy of Lancaster estates, for example, Sir Henry Sacheverell (c.1475–1558), deputy steward of Tutbury, who served under Shrewsbury in 1513 and 1536 and who was recommended to Cromwell by Shrewsbury when he once wanted access to the king,[122] Sir Godfrey Foljambe, Sir Francis Leake. Men turned to the Talbots for advice and assistance, if, for example, the collectors of a forced loan failed to turn up, or to arrange marriages, or to arbitrate their quarrels.[123] Some knightly families were no more and no less than friends. Sir Gervase Clinton added greetings to Shrewsbury and his wife in a business letter of 1550. The fifth earl called Sir Roger Chumley his old acquaintance in 1548.[124]

How far connections with the Talbots furthered the careers of such men is unclear. Henry Sutton (c.1501–59) was commanded by his father to the service of the fourth earl, whom he appointed supervisor of his will. Sutton later became one of Henry VIII's knights of the body. Did Shrewsbury, as Lord Steward, introduce him to court? Possibly Sir Thomas Cockayne's connections with the fifth earl secured his election to parliament in March 1553: the same may be true of Thomas Powtrell of West

Hallam, Derbyshire, MP in 1547 and 1554.[125] A hint of the fifth
earl's influence was given by John Criche in a letter to
Shrewsbury on 13 October 1555 in which he informed his master
that 'Mr Rokeby sendeth your lordshipp word that Mr W ...
doth thinke some vnkindnes in youe ... for that he ... was not
knight of the shyre'.[126] But there is nothing to suggest that
Shrewsbury had influence comparable to that of the earl of
Rutland in Lincoln. On 18 January 1553 Rutland was accorded
the nomination of one of the burgesses of the parliament (with a
present of a tun of claret wine for his goodness); in September
1555 he nominated his secretary to the next parliament.[127] The
fourth earl was consulted over sheriffs. In a letter to Shrewsbury
from London on 3 November 1500 Thomas Jakes said that Mr
Haye of the exchequer had promised that the sheriff of Nottinghamshire and Derbyshire should not be chosen without
Shrewsbury's approval: 'he shead plenly that no shref shulde be
other but such as shuld content yoyr mynde'. Jakes had proposed
three names each for Nottinghamshire and Derbyshire, for
Shropshire, for Staffordshire and for Leicestershire: in each case
the first-named man was pricked sheriff.[128] What such scrappy
evidence does not easily allow is generalisation about the
frequency of such noble influence. Moreover even if it could be
concluded that MPs, sheriffs and JPs were regularly named by
magnates, it would remain to determine how far such choices
simply reflected the realities of gentry landholding rather than
any personal preferences by the earls. It is similarly difficult to use
a list of those serving under the earls in war, such as that of
Shrewsbury's force in 1513, to show the extent of a nobleman's
local power.

What is surprising is that there was little contact between the
earls of Shrewsbury and the cadet branch of the family based in
Shropshire and Worcestershire. The fourth earl's uncle, Sir
Gilbert, was a courageous supporter of Henry Tudor at Bosworth
Field and a deputy of Calais and occasional ambassador from
1489 to his death in 1517. His descendants were country gentry
who served as JPs, subsidy collectors, sheriffs, and occasionally at
court and in war. The earls interfered only in the late 1550s when
there was a minority and the widow of Sir John Talbot (d. 1556)
was suspected of depriving her daughter of the 1,000 marks of his
goods that Sir John, who died intestate, had promised her. Lady

Talbot allegedly sold corn and cattle for money and refused to see Shrewsbury's servant. Lady Talbot's brother declared 'the greffe that the mother bore towardes her dawghter for her vnnaturall workynge agenste her in tymes paste'. Jane's case was not legally sound and Shrewsbury evidently did not get his way. When in 1558 he arranged her marriage with Sir George Bowes, Bowes, while thanking Shrewsbury for promoting the marriage and winning the goodwill of Jane's mother, noted that the sum offered by Jane was very small compared with that due to her given her father's substance.[129]

The earls of Shrewsbury were, then, a midlands landed family with concentrations of manors in Shropshire, Derbyshire and Hallamshire, and a number of manors scattered across several different counties. Their principal residences were Sheffield Castle, Sheffield Manor and South Wingfield. They acquired considerable estates after the dissolution of the monasteries and chantries and were able to consolidate their holdings. Their estates produced, probably, no more in the mid-sixteenth century than they had in the late fifteenth century. A traditional form of administration obtained, and this was not legalistically exploited. Further revenues, and influence, were derived from mining and associated cutlery production, ecclesiastical posts, and crown offices, especially the very important duchy of Lancaster offices which the earls held in Derbyshire and Stafford-shire, and also the chamberlainship of the exchequer. For a long period the earls were in debt to the crown: the fourth earl may have been living beyond his means, but the fifth earl succeeded in improving the financial position of his family by favourable exchanges and by exerting his political influence to secure the remission of debt. The earls, as their expenditure and household stuff show, lived well. There is little evidence of disputes with their tenants or their neighbours. A major concern was the marriage of their sons and daughters, usually involving complex bargains with other noble families: the problems that the landed settlements required by marriage alliances produced occupied much of the energies of the earls and their servants. Both earls were served by many men, from collectors of small revenues to general assistants such as Robert Swyft. Both earls had connections with other families in their sphere of influence and showed just an occasional interest in the affairs of the cadet branch of the family.

Notes

1 A.J. Pollard, 'The family of Talbot, Lords Talbot and earls of Shrewsbury in the fifteenth century', University of Bristol Ph.D. thesis, 1968, pp. 5-34 38-51, 61-5, 104-5, 184, 239.

2 PRO SP1/85/fos. 72-3 (*LP*, VII 991).

3 A.H. Thomas, 'Some Hallamshire rolls in the fifteenth century', *Transactions of the Hunter Archaeological Society*, ii (1920-4), pp. 72-3.

4 J. Thirsk, ed., *The Agrarian History of England and Wales, iv. 1500-1640* (Cambridge, 1967), p. 4.

5 J. Hunter, *Hallamshire: the History and Topography of the Parish of Sheffield*, rev. A. Gatty, (1869), pp. 239-43; D.A. Postles, 'An early modern town: Sheffield in the sixteenth century', *Transactions of the Hunter Archaeological Society*, xii (1983), pp. 61-7 (which puzzlingly treats Sheffield as unincorporated: see *Calendar of Patent Rolls, Mary*, i. 170-2).

6 T. Blore, *An History of the Manor and Manor House of South Wingfield in Derbyshire* (1793), pp. 39-40, 43; Pollard, thesis cit., p. 65 and n. 3; Longleat, N. Johnston, MS Lives of the early lords of Sheffield, p. 249; Talbot Papers, B 227.

7 A.J. Pollard, 'Estate management in the later middle ages: the Talbots and Whitchurch, 1383-1525', *Economic History Review*, 2nd series, xxv (1972), pp. 553-66; Pollard, thesis cit., pp. 336, 339, 348-55; Lambeth Palace MS 709 fo. 128; Shropshire Record Office, Bridgewater Papers (see *A Guide to the Shropshire Records 1952* (Shrewsbury, 1952), pp. 85-90).

8 Leland, *Itinerary*, iii. 47; W.R.B. Robinson, 'The marcher lords of Wales 1525-1531', *Bulletin of the Board of Celtic Studies*, xxvi (1974-6), p. 345; BL Add. MS 11042 fo. 94; Shropshire Record Office, Bridgewater Papers, Box 78.

9 Longleat, Johnston, MS Lives, p. 249; Lambeth Palace MS 695 fo. 111; *Calendar of Patent Rolls, 1467-76*, p. 294 (Notts.); Lambeth Palace MS 700 fo. 89 (Gloucs.); Longleat, Johnston, MS Lives, p. 249 (Staffs.); *LP*, XV 444; Talbot Papers P 39; *Calendar of Inquisitions Post Mortem*, iv. 363-4; *Historical Manuscripts Commission, Marquess of Bath, vol. iv. Seymour Papers*, ed. M. Blatcher (1968), p. 105; Pollard, thesis cit., p. 65 (Oxon.); *Victoria County History, Berkshire*, iv. 532, 538 (Berks.); Longleat, Johnston, MS Lives, p. 249 (Yorks.); Talbot Papers P. 263; E. Williams, *Early Holborn and the Legal Quarter of London*, (2 vols, 1927), i [487], [515] (I owe this reference to Dr C.W. Brooks) (London).

10 P. Hope, *History of the Town and County of Wexford* (6 vols, 1900-11), i. 3; ii. 74, 89; iii. 130, 234; iv. 324, 456; v. 28, 420; Pollard, thesis cit., ch. iv.; *LP*, III i 430; VII 264; XII ii 173, 1310; Talbot Papers P. 7; *Historical Manuscripts Commission, Various Collections*, ii (1903), pp. 310-11 (from BL Add. MS 46457).

11 Bodleian Library, MS Top. Yorks. c.34 fo. 44; Hunter, *Hallamshire*, p. 336; Hunter, *South Yorkshire*, ii. 188; 'Testamenta Eboracensia iii', *Surtees Society*, xlv (1865), p. 373; A.L. Armstrong, 'Sheffield Castle: an account of discoveries

made during excavations on the site from 1927 to 1929', *Transactions of the Hunter Archaeological Society*, iv (1929–37), pp. 7–27.

12 Bodleian Library, MS Top. Yorks. c.34 fo. 44; Talbot Papers O 1; Leland, *Itinerary*, iv. 14; Hunter, *Hallamshire*, pp. 334–5; Cavendish, *Wolsey*, p. 163; F. Peck, *Desiderate Curiosa* (1779), p. 252; P. Beswick, 'Sheffield Manor', *Archaeological Journal*, cxxxvii (1980), pp. 468–9.

13 Leland, *Itinerary*, iv. 14; Blore, *South Wingfield*, pp. 39–40 (engravings and plates between pp. 84–5); *Historical Manuscripts Commission, de L'Isle and Dudley* (6 vols, 1925–66), i. 210, 212; Pollard, thesis cit., p. 334 & n. 1; M. Thompson, 'The construction of the manor at South Wingfield, Derbyshire', in G. de Sieveking, I.H. Longworth and K.E. Wilson, eds, *Problems in Economic and Social Archaeology* (1976), pp. 417–38.

14 Leland, *Itinerary*, iv. 14; *Valor Ecclesiasticus* (5 vols, 1810–34), v. 174.

15 Leland, *Itinerary*, iv. 2; v. 17; Pollard, thesis cit., pp. 239–40; Lambeth Palace MS 707 fo. 64; Shropshire Record Office, Bridgewater Papers, Box 346, item 36.

16 *Royal Commission on Historical Monuments, Herefordshire: i south-west* (1931), p. 74; Leland, *Itinerary*, iv. 15; v. 3; Talbot Papers P 393; Hunter, *South Yorkshire*, ii. 182; *LP*, III ii 3605; BL Add. MS 11042 fo. 96; PRO PROB 11/26 (printed by F. Brodhurst, 'The will of George Talbot, fourth earl of Shrewsbury, A.D. 1468–1538', *Derbyshire Archaeological Journal*, xxxi (1909), pp. 73–8.

17 *LP*, XII ii 1008 (9); Sheffield City Libraries, Arundel Castle MS DD 100; A. Cameron, 'Some social consequences of the dissolution of the monasteries in Nottinghamshire', *Transactions of the Thoroton Society*, lxxix (1976 for 1975), p. 54.

18 *LP*, XVI 1356, 1391 (54); XVII p. 138 fo. 33; Sheffield City Libraries, Arundel Castle MS WD 1741; *Calendar of Inquisitions Post Mortem*, iv. 377 (no. 58); Cameron, art. cit., p. 55; Talbot Papers P 63, 175.

19 *LP*, XIII i 1309 (12); BL Add. MS 11042 fo. 92.

20 *LP*, XX i 125 (12), 282 (40), 1081 (50).

21 Talbot Papers P 125, 171.

22 Lambeth Palace MS 695 fo. 31.

23 *Cal. Pat. Rolls, Edward VI*, ii. 431–2; C.E.B. Bowles, 'The manors of Derbyshire', *Derbyshire Archaeological Journal*, xxvii (1905), pp. 87–125; cf. also J. Hurstfield, 'The Greenwich tenures of the reign of Edward VI', *Law Quarterly Review*, lxv (1949), pp. 72–81.

24 *Cal. Pat. Rolls, Edward VI*, iv. 407; PRO SP10/19/fo. 45ᵥ; Sheffield City Libraries, Arundel Castle MS SD 268.

25 *Cal. Pat. Rolls, Edward VI*, v. 72–3.

26 *Historical Manuscripts Commission, Hatfield, Salisbury MSS* (24 vols, 1833–1976), i. 118 (no. 439); *Cal. Pat. Rolls, Edward VI*, v. 70–2; PRO SP10/19/fo. 53.

27 *Cal. Pat. Rolls, Edward VI*, v. 230–1; PRO SP10/19/fo. 51ᵥ.

28 Talbot Papers A 27, 31.

29 PRO C54/412 (I should wish to thank Mr S.J. Gunn for drawing to my attention the recording of noblemen's lands and debts in this volume).

30 Sheffield City Libraries, Bacon-Frank MS 4, *Valor* of Talbot estates in

pocket of N. Johnston, MS Life of Francis, fifth earl of Shrewsbury (hereafter 'B-F MS 4 *valor*'). For the dangers of *valors* see R.R. Davies, 'Baronial accounts, incomes and arrears in the later middle ages', *Economic History Review*, 2nd series, xxi (1968), pp. 210-29.

31 Shropshire Record Office, Bridgewater Papers, Box 88, *Valor*. Dr A.J. Pollard has computed the total as £490 17s 2¼d. (thesis cit., p. 454).

32 Pollard, art. cit., p. 562; thesis cit., p. 399. Ch. ix of Dr Pollard's thesis is less pessimistic than his later article.

33 Talbot Papers P 115.

34 W.H. St. J. Hope, *Windsor Castle: an Architectural History* (2 vols, 1913), ii. 377-81, 399-405; Bodleian, MS Top. Yorks c.34 fos. 36-8; Sheffield City Libraries, B-F MS 4 *valor*.

35 A.S. Scott-Gatty, ed., 'Liber Finium Custarmariorum', *Transactions of the Hunter Archaeological Society*, i (nos 3 and 4) (1918), pp. 306-7, 313-14, 317; T.W. Hall, ed., *Sheffield Manorial Records* (Sheffield, 3 vols, 1926-34), i. 28, 30, 62, 113-14.

36 S.E. Kershaw, 'To have and have not: the power of an Elizabethan nobleman: George, [sixth] earl of Shrewsbury, the Glossopdale dispute and the council', paper read at St John's College, Oxford, 31 May 1983.

37 I.S. Leadam, ed., *The Domesday of Inclosures 1517-1518* (2 vols, 1897), i. 181, 346; ii. 432, 472, 650; 'The inquisition of 1517. Inclosures and evictions', *Transactions of the Royal Historical Society*, 2nd series, vi (1892), pp. 179-80; PRO C54/395 m. 35 (I owe this last reference to Mr S.J. Gunn).

38 Lambeth Palace MS 705 fo. 128, 707 fo. 64; Talbot Papers P 279.

39 BL Add. MS 11042 fos. 95-6; Talbot Papers B 207 (2), P 55; Lambeth Palace MS 707 fo. 116, 710 fo. 39, 704 fo. 84.

40 I.S.W. Blanchard, 'Economic change in Derbyshire in the late middle ages 1272-1540', University of London Ph.D. thesis, 1967, p. 320.

41 Talbot Papers P 33, A 41; cf. A 45, P 29.

42 J.R. Wigfull, 'Her Majesties manor of Ecclesall', *Transactions of the Hunter Archaeological Society*, iv (1931-7), p. 40; Blanchard, thesis cit., pp. 273-314; J. Rhodes, 'Derbyshire lead mining in the eighteenth century', Local History series, University of Sheffield Institute of Education, vii (1973), p. 26; I.S.W. Blanchard, 'English lead and the international bullion crisis of the 1550s', in D.C. Coleman and A.H. John, eds., *Trade, Government and Economy in Pre-industrial England* (1976), pp. 33-4; R. Meredith, 'The Eyres of Hassop, 1470-1640', *Derbyshire Archaeological Journal*, lxxxiv (1964), pp. 29-31.

43 G.G. Hopkinson, 'The charcoal iron industry in the Sheffield region, 1500-1775', *Transactions of the Hunter Archaeological Society*, viii (1961), p. 123; Blanchard, thesis cit., pp. 351-6.

44 R.A. Mott, 'Early iron-making in the Sheffield area', *Transactions of the Newcomen Society for the Study of the History of Engineering and Technology*, xxvii (1956 for 1949-51), p. 231; 'Testamenta Eboracensia v', *Surtees Society*, lxxix (1884), pp. 65-7.

45 Leland, *Itinerary*, iv. 14; Blanchard, thesis cit., pp. 351-9.

46 T.W. Hall, *A Catalogue of Ancient Charters* (Sheffield, 1913), p. 81.

47. R.E. Leader, *History of the Company of Cutlers in Hallamshire* (Sheffield, 2 vols,

1905-6); G.I.H. Lloyd, *The Cutlery Trades: an Historical Essay in the Economics of Small Scale Production* (1913), pp. 66-70.

48 T.W. Hall, ed., *Sheffield Manorial Records* (Sheffield, 3 vols, 1926-34), ii. pp. vi, 57-8, 66; idem., *A Descriptive Catalogue of Miscellaneous charters and Other Documents Relating to the Districts of Sheffield and Rotherham, with Abstracts of Sheffield Wills Proved at York from 1554 to 1560* (Sheffield, 1916), pp. 87-90, 94, 104; Leader, *op. cit.*, ii. app. p. 1; D. Hey, 'The rural metalworkers of the Sheffield region: a study of rural industry before the industrial revolution', *University of Leicester, Department of Local History, Occasional Papers*, 2nd series, v (1972).

49 R. Somerville, *History of the Duchy of Lancaster* (1953), pp. 515-49.

50 BL Add. MS 46460 (3) fo. 184$_v$; Add. MS 666 fos. 320-61 esp. 358$_v$-60; Lambeth Palace MS 705 fo. 154.

51 C. Black, 'The administration and parliamentary representation of Nottinghamshire and Derbyshire, 1529-1558', University of London Ph.D. thesis, 1966, pp. 156-8, 161.

52 Talbot Papers P 361.

53 *LP*, IV i 1553 (10); W.R.B. Robinson, 'Early Tudor Policy towards Wales: part three: Henry, earl of Worcester, and Henry VIII's legislation for Wales', *Bulletin of the Board of Celtic Studies*, xxi (1964-6), p. 336 & n. 5.

54 Talbot Papers B 63, P 127, 227; Lambeth Palace MS 695 fo. 119.

55 Talbot Papers B 109; Longleat, N. Johnston, MS Life of Francis, fifth earl of Shrewsbury, p. 180; *Historical Manuscripts Commission, Salisbury*, iii. 275; C. Cross, *The Puritan Earl: the Life of Henry Hastings, Third Earl of Huntingdon 1536-1595* (1966), pp. 83, 99-106.

56 *LP*, I i 54 (10) (renewed for Francis 17 July 1529: *LP*, IV ii 3324); cf. *LP*, II i 2736.

57 Longleat, N. Johnston, MS Lives of the early lords of Sheffield, pp. 147-8.

58 Staffordshire Record Office, D (W) 1721/1/1 fos. 241$_v$-244 (Great Cartulary) for Stafford's complaint. (There is another copy in BL Lansdowne MS 106/3/fos. 7-15: ex inf. Mr C.H.D. Coleman, to whom I am grateful for his comments: we agree that internal evidence makes the petition datable to November 1558). For the commission see PRO SP12/33/fos. 2-5 (*Cal. State Papers, Domestic 1547-80*, p. 234); A.H. Anderson, 'Henry, lord Stafford (1501-63) in local and central government', *English Historical Review*, lxxviii (1963), pp. 225-42.

59 Lambeth Palace MS 700 fo. 5 (cf. Talbot Papers P 43, 268, 349, C 155, 175, 183, 191; P.W. Lock, 'Officeholders and officeholding in early Tudor England c.1520-c.1540', University of Exeter Ph.D. thesis, 1976, pp. 38-9; W.C. Richardson, ed., *The Report of the Royal Commission of 1552* (Archives of British History and Culture, vol. iii., Morgantown, West Virginia University, 1974), pp. 15-16; J.D. Alsop, 'The exchequer of receipt in the reign of Edward VI', University of Cambridge Ph.D. thesis, 1978, (I am also grateful to Dr J.D. Alsop for many references to the collectors of the earls' exchequer fees).

60 A.F. Pollard, ed., *The reign of Henry VII from contemporary sources* (3 vols, 1913-14), iii. app. i. 317.

61 A. Savine, 'English monasteries on the eve of the dissolution', *Oxford Studies*

in social and legal history, ed. P. Vinogradoff, ii (1909), pp. 255–6; *LP*, XII ii 411, XIII ii 839; W.F. Munford, *Wenlock in the Middle Ages* (Shrewsbury, 1977), p. 46.

62 T. Stapleton, ed., *Plumpton Correspondence*, Camden Society, 1st series, iv (1839), pp. 65–6, 264–5.

63 *LP*, IV iii 5964; VII 177, 247; VIII 56; cf. XI 326.

64 A. Raine, ed., 'York Civic Records, iv', *Yorkshire Archaeological Society Record Series*, cviii (1945 for 1943), p. 120; 'York Civic Records, v', *ibid.*, cx (1946 for 1944), pp. 25, 35, 80, 88, 92–5, 104, 150–1, 162; D.M. Palliser, 'Epidemics in Tudor York', *Northern History*, viii (1973), p. 61; *idem, Tudor York* (Oxford, 1979), pp. 218, 221.

65 PRO E36/215 pp. 21, 253, 591, 605 (*LP*, II ii pp. 1443, 1461, 1481–2); PRO C82/443 (*LP*, II ii 2954).

66 PRO SP1/21/fos. 195–9 (*LP*, III i 1153); SP1/29/ fos. 163, 166 (*LP*, III i 3694).

67 PRO SP1/58/fo. 285 (*LP*, IV iii 6792); PRO SP1/85/fos. 72–3 (*LP*, VII 991).

68 Sheffield City Libraries, Arundel Castle MS, SD 112.

69 PRO PROB 11/26.

70 Talbot Papers P 341; PRO E315/29/fo. 51 (I am very grateful to Dr J.D. Alsop for drawing my attention to this volume); cf. also Talbot Papers P 119, 121, 341; Lambeth Palace MS 695 fo. 49.

71 Talbot Papers A 27, 28, 31, 41, P 29.

72 *Historical Manuscripts Commission, Hastings* (4 vols, 1928–47), i. 313–14.

73 PRO SP1/85/fos. 72–3 (*LP*, VII 991); Lambeth Palace MS 695 fo. 29; Black, thesis cit., pp. 447–8; *LP*, XIII i 1543; *Cal. Pat. Rolls, Philip and Mary*, ii 446; Shropshire Record office, Bridgewater Papers, Box 346, item 36.

74 Talbot Papers P 93, 71, 85; A 31, 45, 29; cf. H.R. Trevor-Roper, 'The Elizabethan aristocracy: an anatomy anatomised', *Economic History Review*, 2nd series, iii (1951), pp. 279–89.

75 Cf. R.A.C. Parker, *Coke of Norfolk: a Financial and Agricultural Study 1707–1842* (Oxford, 1975), p. 286.

76 Lambeth Palace MS 709 fo. 14.

77 PRO SP46/1/fos. 196. 198 v; Sheffield City Libraries, Bacon-Frank MS 2/11; Talbot Papers P 37 (grains); Sheffield City Libraries, Bacon-Frank MS 2/282 (20 dozen) and Talbot Papers P 29 (8 dozen) for quails; Longleat, Johnston, MS Lives, inventory, for lings; Sheffield City Libraries, Bacon-Frank MS 2/283 (capons); Talbot Papers A 35, 41, P 25, 33 (congar).

78 Talbot Papers A 45, P 33, 67, 167; Longleat, Johnston, MS Lives, inventory; Lambeth Palace MS 704 fos. 84, 147; Sheffield City Libraries, Bacon-Frank MS 2/282.

79 Arundel Castle MS, Autograph Letters 1513–85, no. 2; Talbot Papers A 33, 41, C 183, P 33; Longleat, Johnston, MS Lives, inventory; PROB 11/26.

80 Talbot Papers A 39, C 175, 183, P 25, 29, 33, 67; Sheffield City Libraries, Bacon-Frank MS 2/259; Longleat, Johnston MS Lives, inventory, pp. 226–7; PRO PROB 11/26.

81 Cavendish, *Wolsey*, p. 167; Talbot Papers A 415.

82 *Historical Manuscripts Commission, Middleton, Wollaton Hall* (1911), p. 328;

Historical Manuscripts Commission, Rutland, iv. 294, 371.
83 Talbot Papers A 35, 39, P 33; Arundel Castle, Autograph Letters 1513–85 no. 15.
84 *LP*, I i 1415 (27).
85 G.C. Moore-Smith, 'Sheffield Grammar School', *Transactions of the Hunter Archaeological Society*, iv (1931-7), p. 152; J. and J.A. Venn, *Alumni Cantabrigienses Part i to 1751*.
86 Talbot Papers P 185.
87 F.B. Williams, jr., *Index of Dedications and Commendatory Verses in English Books before 1641* (1962), nos 3480, 24361.
88 Staffordshire Record Office, D (W) 1721/1/10 after p. 434.
89 Longleat, Johnston, MS Life of Francis, pp. 228-9; Talbot Papers O 15.
90 *LP*, III ii 3321, 3322, 3334; IV i 1201; E.B. de Fonblanque, *Annals of the House of Percy* (2 vols, 1887), i. 385-6; BL Cotton MS, Caligula B I fo. 127 (*LP*, IV iii 5920; de Fonblanque, *Annals*, i. 401-3).
91 PRO SP1/102/fos. 201, 203 (*LP*, X 459) (Bodleian Library, MS Top. Yorks. c. 36 fos. 221ᵥ-2 is a draft: I owe this reference to Mr S.E. Kershaw); de Fonblanque, *Annals*, i. 457, 470-1, 576; *LP*, XI 1048 (i and ii), XII ii 954, 989; XIII i 96, 451-2, 976; Talbot Papers A 63, 63 (2), C 203, O 8, P 39, 55, 67; Lambeth Palace MS 695 fos. 49, 73, 704 fo. 84.
92 PRO SP1/42/fo. 6 (*LP*, IV ii 3119).
93 Lambeth Palace MS 709 fos. 174, 193; cf. *LP*, III i 238.
94 *See above*, p. 13.
95 *Historical Manuscripts Commission, Rutland*, iv. 288-9.
96 *LP*, XVII 880 p. 474; Talbot Papers P43, 47, 113, 121, 279, 309; Lambeth Palace MSS 695 fo. 73; 696 fos. 27, 29, 116; 707 fo. 110; Anon., 'The Brays of Shere', *The Ancestor*, vi (1903), p. 6; *Historical Manuscripts Commission, 3rd report, appendix, Bedingfield MSS, Oxburgh* (1872), pp. 238-9; *Historical Manuscripts Commission, 15th report, appendix, part v., Savile Foljambe* (1897), p. 6.
97 Peck, *Desiderata Curiosa*, p. 252; Talbot Papers B 217 (1); D 157; E 9; Lambeth Palace MS 696 fo. 49.
98 Talbot Papers E 47, 91, O 22, 24, P 353, 355; *Historical Manuscripts Commission, 11th report, appendix, part vii*, (1888), p. 121.
99 *LP*, III ii 3604, 3628.
100 *Historical Manuscripts Commission, Calendar of MSS of the Marquess of Bath at Longleat, Talbot, Dudley and Devereux papers 1533-1659*, ed. G.D. Owen (1980), p. 58.
101 Talbot Papers D 250.
102 On the family see A.H. Thomas, 'Some Hallamshire rolls of the fifteenth century', *Transactions of the Hunter Archaeological Society*, ii (1920-4), p. 225; Sheffield City Libraries, Arundel Castle MS WD 897. On Swyft: Talbot Papers P 113; Lambeth Palace MS 695 fos. 81, 84; Talbot Papers P 175; Lambeth Palace MS 695 fo. 73; Talbot Papers P 119, 171, 387, C 23; Sheffield City Libraries, Bacon-Frank MS 2/5, 2/8; Talbot Papers P 279, 349; Lambeth Palace MS 696 fo. 116.
103 I.H. Jeayes, *Descriptive Catalogue of Derbyshire Charters* (1906), p. 288, no. 2280; Hunter, *Hallamshire*, pp. 239-41, 363-5; *LP*, XIX i 610 (46), p. 375; ii 527 (43);

690 (67); XXI i 302 (65); *Cal. Pat. Rolls, Edward VI*, i. 144, 388–91, v. 292–5.
104 *LP*, XX i 116, ii 109; Talbot Papers B 107; Lambeth Palace MS 696 fo. 1.
105 Lambeth Palace MS 704 fo. 102.
106 *Cal. Pat. Rolls, Philip and Mary*, iii. 342, 471.
107 Hunter, *Hallamshire*, p. 492; J. Eastwood, *History of the Parish of Ecclesfield* (1862), p. 178 & n. 1; Talbot Papers P 43, 47, 55; Lambeth Palace MS 704 fo. 84.
108 Hunter, *Hallamshire*, p. 485; Lambeth Palace MS 698 fo. 5; Talbot Papers P 37.
109 PRO PROB 11/26; Black, thesis cit., p. 166; Lambeth Palace MS 704 fo. 78, 705 fo. 154, 709 fo. 146; BL Add. MS 11042 fo. 96.
110 *Calendar of Ancient Deeds*, v. A 13345; BL Add. MS 11042 fos. 92–3.
111 Lambeth Palace MS 695 fo. 41.
112 Bodleian Library, MS Top. Yorks c. 34 fos. 36–8.
113 W.R.B. Robinson, 'The officers and household of Henry earl of Worcester, 1526–49', *Welsh History Review*, viii (1976), p. 27; J. Nichols, *The History and Antiquities of the county of Leicester* (4 vols, 1795–1800), iii. part ii. 575.
114 Talbot Papers P 333.
115 T. Cockayne, *A Short Treatise of Hunting*, ed. G.E. Cockayne, Roxburghe Club (1897), sigs. A 2–3, C 1; cf. Talbot Papers N 7; Talbot Papers P 153; Peck, *Desiderata Curiosa*, pp. 252, 255.
116 Smith, *Land and Politics*, pp. 136–7; *Historical Manuscripts Commission, 11th report, appendix, part vii* (1888), p. 120.
117 PRO PROB 11/14/8; Talbot Papers A 415, P 303; Nichols, *County of Leicester*, iii. part ii pp. 574, 576; 'North country wills 1383–1558', *Surtees Society*, cxvi (1908), pp. 75–7; *LP*, I i 1804 (28); *Historical Manuscripts Commission, Hastings*, ii. 2.
118 *Historical Manuscripts Commission, Hastings*, ii. 2; Talbot Papers P 315; Nichols, *County of Leicester*, iii. part ii p. 579.
119 Black, thesis cit., pp. 243; Talbot Papers B 113, P 193, 259; S.T. Bindoff, *The History of Parliament: the House of Commons 1509–1558* (3 vols, 1982), i. 396.
120 Talbot Papers C 1, 274, 274 (2), 276, P 211.
121 Lambeth Palace MS 695 fo. 115.
122 Somerville, *Duchy of Lancaster*, p. 541; Black, thesis cit., pp. 428–9; Lambeth Palace MS 698 fo. 5, 709 fo. 193; *LP*, XII ii 209.
123 Black, thesis cit., pp. 412–15; Lambeth Palace MS 698 fo. 15; Talbot Papers P 303.
124 Talbot Papers B 63, P 201; Arundel Castle MS, Autograph Letters 1513–85, no. 20.
125 Black, thesis cit., pp. 317–18, 421–2, 494–5; Bindoff, *History of Parliament*, i. 667–8; iii. 522.
126 Talbot Papers C 155.
127 *Historical Manuscripts Commission, 14th report, appendix viii* (1895), pp. 47–9.
128 Lambeth Palace MS 695 fo. 77; *PRO Lists and Indexes. ix List of Sheriffs for England and Wales* (1898).
129 Lambeth Palace MS 695 fos. 25, 47, 90.

PART FOUR : CONCLUSION

6 The power of the early Tudor nobility

The sources of noble power

'The nobles and gentlemen live for the most part on the yearly revenues of their lands and fees given them of the king.'[1] Noble power depended upon wealth. Noble incomes consisted above all of rents drawn from agricultural production, profits from mining and industrial production, fees from local and national offices, and, for the more important nobles, occasional pensions from the rulers of France and Spain. These incomes were considerable. A *valor* of c.1560 suggests that the yearly landed income of the fifth earl of Shrewsbury was over £1,500.[2] In 1523 that of the fifth earl of Northumberland was above £3,900;[3] in 1525-6 that of the third duke of Norfolk £2,800;[4] the first earl of Rutland at his death £2,600.[5] A fiscal assessment of 1558-60, presumably an underassessment, put the earl of Shrewsbury and his family at over £2,000, the earl of Oxford at £1,600, the fourth duke of Norfolk, the marquesses of Winchester and Bath and the earls of Rutland and Pembroke at £1,200 each.[6] By contrast the net annual income of one of the wealthiest monasteries, Westminster Abbey was £2,827 in 1535,[7] and that of the bishopric of Worcester £1,074 in 1539-40.[8] The annual income of the crown was some £40,000 from lands and £40,000 from customs in the later years of Henry VII's reign and some £160,000 from both sources combined in 1558-60.[9] The average wage of a building labourer was 4d a day, possibly 6d a day by 1560, or an annual income of £2-3.[10] Noble incomes of this order of magnitude—the largest individual shares of wealth and income after the king—gave their recipients the ability to raise and to pay armed forces, to build large and impressive buildings, to entertain lavishly and to live in luxury. Not only did such wealth give power over lesser men: if soundly husbanded it could produce greater wealth and greater power. At the time same noblemen were never much bothered by material concerns, nor did they examine their finances closely before embarking on any action. Carefully calculated long run motives (as opposed, in some cases, to simple greed) did not play a prominent part in noble livelihoods. In any event the relationship between wealth and power was not straightforwardly mechanical.

There is no reason to suppose that there was any decline in the fortunes of the nobility as a whole c.1485–1560: there was no early Tudor 'crisis of the aristocracy'.[11] Appearances can be deceptive, as, for example, when debt is cited as an indicator of the financial difficulties of the nobility. The first earl of Rutland died owing £8,400—but his executors were able to pay this off by selling woods and lands from his newly acquired monastic estates.[12] The third duke of Buckingham died owing £6,840— but this was no more than the equivalent of two years' net revenue.[13] Debts owed by noblemen to the crown were often unpaid taxes, partly paid purchases of crown (and former monastic and chantry) lands and wardships; sometimes such debt could be more political than financial, for example when noblemen were bound in large sums to be of good behaviour. Such debts might never be paid. Charles Brandon, duke of Suffolk, indented to pay off a debt of £24,000 in instalments from 1515; by 1534 his debt, far from diminishing, had grown to £25,853. It was then cancelled. For twenty years Suffolk had never been less than £24,000 in debt to the king, who, it seems, had not the slightest intention of doing anything about it.[14] A change of regime could secure the remission of debt. Many benefited from this after the death of Henry VII. At a crucial moment in the power struggles after the fall of Protector Somerset, the fifth earl of Shrewsbury had debts to the crown of over £1,360 remitted in November 1549 'for the great seruice' he had done the king.[15] It was thus always in a magnate's interests to roll over debts. No conclusions of general noble decay should be drawn from this: in the sixteenth century, as in the nineteenth, debt, but not ruinous debt, was a common feature of life for many noble families.[16]

The sparsity of surviving estate records makes it difficult to judge the movement of landed incomes in this period. Only a few instances of vigorous estate policy are known. The third duke of Buckingham was increasing—or attempting to increase—rents in the 1510s.[17] The first earl of Cumberland (on some, but not all, of his estates), William, lord Conyers, and Sir James Leyburn were increasing rents in the 1520s.[18] Rents were rising on certain of the estates of the *parvenu* earls of Pembroke in the mid-sixteenth century, possibly in the 1530s, definitely in the 1550s.[19] Criticisms of the enhancement of rents expressed in contemporary literature and in the demands of the rebels of 1549 are further signs that some landowners were—or were thought to be—raising rents, so exploiting an economic conjuncture of rising population and rising arable prices that should have favoured landowners. But noblemen of ancient lineage, such as the earls of Shrewsbury, on whose estates rents do not seem to have risen much before 1560, may have subordinated the search for profit to their local and regional ambitions and to contemporary notions of good lordship: or possibly they were just too rich to notice, or to worry about, inflation at its mid-sixteenth century rate.[20] Landownership could in some senses prove a nebulous blessing. The rights and privileges of customary copyholders made it difficult (should the attempt be made) for a landowner quickly and radically to change conditions of tenure in his favour. The lack of obvious upward movement of rents and the longevity and hereditary succession of some manorial office-holders on the Talbot estates suggest that it was not the earls but some of their more fortunate tenants that benefited from any early sixteenth century agrarian prosperity. Custom rivalled, even superseded, the rights of a landowner, at least making the assertion of those rights more difficult. Or perhaps the Talbots preferred to concentrate their patrimony into a more compact and easily managed whole and to increase their total holdings of land, doing especially well out of the redistributions of crown and church lands in the 1530s to 1550s. Here it is worth noting that had the earldom been held by a minor, or a feckless adult, it is unlikely that the fortunes of the family would have been advanced by such a windfall: the Berkeleys, for example, got nothing, Henry, lord Berkeley, being born nine weeks after the death of his father in 1534, two years before the smaller monasteries were dissolved, and coming to his independence on his marriage in 1554, just after the accession of Queen Mary, when the distribution of church lands ceased.[21] Many families prospered, or suffered, according to the chance of inheritance and their fortunes in the marriage market. Individual reality was more complex than social models allow.

Such considerations foster scepticism towards the grander social explanations of sixteenth and seventeenth-century history: the rise, or the decline, of the gentry, the crisis of the aristocracy. Examples can of course be found to support, but not prove, any of these. Attempts at a more solid statistical analysis are bedevilled by problems of definition. Strictly, a nobleman was a man summoned by king by personal writ to sit in the House of Lords when a parliament was held. But to undertake a study of the nobility focussed exclusively on the parliamentary peerage is to begin with a distortion. Is the sixth earl of Northumberland to be counted noble and his younger brothers Sir Thomas and Sir Ingram Percy to be counted gentry when the earl, especially in his later years, was weak, gullible and ill, and his younger brothers wielded much of the traditional influence of the earldom? Is Sir Henry Vernon of Haddon Hall, so powerful in Derbyshire in the early sixteenth century that he was known as king of the Peak, to be classified as gentry just because he did not have a title? Just how should one count the fortunes of rising families, non-noble in one century, noble in the next? How should one treat great families whose line becomes extinct or who crash in unsuccessful rebellion: their inclusion or exclusion can make the statistics give opposite conclusions. Moreover the nobility was not, could not be, a constant, static group: its composition was always changing for in an age of high mortality rates and low expectation of life, noble families, like other families, would tend to die out. K.B. McFarlane calculated that a quarter of noble families in the fourteenth and fifteenth centuries became extinct in the direct male line every twenty-five years.[22] However uncertain the precise rate, what is clear is that if new nobles were not created, the total number would always be falling, and the condition of the nobility as a group would depend on the rate at which new creations were made, which could vary considerably. As for the gentry, it is likely that by 1640 there were *more* gentlemen than there had been in 1450 or 1540 but it does not follow that such an increase was necessarily at the expense of the nobility (to accept for the moment such distinct categories).

As rents and the volume of agricultural production rose in the later sixteenth and early seventeenth centuries, it may well be that land that earlier could have supported one gentleman could now support more, that less land was now needed to live like a gentleman.[23]

Perhaps for a nobleman (if not for his steward) the revenues produced by his land were less important than the opportunities that landownership gave for building or consolidating his social and political influence within his 'country'. Stephen Tempest remarked, 'I look upon every man possessed of a great landed estate as a kind of petty prince in regard to those that live under him.'[24] At the end of the sixteenth century the seventh earl of Shrewsbury was reminded that 'you are a prince (alone in effect) in two countries in the heart of England'.[25] Tenants, servants, adjacent gentry and neighbouring towns came under his sway. A nobleman exercised patronage on his estates and on crown lands of which he was steward, nominated or influenced the nomination, of local and country officials, arbitrated his neighbours' quarrels and raised troops in emergency, an obligation which gave him further opportunities for the exercise of patronage in appointing captains and petty captains, and in general symbolised, and vividly publicised, his leadership of local society. An English nobleman spent most of his time on his estates.[26] He kept a large household. Principal residences were built or improved so that they might be the most comfortable places in which to live: the fourth earl of Shrewsbury built Sheffield Lodge and spent lavishly on tapestries.[27] Buildings were also an assertion of landownership and power, visible evidence that the noblemen who lived in them were members of the ruling class, reflecting and reinforcing 'lineage society'. Noblemen's buildings were usually the largest, tallest, most fashionable, most beautiful, most striking houses in the region. Robert Southwell thought that the castles of the earls of Northumberland were 'as mirrors or glasses for the inhabitants for the 20 miles compass every way from them to look in and to direct themselves by'.[28]

Noblemen not only owned much land; they tended to concentrate their holdings. Thomas, lord Berkeley (d.1534), 'his affection and desire of being a meer Gloucestershire man, of being imbowelled into the soil of that county' ... 'having many fair possessions in other counties, which he accounted as foreigne, hee entertained sundry communications with divers gentlemen of other shires having lands in this county of Gloucestershire, of exchanging such his lands with them as lay in the counties where they dwelt, and more commodiously for them'.[29] The earls of Shrewsbury certainly consolidated their patrimony around their principal holdings in south Yorkshire, Derbyshire and Nottinghamshire. In 1537 the fourth earl was granted Rufford Abbey, and virtually all its estates including Worksop and Rotherham, in recognition of the confiscation of Shrewsbury's Irish properties in 1536. In 1541 the fifth earl exchanged Farnham Royal, Buckinghamshire, and other lands, for a cash payment and a package of monastic lands, including plots in Crich, Dronfield and Rotherham; in the same year his sister was granted a package of rectories including Sheffield, Ecclesfield and Bradfield (of which the fifth earl was later granted the reversion). These exchanges and acquisitions reinforced the position of the Talbots as northern midlands magnates.[30]

What is remarkable is that the development of such concentrations of landholding was advanced by successive monarchs. Edward IV created and delineated areas of territorial influence in which his chosen men should rule the shires: the Nevilles in the north, Herbert in south Wales and Stafford in the south-west in the 1460s; Gloucester and the Percies in the north, the Stanleys in Lancashire and north-east Wales, and Hastings in the Midlands in the 1470s.[31] Charles Somerset, first earl of Worcester (d.1526), received a series of grants in the Welsh marches in the late 1490s, 1500s and 1510s that indicates that 'it was the kings' policy to make him the dominant figure in that region'.[32] Sir William Compton (d.1528), one of the greatest courtiers of the early part of Henry VIII's reign, used his influence at court to build up, with royal blessing, a considerable patrimony in the southern Midlands. By the end of his life this son of a Warwickshire farmer worth £5 p.a. had an annual income of some £1,500.[33] The striking endowment of John, lord Russell, later first earl of Bedford (d. 1555), in the south-west is a further illustration. A favourite and trusted servant of Henry VIII for nearly three decades, Russell was in July 1539 granted the site of the abbey of Tavistock, Devon, together with various lands, lordships and messuages; and the stewardship of all duchy of Cornwall lands in Devon and Cornwall, and the wardenship of the court of stanneries in these counties. Before these grants his landed income had been £557 p.a.; these grants added £649 officially, possibly as much as £1,000. What is especially interesting here is that Russell's endowment by the crown followed soon after the downfall of the marquess of Exeter, previously the dominant magnate, in 1538. It is revealing that Henry VIII chose to fill the vacuum of power left by Exeter's execution by creating a new nobleman to rule the south-west. His trust was shown to be well founded when Russell served against the western rebels in 1549. But it is also worth noting that Russell had been endowed in perpetuity, not merely given a life commission; and while he, as a new noble, was loyal and diligent in the service of the Tudor dynasty, his descendants included the Elizabethan earl who patronised puritan preachers and the Caroline earl who was a prominent critic of Charles I and a protector of Pym. New men soon became old nobles.[34] Others lavishly endowed included the Herberts earls of Pembroke in Wiltshire and in south Wales, and courtier-administrators like Thomas Wriothesley, earl of Southampton (d.1550) in Hampshire and Thomas Audley in Essex and north-east Hertfordshire.[35]

The consequence of this noble devolution was that England was divided into spheres of influence.[36] In 1549 Sir William Sharington told how Sir Thomas Seymour

> would divers Tymes loke vpon, a charte of England whiche he hath, and declare to this Examinate, how strong he was; and how far his lands and Domynions did stretche; and how it lay all to gither betwene his House and the Holt; and what Shire and Places wer for hym; and that this way he was emong his Friends; so notyng the Places; And when he cam to Bristow, he would say, this is my lord Protector's; and of other, that is my lord of Warwik's; to the which two, this Examinate knoweth he had no great Affection.

On another occasion Seymour showed the countries round about to Sharington saying 'all that be in thies Partes be my Frendes'.[37] Writing to the earl of Rutland, William Horsley said that in Leicestershire —— and the earl of Huntingdon had the rule; in Lincolnshire Lady Suffolk; and went on to say that if Lord —— had all of an unnamed shire, there would be but Nottinghamshire for Rutland.[38] In 1560 the fifth earl of Shrewsbury's pre-eminence in the northern Midlands was matched by that of the earl of Bedford in the south-west, the earl of Pembroke in south Wales and central southern England, the earl of Arundel in Sussex, the duke of Norfolk in East Anglia, the earl of Huntingdon in the south Midlands, the earl of Derby in the north-west and the earl of Northumberland in the north-east.[39] In some senses early Tudor England was a federation of noble fiefdoms. Moreover this was the direct outcome of the tendency of successive monarchs to entrust the general supervision of a region to a nobleman and to buttress the authority of that nobleman by grants, often on a lavish scale, of crown and church land and crown offices.

'The polityk rule of every region wele ordeigned stondithe in the nobles', wrote Bishop John Russell in 1483.[40] To their concentrated ownership of lands were added the local offices they held on behalf of the crown, especially on crown lands. From 1509 the fourth, and later the fifth, earl of Shrewsbury was steward of Tutbury, Newcastle-under-Lyme, Ashbourne, Wirksworth and High Peak and constable of the castles of Tutbury, Melbourne and High Peak. These offices on the crown's Duchy of Lancaster lands reinforced the authority of the earls in their home area.[41] In 1548 the fifth earl was appointed chief justice in eyre north of the Trent, an office which gave him the opportunity, as he himself put it, to give preferment to the offices belonging to the justiceship 'unto suche of my servantes as haue contynued long with me and haue taken great paynes in my service'.[42] Noblemen were frequently used as *ad hoc* commissioners by the central government.[43] This practice was codified and formalised in the mid-sixteenth century with the emergence of the lieutenancy. Originally (as in May 1547 when the fifth earl was appointed lieutenant in seven counties) intended to facilitate the raising of troops, and then to quell, or to prevent, rebellions and riots, lords lieutenancies developed (after a period of abeyance in the mid-1550s) into wide-ranging supervisory offices. The formalisation of the lord-lieutenancy in the mid-sixteenth century acknowledged, and reinforced, the social, political and military power of the nobility in their countries: later Tudor and early Stuart rule would be based on noble lieutenants rather than royal intendants.[44]

Wealth and lands (including those on which noblemen were crown officers) combined to give noblemen the power to 'make men'. They had large personal followings. In 1551, when the fifth earl of Shrewsbury was suspicious of the intentions of the government, he arrived in London with 'vii$_{xx}$ horse and a-for hym xl welvet cotts and chynes and in ys own leveray'. In October 1554 he rode into London with 120 horse and thirty gentlemen in velvet caps and then accompanied Cardinal Pole with his men in blue coats, red hose, scarlet caps and white feathers.[45] Nobles could raise large armies. The fourth earl of Shrewsbury's retinue in the army royal of 1513 was 4,437 men.[46] In 1536 he raised 3,947 soldiers on horseback to resist the Pilgrimage of Grace. These forces could be raised quickly. Shrewsbury heard of this rebellion on 4 October. By 8 October he had 2,470 men prepared, by 10 October 3,659.[47] Long-standing loyalties continued to help in war. In 1557 the earl of Westmorland recommended to the fifth earl of Shrewsbury that he brought with him to defend the northern borders[48]

all the worshipfull and wealthiest of the countrie so that every man of worship may haue the conduction and guyding of his owne freindes and tenantes; to thintent that if any murmor or grudg shuld arise amongest the soldiers for lak of money before the same may be provided, every man of worshipe may helpe to releve his own company and as I think the hertes of the people is such that they wold soner be persuaded by their owne naturall lords and maisters and more willinglie serue under theym for love then with straungers for monye.

At the same time it should not be concluded from this that the early Tudor nobility were great overmighty subjects on the (alleged) lines of their French or German peers. Noble concentrations of land, such as that of the Talbots, were indeed extensive, but they could never be compared to the possessions of a fifteenth-century duke of Burgundy or a sixteenth-century duke of Guise. Few, if any, of such concentrations of land were associated with definite regional feeling.[49] English noblemen did not treat the secular church as a source of benefices with which they could endow their younger sons as if they were part of their patrimony. There has, perhaps, been a tendency to underplay the continuing influence of the church: the large sums expended on church building and rebuilding in the later fifteenth century and in the sixteenth century up to the 1530s suggest that the church had maintained its attraction to lay society, even if the superior power of the lay landowning classes was clearly demonstrated in 1554 when Mary's efforts to secure the restoration of

church lands were foiled.[50] Of the land in the kingdom the
proportion owned by the nobility and the greater non-noble
landowners was around 20–25 per cent: neither in 1436 nor in
1523 were they a majority of great landowners.[51] Moreover one
should not overestimate the power of a nobleman over those
whom he hoped to lead: that was always a two-way relationship.
The raising and commanding of soldiers was never simple: the
men raised were not puppets. If they were to serve effectively,
they had to be convinced that their cause was worthwhile, that it
would be successful and that they would be paid. In 1536 the
fourth earl of Shrewsbury succeeded in leading his men against
the Pilgrims of Grace despite their likely sympathies for the
rebels.[52] In 1525, however, the duke of Suffolk's household
servants said that while they would defend the duke himself
against attack, they would not help him assault those up against
the Amicable Grant.[53] The earls of Westmorland and Northumberland failed to mobilise their tenants in 1569: only between
80 and 100 turned out for Percy in Northumberland.[54] A
nobleman was not absolute in his region: his competence, his
powers of leadership, mattered; his patronage was not limitless.
Patronage alone could not buy support.[55] But this was not a sign
of any long run structural decline in seigneurial authority or of
any transformation in ideas of service and honour.[56] What
counted were the immediate political circumstances, the
efficiency of a nobleman's planning, the quality of his leadership,
attitudes to his cause. Moreover it was always thus. A
preconception most damaging to the proper understanding of
noble power in Tudor England is a romantic exaggeration of the
greatness of noble power in earlier periods. But the world of
lordly dominance and unqualified service imagined by some
historians (and some Elizabethans) never existed. It was never
true, for example, that the north knew no lord but a Percy. In
1471 the fourth earl of Northumberland was unable to persuade
his retainers to join with him in support of Edward IV; in 1489
they failed to protect him and prevent his murder by angry
commons rioting against taxation.[57] Earlier even John of Gaunt
has been seen as facing real limits on his control over his retainers,
and the late fourteenth-century parliamentary complaints by the
commons against the abuse of magnate power have been seen as
attempts by the gentry to seize a moral advantage rather than as

a credible description of reality.[58] It is worth remembering that a nobleman may have had less choice in recruiting his affinity or in nominating MPs or local officials than might appear: some prominent gentry could hardly have been avoided.[59] In assessing relations between nobles and gentry what should be emphasised is the 'interdependence and co-operation, and constant effort of reconciling and accommodating a variety of changing and conflicting interests'.[60]

The power of early Tudor noblemen did not depend exclusively on their role as large rentier landowners and rulers of their countries. They were also expected to attend regularly, if briefly, at court where they played an important part in ceremonial. This was highly important. The impression that it made on contemporaries is evident in the space that the chronicler Edward Hall devoted to loving accounts of pageants and tournaments.[61] It was crucial for a king whose throne was weak, challenged or newly acquired to demonstrate to his more powerful subjects that he was strongly supported and well fitted to rule. It was important for any king to display to visiting monarchs and foreign ambassadors the strength that he could command. The absence of noblemen such as the fourth earl of Shrewsbury when the Queen of Scots was at court in 1516 was highly embarrassing for the king.[62] In 1547 it was vital for noblemen of ancient lineage such as the fifth earl of Shrewsbury to take part in the ceremonies in which Edward Seymour, earl of Hertford, was created duke of Somerset and William Parr was created marquess of Northampton: so the old nobility legitimised the new, an especially important proceeding when the justifications for the elevations was not beyond reproach.[63]

Noblemen were also important counsellors. It is true that they were not prominent members of successive royal councils. It is also true that noblemen, especially those of ancient lineage, are not usually found holding any of the great executive offices of state. But these facts should not be misinterpreted: as K.B. McFarlane pointed out, the king's greatest subjects were counsellors, not aspirants for office.[64] Only at times of national crisis, as in 1641, during what Conrad Russell once described as 'the last baronial revolt but one in English history', did noblemen seek specific office.[65] A great deal depended on the business of government.[66] Routine administration—even the execution of a potentially controversial policy such as war, so long as matters went well—was carried on by professional officials and administrators: noblemen for the most part would not want to become involved in this kind of administration. They might sit on the council from time to time when they were at court, but otherwise they would prefer to be in their 'country', enjoying their wealth, devoting more time to hunting than to politics. If circumstances changed the need for noble counsel grew. Henry VII, anxious about security and desiring support for his foreign policies, held *magna consilia*—meetings of noblemen—in 1485, 1487, 1488, 1491, 1496, c.1502, 1504.[67] Henry VIII, wishing to intimidate the pope, summoned the nobility to subscribe to a threatening letter in summer 1530.[68] Queen Mary broke the news of her betrothal to Philip to a similar group of noblemen after the dissolution of her first parliament. A *magnum consilium* discussed Mary's plans for the coronation of Philip in 1557.[69] During a royal minority, such as that of Edward VI, noblemen and professional administrators ran the country: the councils of that reign are more aristocratic. Major matters—war, rebellion—necessarily concerned noblemen. It is therefore misleading to write of the council as if it were an unchanging institution, or as if variations in its functions and activities were merely signs of institutional development. It is also misleading to see those who called for greater noble membership of the council as either correct in their claim that few nobles were counsellors or as exponents of a coherent conciliar ideology when this rhetorical cry was rather a means to secure what was really wanted by those who used it, removal of a royal minister or a change of policy.[70]

Nobles moreover played an important part in parliaments in the House of Lords, which was in many respects as important, if not more important, than the House of Commons. Parliaments are now rightly seen not as seeking power or sovereignty, not as opposed to the crown, but rather as events not institutions, as occasions which provided opportunities for the crown and ruling groups to meet to discuss matters of mutual concern.[71] Parliaments were more than makers of legislation. Political conflict was possible. A parliament could even be wrecked by noblemen but this was power that was rarely used. In 1547-8 Thomas Seymour, lord Sudeley, recruited supporters, aimed at promoting a bill to make himself governor of the king and threatened to make the blackest parliament that ever was in England.[72] In 1554 Paget, anxious to become the Queen's chief minister, exploited noble fears about the restoration of church lands to engineer the loss of government bills against heresy and extending the protection of the treason laws to Philip, in the hope that this would make him indispensable to Mary.[73] Here opposition in Parliament was self-interested if not factious, but opposition could be principled too, as, for example, when the fifth earl of Shrewsbury dissented from the Elizabethan religious settlement in 1559. If noblemen did, then, have the power to use parliament, it was more a latent power to be used in certain circumstances: most of the time most noblemen wished to co-operate with the crown and its ministers.

Attitudes to nobility

Obviously it is correct to argue with Sir John Fitzherbert who answered his question 'howe and by what maner doo all these great estates and noblemen and women lyue, and maynteyne theyr honour and degree?' by saying, 'by reason of their rentes, issues, reuenewes, and profyttes that come of their maners, lordshyps, landes and tenementes to theym belongynge'.[74] And yet this does not explain why noblemen were allowed to possess so unequal a share of lands and resources in money and men. Their power did not rest, indeed given the inadequacy of the means of repression available to the nobility, could not rest on force alone. Ultimately it had to rest on consent. Men who obeyed their masters may have obeyed because they feared that they would be punished if they did not but at the same time most obeyed because they had been told, and very largely accepted, that it was morally right that they should obey.[75] In the context of medieval towns 'much willing submission' has been noted, 'most of all by those who according to our standards were most unjustly treated'.[76] The issue of noble privileges was aired in contemporary literature. But almost always criticisms of nobility gave way to vigorous justifications, a triumph that both reflected and reinforced noble power. The nobility drew enormous strength from the common acceptance of the belief that its

inherited position conferred a special and privileged place upon
it.

There are obvious difficulties in considering contemporary
attitudes to nobility. The views expressed in what is overall a very
small number of books cannot be taken as definitive. They were
not written by noblemen. That they were representative of those
who thought about the matters with which they deal must be
taken on trust. That these attitudes reflected and influenced the
outlook of kings, administrators and noblemen, and percolated
through society, may only tentatively be suggested. Some of the
works cited below were dedicated to noblemen. Some noblemen
did collect books: most notably, perhaps, in this period, Henry,
lord Stafford.[77] It is not possible to connect the Talbots with any
of these writers and it is not possible here to show connections and
interactions between ideas and politics, between intellectual
interests and political ideals, as has been attempted, for example,
for the earl of Arundel in the 1620s.[78] It would be foolhardy to
point to any specific instance in the lives of the fourth and fifth
earls of Shrewsbury in which attitudes counted. And yet such a
minimalist approach, which might undermine any study of the
history of ideas, does leave large questions unanswered. It is
misleading to suppose that what cannot be shown precisely
cannot be evaluated at all.[79]

Criticisms of nobility were expressed. Rebels, or potential
rebels, did so. Richard Fulmerston reported to Somerset from
Bath in May 1549 that he had heard 'lewde and unfyttinge
talke', such as 'why shulde oone manne have all and another
nothing'.[80] Edmund Dudley devoted some space in the *Tree of
Commonwealth* to the refutation of the arrogant messenger who
contrasted worldly inequality with the natural equality of men.[81]
Laurence Humfrey believed 'there be neither fewe, nor those
altogether euel, that think this nobilitye ought to be banished
and not borne in the commen wealth'; it was 'muche doubted . . .
whether nobles oughte to be borne in a wel ordred and christian-
like state'.[82] The extent of class conflict, even of class con-
sciousness, was not great: certainly there was nothing on the scale
of late eighteenth-century Languedoc where seigneurs lived in
fear of their peasants, seeing their pigeons strangled and their
places in church taken by dissident tenantry.[83] But is should not
be supposed that noble privileges were unquestioned.

Criticisms of nobility were implicit in discussions of the definition of nobility and of what constituted true nobility. The problem here was that in theory the nobility were the virtuous, while in fact nobility was derived from birth, inheritance, wealth and favour. Clearly there was in early Tudor society, as in any society, no visible connection between virtue and nobility.[84] The ideal was a nobleman at once virtuous in his actions and rejoicing in ancient lineage. Humfrey thought that 'the hawtiest, worthiest and honourablest nobilitye is that whyche with the renoume and fame of auncestrye hath coupled excellent chrystyan and farre spred vertue'.[85] Nobility solely dependent on ancient lineage was generally criticised. 'For the onely noblenes of birth and lignage, there is no honour nor prayse to be gyuen vnto a man,' argued *The Boke of Noblenes*.[86] The emphasis that Elyot gave to education in *The Governor* tended to undermine any belief in the sufficiency of good birth.[87] A major source of criticism of nobility was the medieval christian tradition. 'Everyone came of Adam and Eve' noted Rastell's ploughman, who then asked the old question, 'for when adam dolf and eue span who was then a gentylman'.[88] The arrogant messenger whose subversive arguments were outlined by Dudley in his *Tree of Commonwealth* took this line further:[89]

He will tell you that ye be the childeren and righte enheritors to Adam aswell as thei. Whie should thei haue this great honours, royall castelles and manners, with somotche landes and possessions, and ye but poore cottyges and tenementes? He will shew also how that Christ bought you as derely as the nobles with one maner of price, which was his preciouse Bloude. Whie then should ye be of so poore estate and thei of higher degre, or whie should you do them somotche honour and reuerence with croching or knelyng and thei take it so highely and stately on them? And percase he will enforme you how conserning your soules and theres, which make you all to be men or els ye were all but beestes, god creatyd in you one maner of noblenes without any diuersitie and that your soules be as precious to god as theires. Why then should thei haue of you so greate auctoritie and power to commytt you to prison, and ponishe and iudge you?

The Booke of Noblenes observed that all men had the same celestial father.[90] Humfrey pointedly remarked that it was Joseph the carpenter and Mary the humble maid that Jesus had chosen for his parents. Nor had he borne arms.[91] All in all, christian ideals made it difficult to argue that vice or virtue corresponded to differences in social status: if the first chapter of the first gospel was devoted to a genealogy of Christ, tracing his royal descent from King David, and if Saint Paul, Roman citizen, might be regarded as noble, nonetheless the Bible made no explicit reference to nobility.[92] Arguments supporting equality might also be drawn from parallels with the body. Dudley was eloquent: 'loke when our glorious garmentes be don off, and we nakyd, what differens is then between vs and the poore laborers. Peraduenture a more foolle and shamefull karcase'.[93] Rastell's ploughman told the knight 'thy blood and the beggars of one colour be/, Thou art as apt to take sekenes as he'.[94] That we were all born the same way was a commonplace: 'Beginne we not all our life with wrallyng, and cryes?'[95] After death everyone would be powder and dust: once buried there was no difference between nobles and others.[96] (The notion of 'fame' that would outlive the decay of the body seems to have developed later in the century.) There were also complaints that noblemen were misusing their privileges—enclosing, engrossing, enhancing rents—but most often (with the interesting exception of Rastell's ploughman) such criticisms tended to be expressed as censure of wicked individuals who had failed in their duty and who were called upon to reform, and not as a fundamental critique of the social order. Nonetheless the force of this questioning of the nobility may be measured by the volume of efforts devoted to justifying it at a time when Humfrey believed that men neither wrote nor spoke freely of the state of the nobility.[97] What weakened these criticisms of nobility as expressed in contemporary writing was not that their authors neutralised the supposedly radical implications of their emphasis that true nobility came from virtue—which was hardly a novel idea—by claiming that, in empirical fact, virtues were most fully displayed by the traditional ruling class.[98] At most writers such as Elyot and Humfrey admitted that nobles begin with the advantage of the example of their illustrious forbears,[99] but often they castigated noblemen precisely for not behaving as virtuously as they ought. What did undermine their criticisms was first, that the very fact of criticising noblemen for behaving badly tended to imply that nobles ought to behave better than other men, that they were somehow intrinsically or potentially superior, that when they were virtuous, virtues glittered more brightly in them than in other men,[100] and secondly, that the emphasis placed on virtue, and on learning, as a sign of true nobility, was easily compatible with the defence of an hierarchical society at the apex of which noblemen—virtuous noblemen—were still properly to be found.[101] Moreover, however much early Tudor writers were prepared to cajole, and to report the arguments of those hostile, ultimately they defended nobility with vigour.

Nobility was a singular grace of God, asserted Humfrey.[102] God 'hath ordeyned dyuers estates and degrees in his people and creatures' wrote Fitzherbert.[103] Edmund Dudley declared that God had set an order between man and man, and man and beast.[104] More specific Biblical justification was offered by the knight in Rastell's dialogue who cited Noah's curse, referring to the malediction of Canaan son of Ham who had seen the nakedness of his father Noah and to the blessing of Noah's sons Shem and Japheth who were to be served by Canaan. Canaan's posterity became commoners, Shem and Japheth were the ancestors of noblemen and gentlemen.[105] Parallels were drawn from the body to justify inequality. Rebellion by the commons was seen as the contention of 'the vyler partes of the bodie' with the 'fiue wittes'.[106] Parallels were also drawn from the natural world. Humfrey declared 'howe muche men passe beastes, so muche the nobles to excell the rest'.[107] Elyot argued that bees, cranes, red deer and wolves all had governors and leaders.[108] Gradation was implied in a view of the world that ranked fire, air, water and earth. Considerable emphasis was placed on blood. Some men, and races, were seen as superior to others. Elyot wrote of 'Irisshemen or Scottes, who be of the same rudeness and wilde disposition that the Suises and Britons were in the time of Cesar'.[109] Rastell's knight noted that artificers made things for lords 'because comenly they haue lytell wyt'.[110] 'As it becometh neither the Man to be Governed of the Woman, nor the Master of the Servant', wrote William Thomas, 'even so in all other Regiments it is not convenient the Inferior should have power to direct the Superior.'[111] In France there was a greater emphasis on racial criteria for nobility. Some writers argued that those qualities which placed a man in society were transmitted hereditarily and that therefore the children of nobles and those of *roturiers* had inherently different capacities. Much was made of the mysterious potency of *sang* and *semence* and no little ingenuity was deployed in parrying obvious objections. In the later

sixteenth century it became common to see the French nobility as
descendants of warrior Franks, while the *roturiers* were the
posterity of the vanquished Gaulois Gauls.[112] No such clear cut
racial theory evolved in England: the 'Norman Yoke' theme does
not seem to have been used in this way.[113] Mythical or quasi-
historical origins of nobility were discussed, however, and were
used to justify nobility. Elyot told how in the beginning people
had everything in common and were equal but they had agreed
to give their possessions to men 'at whose vertue they meruailed'
whom they regarded as fathers. 'Of those good men were
ingendered good children who were brought up in virtue, strove
to equal the virtue of their ancestors, and so retained the favour of
the people.'[114]

A different kind of justification of nobility was the contention
that the social order depended on hierarchy, and, as a corollary,
that rebellions, the aim of which was to produce equality, were
the greatest of evils, leading to anarchy. 'Wherfore yf we shuld
dystroy enherytaunce, We shuld dystroy all good rule and
ordynaunce.'[115] The Doctor in *A Discourse of the Commonweal of this
realm of England* asked 'what ship can long be safe from wreck
where every man will take upon him to be a pilot; what house
well governed where every servant will be a master or
teacher?'[116] Elyot praised 'the discrepance of degrees, wherof
procedeth ordre'. Without order there would be chaos. 'Where
there is any lacke of ordre needes must be perpetuall conflicte.'
Without government and laws the stronger would force the
weaker to be their servants. Equality would be destroyed. Worse
would ensue—manslaughters, ravishments, adulteries and other
enormities—unless those who sought equality 'coulde perswade
god or compelle him to chaunge men in to aungels'.[117] Without
the spur of poverty, men would do no work.[118] A crucially
important extension of such attacks against rebellions was to
point out, as Cheke did,

> how can ye keepe your owne if ye keepe no order, your wife and children, how
> can they be defended from other mens violence, if ye will in other things breake
> all order, by what reason would ye be obeyed of yours as seruauntes, if ye will
> not obey the king as subiectes, howe wold ye haue others deale orderly with you,
> if ye will vse disorder against all others?

In an hierarchical society only those at the very bottom had no one to obey them. 'The existing social order was accepted as natural, immutable: its property-orientated, patriarchal, authoritarian character in fact harmonising with much of the peasant's own experience in relation to his family and land-holding.'[118] Moreover noblemen provided support and employment for those around them: the Doctor in *A Discourse* noted that spending on building and trimming of houses provided revenues for carpenters, masons and labourers. 'The household worked as part of the local, and to some extent national, economic system, providing a major stimulant in the market economy.'[119] Nobility was then defended because it was ordained by God, paralleled in the body and natural world, sanctified by blood, demonstrated by myth and history, necessary if social order and prosperity were to be maintained, advantageous to society and reckless to overturn.

At the same time the apparent harshness of inequality was mitigated by the tacit or explicit recognition of the possibility of social mobility. If Humfrey attacked 'lewde cutters and roysters who in theyr vtter behauiour, apparayle, practises & talke, counterfaite a maner nobility', he nonetheless defended new nobles who 'by theyr owne vertue and commendacion of wisedome ... atteynde to this higher room, as many at this day both singulerly learned and guyltles and sincere in life'.[120] *The Institucion of a Gentleman* vigorously defended the 'vngentle gentle'. Born of a low degree, of a poor stock

which man taking his beginninge of a poore kyndered, by his vertue, wyt, pollicie, industry, knowledge in lawes, valliency in armes, or such like honest meanes becometh a welbeloued and high estemed manne, preferred then to great office, put in great charge and credit, euen so much as he becommeth a post or stay of the commune welth, and so growing rich, doth thereby auaunce and set vp the rest of his poore line or kindered: then are the chyldren of suche one commonly called gentlemen, of which sorte of gentlemen we haue nowe in Inglande very many, wherby it should appeare that vertue flourisheth emong vs.

'Suche as worthynes hath broughte vnto honor' should be defended from the charge of being upstarts: 'no man oughte to contempne or dispise that man whom virtue hathe set vp more hygher then his parentes wer before him'.[121]

What moralists taught, the day-to-day manifestations of

hierarchy reinforced. Even if sumptuary legislation failed to impose appropriate clothing for different ranks in society, the successive acts and proclamations did publish the hierarchy and a man's dress did broadly correspond to his social status.[122] The extreme deference adopted in ceremonies or in the addressing and writing of letters to the great also reinforced hierarchy. Royal letters, proclamations and parliamentary statutes usually distinguished noblemen from the rest.[123]

Of course, the nobility survived, and, in short, the fundamental values of early Tudor society were aristocratic. In two important respects the justifications of nobility triumphed. First, the poor turned to resignation, receiving advice from Humfrey to pay to God 'the stout auengeour of the poore', or waiting, as did Rastell's ploughman 'tyll god wyll send/ A tyme tyll our gouernours may intend/ Of all enormytees the reformacyon/ . . . / For the amendment of the world is not in me'.[124] Secondly, noble values permeated lower levels of society. Popular culture, based on mythical, medieval and chivalric societies, was imbued with aristocratic values which, however much modified by this 'sinking', influenced even the uneducated and the poor.[125] At a higher level, ambitious men were constantly striving to be accepted as gentlemen, and then to establish their families within the gentry. Prosperous yeomen sought the trappings of gentility. Courtiers such as Sir William Compton built up a landed inheritance that would serve as a power base for his heirs and lead to a title of nobility for his grandson, testifying eloquently to the attractions of the noble way of life to ambitious men in early Tudor England.[126] Royal administrators did the same. Lawyers 'as soon as they were able . . . acquired the lands and interest of the country gentleman'. The objectives of common lawyers were 'nowhere more obvious than in the widespread refusal of families to forge continuing links with the profession'. There were few legal or administrative dynasties: such posts offered 'lucrative careers for individuals'.[127] Few lawyers, or merchants, who could afford to set themselves up as gentry (and of course not all could) failed to do so. Once advanced, such social climbers had a vested interest not only in raising the drawbridges but also in defending nobility and gentility as such. 'Quel meilleur signe de la vigueur de la noblesse que "la trahison de la bourgeoisie"?'[128] Such aspirations survived well into the nineteenth century and beyond.[129]

Contemporary writers also emphasised the duties of the nobility. 'To be a perfect soldier or Captaine in the warres or to haue knowledge in the feates of armes', wrote the author of *The Institucion of a Gentleman*, 'is so honourable in a gentleman that there can be nothyng more prayse worthy, nether is there any thing which hath reised nobilitie to higher honour then valiency in armes hath done.'[130] *The Book of Noblesse* was a clarion call to chivalry to put forthe youre silf, avaunsing youre corageous hertis to werre, and late youre strenght be revyved and waked agen, furious, egre, and rampanyng as liouns woulde put you frome your said rightful enheritaunce'.[131] To some extent this noble ideal was challenged by early sixteenth-century humanists but their immediate influence has been exaggerated. If Dudley acutely observed that 'warr is a greate consumer of treasure and riches ... Ther are many waies to enter into yt, and the begyning semeth a greate pleasure, but the waie is verie narroo to come honorablely owt therof', he nonetheless also believed that chivalry's reward was to defend prince, church and realm.[132] If it is remembered that chivalry was always an ideal, an aspiration, not a reality, then laments such as those by Caxton may be seen in proportion and not as evidence of noble decline.[133] If Erasmus and Colet wrote against war, their stand was isolated. The Knight in *A Discourse of the Commonweal of this Realm of England* could assert that 'we that be gentlemen will with our policy in war provide that we come not in subjection of any other nation' and many mid-sixteenth century writers were preoccupied by the country's lack of military preparedness.[134]

Noblemen were to serve their king. For Castiglione 'the final end of a courtier ... is to become an Instructor and Teacher of his Prince or Lorde, inclininge him to vertuous practices'.[135] As William Turner pointed out, kings required the service of noblemen in order to govern: even Moses had not ruled alone.[136] Humfrey thought that all countries 'staye on the counsaile wit & authority of the nobility' ... 'for they be both the eyes and eares of prynces'.[137] More precisely such service included attendance on the king. Lydgate wrote 'howe it longeth to a kynge ones in the yere to shewe hym in his astate royall and beste array and his lordes in the same wyse to shewe them selfe in his presence'.[138] Well born men were particularly suited to serve as ambassadors[139]

because gentlemen doe know how to beare countenaunce & comly gesture
before the Majestye of a king better than other sortes of men: also gesture before
the Majestye of a king better than other sortes of men: also they know how to
receiue and interteigne others, and how they themselues oughte to be
interteined.

Noblemen and gentlemen were also expected to be social and
political leaders in their own communities. 'As they be the
subiectes of kinges so be they in maner the lordes of the people.'
Rastell's knight had 'holp to ponysshe theuys & brybers
alwey/To the grete tranquylyte of my contray'.[140] Asking 'how a
gentleman dwelling in the cuntrie, may profitt others bi his office
or otherwise', the author of *The Institucion of a Gentleman* wrote:[141]

To bee a iustice of peace in the cuntrye, as a stay for symple men & helper of
theyr causes by way of arbitrement, or otherwise to end their contentions, and
stynt theyr stryues, it is a goodly ministracion and office for a gentleman wherin
a man may doo muche benefite to the commonwelth & purches great loue
emong his neighbours.

There was an apparent growth in demands for the nobility to
acquire an education. There is an obvious contrast between *The
Book of Noblesse* which regarded education as inappropriate to
nobility and Elyot's *Governor* which insisted upon it.[142] Many
writers complained that the nobility were not learned. 'For
veryle I feare me, the noble men and gentlemen of England be
the worst brought vp for the most parte of any realme of
Christendom.'[143] 'The moste parte of the noble men and
gentlemen in England is not learned', wrote William Turner.[144]
Humfrey sighed: 'nor is oughte at this daye more lamentable,
then the ignorance of magistrates and nobles, head cause of all
euils, both in the state and religion'.[145] Clearly it is not true of the
early Tudor period as it was true of the early seventeenth century
that 'cultural attainment was of the essence of nobility'.[146] But
some points may be made in mitigation. The standards of
learning demanded by the humanists were higher than those
prevailing earlier, and they were certainly different. In as much
as this was a matter of changing fashions, noblemen would soon
catch up. Late medieval noblemen were not, moreover, as
unlearned as legend has it.[147] The Burgundian court, imitated in

England under Henry VII, combined chivalry with learning.[148]
The literate office-holding layman was not an invention of the
sixteenth century. While denouncing education as distracting
noblemen from their true vocation, that of bearing arms, *The
Boke of Noblesse* described how many noble born

set him sife to singuler practike, straunge faculteez frome that set, as to lerne the
practique of law or custom of lande, or of civile matier, and so wastyn gretlie
theire tyme in such nedelesse besinesse, as to occupie courtis holding, to kepe
and bere out a proude countenaunce at sessions and shiris halding

behaviour that current searches for 'county communities' and
'gentry' as far back as the thirteenth century suggest was already
old by the early Tudor period.[149] It is also important to beware
the 'optical illusions' created by the sudden abundance of
evidence in late Tudor England: before then there may have
been more noble and gentry university students than formal
records suggest,[150] the proliferation of books of manners in the
later sixteenth century need not necessarily reflect any change in
ideals or in behaviour.

One apparently new task was given to the nobility in the mid-
sixteenth century. In 1555 William Turner addressed *A New
Booke of Spirituall Physik for Dyuerse Diseases of the Nobilitie and
Gentlemen of England* to the dukes of Norfolk and Suffolk and the
earls of Arundel, Cumberland, Derby, Huntingdon, Pembroke,
Shrewsbury, Warwick and Westmorland. 'The proper office and
worke of a ryght noble man', he wrote, 'is to set forth and defende
the true religion of almyghty God' and to destroy false
doctrine.[151] Humfrey thought that nobles must 'call, leade &
allure by al meanes their princes to christian doctrine'. 'This is
peculyer to noble men', he argued, 'to relieue the cause of the
gospell faintinge and fallynge, to strengthen with theyr ayde
empoeryshed religyon, to shield it forsaken with theyr
patronage'. 'They be in maner the pastours of the people.'[152]
Obviously the emergence of religious diversity by the mid-
sixteenth century created a new situation: noblemen did, like the
Elizabethan earls of Bedford, Huntingdon and Leicester, take up
such advice, though not always, as the opposition to the
Elizabethan settlement of the fifth earl of Shrewsbury shows, in
the way that protestant writers wanted. And yet there are echoes

of an earlier crusading tradition here. In Dudley's *Tree of Commonwealth* the 'chivalry' were thus described: 'thies be the very trew christen knightes of whom all we may lerne to do our dewties in the defence of the faith of the churche of Christ'.[153]

Nobles were urged to be liberal and hospitable. Elyot thought that 'liberaltie, in a noble man specially, is commended'.[154]

To gentlemen of the cuntry which haue landes or lyunge there to, it hathe been a greate prayse in tymes past, and is trulye a thyng prayse worthy, to be good houskepers, to reliue their neighbours with meate and drynke, to fede many and be themselues fed of few, to seke London seldome, and at theyr owne houses often to be sought, to haue their smokye kytchens replenysshed wyth vytayle.'[155]

Humfrey urged noblemen to follow the example of his patron Sir Antony Cave and secure provision for the weak, widows, orphans and the aged, reduce vagabondage, compel the idle to labour and repress ravenours and extortioners.[156] Noblemen were also exhorted to do nothing unworthy of nobility. Fitzherbert urged landowners not to 'heyghten their rentes of theyr tenantes, or to cause them to pay more rent, or a greater fyne, than they haue bene accustomed to do in tyme past'.[157] Noblemen should avoid quarrels among themselves. Humfrey cried woe to the nation 'where one man is hangman or butcher to another or rather to himself'. Such divisions had facilitated the invasions of Caesar and William the Conqueror. 'Nothing plageth England but the many breaches, and euer vnsure, neuer faithful, frendshyppe of the nobles.'[158] Nobles were not to demean themselves. For Elyot 'a gentilman, plainge or singing in a commune audience, appaireth his estimation: the people forgettinge reuerence, when they beholde him in the similitude of a common seruant or minstrell'.[159] *The Institucion of a Gentleman* criticised those who knew too much about husbandry, clothmaking and merchandise: 'by continuance of bying & selling they are not estemed as gentlemen but marchantes'. Gentlemen should rather hold offices 'wher in may be no apperaunce or likely hode of disonestie'.[160] French writers, following Xenophon, believed that the work of artisans corrupted and spoilt their bodies and diminished their intellectual faculties. Merchants could not be gentlemen because they were unable to avoid lying in the practice of their trade.[161]

Thus noble power was conditioned by the values of this society. Noblemen were to serve in wars, forgetting their own ease: this the fourth and fifth earls of Shrewsbury certainly did. Noblemen were to be counsellors of their princes, again a task undertaken by the earls of Shrewsbury. Noblemen were to attend kings at court and act as ambassadors: the earls of Shrewsbury did, although in 1516 the fourth earl expressed his disquiet at the current state of court politics by staying on his estates. Noblemen were to rule their countries: this the Talbots did. The demands for education largely passed them by but they defended 'true religion' as they saw it, even if their definition was not that of the reformers. Only glimpses of what they thought of their responsibilities may be seen. Warning his fellow peers in a deputation due to visit Catherine of Aragon in June 1531 not to speak roughly against her, the fourth earl of Shrewsbury said that 'they represented the nobility of the kingdom and ought to behave as such, not to use unbecoming words, or swerve from truth and justice to the detriment of princes or private persons'.[162] By contemporary standards the Talbots did nothing to stain their nobility.

Noble power in perspective

Noble power, then, depended upon wealth and income, on the ownership of land, on command over men, on local and crown office, on attendance at court and counsel to the king, and on contemporary acquiescence in noble power and noble privileges. A final assessment of the power of noblemen as individuals, and the power of the nobility as a whole, must be made by contrast with royal power.

England was a monarchy. Monarchy was unquestioned as a system of government. Monarchs were seen as supernatural beings: anointed with holy oil at their coronation, they touched for the king's evil. In ceremonies and pageants they were portrayed as classical and Biblical heroes. There was in early Tudor kingship a good deal of moral authority: kings were God's lieutenants whose will was not to be resisted. That was reinforced by physical resources: monarchs were in this period by far the wealthiest individuals in England, possessing the largest estates,

revenues, palaces, retinues. In theory royal power greatly
outweighed that of any nobleman. In practice matters were not
so clear-cut. There has been a tendency to 'reify' monarchy: in
fact monarchical authority had to be created and constantly
adjusted and maintained by Tudor monarchs. Henri IV of
France, it has been suggested, 'had consciously to create the
stability of his regime after the wars. There was nothing natural
or automatic about it. It was a deliberate, in some senses artificial
creation, which could have easily been overturned, and which
was constantly being tested, but which became stronger the
longer it lasted.'[163] Much the same was true of early Tudor
monarchy. That meant that circumstances were highly important. The monarchy was weakest on the death and accession
of a king, or during the reign of a usurper or a minor. A young
king such as Edward VI could not rule like an adult: popular
rebellions, courtly intrigue and noble coups mark his reign. Usur-
pers of doubtful legitimacy like Henry VII had to fight, and to
win, their battles before they become fully accepted within their
realm and without: it is striking how much support Perkin Warbeck received from the kings of France and Scotland. Even kings
who acceded without challenge might find it prudent to sacrifice
the unpopular ministers of the former regime.

Royal personality and luck were crucially important in
determining the nature of power exercised by a monarch. Once
established, once they had convinced their leading subjects that
they were not to be disobeyed, then monarchs had little to fear,
unless they provoked dissent and disturbance by their blatant
incompetence, partiality, corruption or innovation. Henry VII
from 1500, Henry VIII after he had discovered Wolsey, Mary
after 1555 each achieved such a dominant position. Then power
could make power. Then the theoretical prerogatives of
monarchs could be exercised, especially by the distribution of
their large reservoirs of patronage, by ceremonial and by their
command of propaganda, to inculcate habits of loyalty. It would
become difficult for a nobleman to refuse a service requested by
the crown. It would be easier for a king or a minister to browbeat
a nobleman before the council for some minor misdemeanour.
Provided that the crown did not take on too many interests at
once, royal power was formidable. Reigns could acquire a
despotic flavour, as in the world of bonds and obligations of

Henry VII's later years or amid the treason laws and interrogations of the age of Thomas Cromwell.[164] A long reign could have profound consequences in such developments. The absence of civil strife could in itself make the recurrence of civil strife less likely.

But there was no long-run policy against the nobility. If at first glance Henry VIII appears the most anti-baronial king since Edward I, vindictively pursuing any noble with a tenuous claim to the throne and securing the judicial murder of magnates such as the third duke of Buckingham or the marquess of Exeter, closer examination shows the absence of policy and the importance of emotional reactions to particular circumstances. Those prosecuted were not obviously innocent; attacks on individual noblemen were not part of any general onslaught. It would be wrong, for example, to suppose that the third duke of Buckingham, the wealthiest nobleman of his day, tried and convicted by his fellow peers and executed for high treason in 1521, was the guiltless victim of charges trumped up against him by Henry VIII and Wolsey. He was accused on several counts. It was claimed that he had intended to exalt himself to the crown. It was claimed that he had imagined and compassed the death of the king by listening over a period of ten years to the prophecies of a Carthusian monk in Somerset that Henry would have no male heir and that Buckingham would be his successor. It was claimed that he had spoken critically of both Henry and Wolsey. It was claimed that he had asserted that if he had been put in the Tower for retaining, he would have done to Henry VIII what his father had intended to do to Richard III, namely to stab him with a knife. By contemporary standards these charges were quite damning: the noblemen on the jury consulted with the lord chief justice on precisely this point of law. The court of peers was not specially hand-picked and it could (and in 1534 did) acquit noblemen charged with treason.

If it is argued that Buckingham was brought down because of some long term policy, it is hard to explain the timing. Why did the king or Wolsey not strike earlier than 1521? In fact Henry VIII and Buckingham seem to have got on fairly well in the 1510s. Henry gave him gifts and visited him at Penshurst in 1518; and Buckingham attended the king at the Field of Cloth of Gold in 1520. There is no reason to think that this was intended to ruin

him financially. At most, through the 1510s, there was some
reluctance by Buckingham to play the fullest part in counsel and
ceremonial, some sense that he had not quite got his due, that his
merits were not properly recognised. Hence his intemperate
outbursts against Wolsey and the king. No doubt Buckingham
spoke and listened unwisely. But he was no dangerously overmighty subject. He was not planning rebellion, nor had he
plotted with others. His splendid new manor house at Thornbury
was conventional and in no sense intended as a threat. He had
difficulties with his tenants, especially in the marches. Perhaps
Buckingham was not long one of Henry's very closest
companions but on Henry's part there is no sign of any
fundamental or lasting mistrust. Nor were relations between
Wolsey and Buckingham bad, judging from the marriage
alliances which Wolsey promoted for him. The explanation of
Buckingham's downfall is more readily to be found in the
comment of Thomas More that he had died 'for secret treason,
lately detected to the king'. It was only in late 1520 that information about Buckingham's rashness was received by Wolsey. That
damning information came from three former household
servants whom Buckingham, notorious as a harsh master, had
not treated well. Wolsey had not sought it out and did not pursue
it with enthusiasm. He even let Buckingham know that he did
not mind what Buckingham said about him but warned him to
watch his language when talking about the king. Yet so insistent
was the gossip that it could scarcely be ignored. Once Henry
knew he acted characteristically swiftly, seeing witnesses himself.
The trial then followed. Buckingham fell not because that was
the culmination of some royal policy but quite simply because of
what Henry had just learned of his doings and sayings.[165]

It would be misleading to interpret such incidents as evidence
that kings and ministers were bent on destroying, or undermining, the nobility. If Thomas, Lord Dacre was removed from
border office in 1524, that was not an attack on the nobility.
Dacre had long wished to retire, was acutely aware of the limits
to his authority in the east and middle marches, where he held
little land, and continued to be consulted by the king and Wolsey
until his death.[166] If the tenth Lord Clifford was replaced as
warden of the west marches in 1526 after just two years, that was
not an attack on the nobility. Clifford lacked influence on the

borders and had proved ineffective.[167] If the fifth earl of Northumberland was denied traditional Percy offices, that was not an attack on the nobility. His son the sixth earl did receive all these posts, showing that it was the fifth earl as an individual, not the Percy family or nobles in general, that failed to win the fullest confidence of Henry VIII.[168] If kings or chief ministers interfered wholesale with a nobleman's lands, that was not an attack on the nobility. When Henry VII took order for the lands of the third earl of Kent, and when Wolsey did the same for the fourteenth earl of Oxford, it was because the crown wished to preserve, rather than to destroy, the patrimony of noblemen whose conduct was not worthy of their office.[169] If some noblemen were fined, or briefly imprisoned, that was not an attack on the nobility. It was rather to show that no one, not even a nobleman, could break the law with impunity. And fines, such as Henry VII's bonds and obligations, were not directed especially against the nobility.[170] If franchises were removed, that was not an attack on the nobility. Noble power there had never been unlimited and royal interference had been considerable. What happened in the early sixteenth century was more a formalisation of earlier attitudes: considerations of revenue, patronage and, in the 1530s, security, were paramount.

Moreover it would be wrong to see any extension of royal justice as an attack on noble power. Litigation is sometimes seen as a challenge to noble power, or at least as leading to a reduction of it. Instead of resorting to feud noblemen turned to the law courts. But this is misleading. Royal justice did, it is true, restrain men. Henry, earl of Westmorland concluded a description of attacks against him by saying that 'were ytt not for the dangers of the lawes, I wolde sone recompennse their doinges'.[171] But if law fostered order, that order was probably a greater gain to magnates than the reduction of their ability to stir up troubles was a loss. Yet it is easy to exaggerate the impact of royal justice. It is unlikely that violence was as endemic in late medieval society as an insensitive reading of legal records might suggest. Many allegations of violence may have been formal or rhetorical.[172] Moreover in the early sixteenth-century noblemen still had the potential to use their influence in pursuit of their local and personal interests: if there was a shift from feud to law it was very gradual. It is a myth that the court of star chamber was used by the crown against lawless noblemen: it was rather employed, as were other courts, by noblemen against other noblemen as another weapon, complementing the use of force locally, to assert their rights. It is interesting to consider the ambiguities in the attitudes of the earls of Shrewsbury and their servants when they were pursuing a matter at law. They seemed entirely convinced that their claims were just and they put pressure on royal legal officers to come speedily to the right decision. High volumes of litigation could, in any case, co-exist with much local feuding, as in the later fourteenth century and in the 1440s and 1450s.[173] The practical impediments on effective and impartial administration of justice remained throughout the sixteenth century: there was no organised police force, no local or national prosecuting authority; juries and sheriffs were vulnerable to bribery and intimidation. Informal arbitration by noblemen of gentry quarrels was and remained important.[174] But so were feuds. Quarrels over property could often be furthered by forcible entry. Men went about armed. Sir George Throckmorton admitted that he went to a disputed manor house with five servants on horseback and five on foot: 'himself a swoorde & a dagger & thother v on horseback hadd iii jauelyns & iii bowes & euery of theim a swerd & a bocler & the six on foote oon of them hadd a bowe & swerd & a bocler, ii billes & swerds & buclers & thother iii euery of theim a swerd & a bucler'.[175] A bitter dispute raged between the Crofts and Coningsbys in Herefordshire in the 1580s and 1590s.[176] In a quarrel between Gilbert, seventh earl of Shrewsbury, and Sir Thomas Stanhope, Shrewsbury stirred up rioters to attack a weir Stanhope had just built, to invade a deer park and to pull down his enclosures; Stanhope's son was attacked by sixteen armed men in Cheapside, London.[177] True, the struggles at court in the mid-century do not seem to have produced or been the result of lengthy local feuds, in contrast to those of the mid- fifteenth century,[178] but, disregarding possible differences in the surviving and exploited evidence, it may be that what saved mid-Tudor England from civil war was the fortunately brief resolution of quarrels in 1549 and 1553, and it is worth noting that these conflicts were resolved by political and military force, not by recourse to law. Too stark a picture should not be drawn. Law and order in general were in the interest of most noblemen most of the time, especially after 1549, year of popular rebellions. Local violence was not indiscriminate; there were misdemeanours by individuals, not by coalitions of families, and there were few cruel vendettas. In the long run, the lack of civil war in the sixteenth century, the fact of external peace between 1560 and 1585, the political stability of Elizabeth's forty-five year reign were all important in contributing to a climate in which new courts and procedures could develop; in which the worst sort of manipulation of local courts could be avoided; in which order, obedience and the humanist emphasis on learning and magistracy became more important; in which the way of thinking of the governing class was increasingly conditioned by law. Yet even here it is important to emphasise how gradual any change was and to remember that in the 1640s a civil war would take place in which the landed classes were prominent.

It has been argued that in this period the power of the crown was greatly strengthened (and, implicitly, that the power of the nobility was diminished) by administrative reforms. Government is said to have become more intrusive, efficient, professional, 'modern'. Criticisms of such a view on purely administrative grounds will not be discussed here. What should be emphasised is the continuing importance of patronage and the problem of enforcement. No significant change in the mechanism of office-holding occurred during Cromwell's ascendancy. Patronage was indispensable. 'Every civil servant who obtained a post ... did so as a result of the successful operation of patronage by an official or social superior.' Offices were sold. There was no career structure: few posts were a springboard for promotion.[179] The central administration remained very small in numbers.[180] Moreover in an age of inadequate retrieval systems and undeveloped communications enforcement was the greatest problem.[181] There is a danger of exaggerating the importance of administration as such: a bureaucratic system could not guarantee efficiency, as the difficulties of providing supplies to armies show.[182] Even Thomas Cromwell relied on noblemen and gentlemen for the implementation of his religious and social reforms, making no effort to introduce 'modern' administration (not least, full-time salaried officers) in the localities.[183] Landowners remained rulers of their 'countries' and agents of the central government. A

'Tudor revolution in the central administration', if there were one, could have had only limited effects in the realm as a whole, particularly perhaps in those regions dominated by larger landowners. 'Administration' is not, perhaps, synonymous with 'government'.

That administrative changes were not intended to curb noble power may be seen in the development of the council in the north. This is often seen as part of a long-term, rational policy by the crown to tame the 'backward' north, and to restrain or to replace the supposedly wild barons of that area by the modern bureaucratic rule of a council composed of royal nominees of inferior social origins. Such a view is misleading. The immediate border areas were indeed lawless, though not anarchic, but it would be quite wrong to see them as characteristic of the bulk of the country north of Trent. Yorkshire, Durham and the lower-lying coastal areas of Northumberland had more in common with the rest of England than with the borders.[184] Border lawlessness continued throughout the sixteenth century: it was as great a problem in the 1580s as in the 1520s. Royal intervention there was old by the early Tudor period: for some two centuries the crown had appointed wardens of the marches. The emergence of the council in the north lies rather in particular circumstances. The crown generally preferred to entrust the overall supervision of a region to a local nobleman. But the supply of competent, adult nobles was obviously limited. After 1537 there was no great nobleman in Northumberland, Durham or most of Yorkshire capable of exercising such a role. The earldom of Northumberland was in abeyance. Thus the council in the north was something of a makeshift, a second best arrangement. It is worth noting that Lancashire was excluded from the jurisdiction of the council: that was where the earl of Derby held sway.[185] Moreover noblemen were involved in the running of the council in the north, showing that thoroughgoing bureaucratic rule by non-nobles was not an aim of successive monarchs. As lord president from 1549 to his death in 1560, the fifth earl of Shrewsbury was impartial and took his responsibilities seriously. He and his deputies dealt with a wide range of business as the council in the north came to function as a convenient, because geographically closer, regional branch of the king's council and as a court of law combining elements of

quarter sessions and assises.[186] Shrewsbury's presidency showed
that noblemen were both able and willing to carry out public
duties and paved the way for future noble lord presidents.

Was the nobility weakened in any way (whether deliberately
or not) by the court in early Tudor England? Was power and
patronage to be found exclusively at court? Were monarchs
manipulated by courtiers? It is certainly true, and has long been
neglected, that those physically closest to kings were neither the
great nobles nor the great ministers but rather the principal body
servants, men like Sir William Compton or Sir William Brereton.
Whether such men were in any sense a threat to noblemen of
ancient lineage is doubtful. 'More attentive to his profit then
publique affairs', Compton exploited his friendship with the king
to build up a patrimony in the southern Midlands. Self-
enrichment, not politics, was his preoccupation. Of course he
might prey on some feckless noble such as the third earl of Kent
but that shows no more than that noble power, like royal power,
had to be husbanded if it were to survive intact. And it is highly
significant that it was to the noble way of life that men like
Compton aspired. That the fourth earl of Shrewsbury married
one of his daughters to Compton's son is a telling comment on the
essential cohesion of early Tudor society and shows that
noblemen knew how to benefit from the rise of courtiers.[187]

Moreover the court was not as important for a great noble as it
was for someone whose lands were still small and whose fortune
depended on continuing royal favour. Attendance at court was
not essential for a magnate in search of preferment for his friends.
Obviously men of the privy chamber had day-to-day access to
the king but this was not all-important. They might influence the
king, knowing just when to present a bill for his signature. But
others were influential too. A Wolsey or a Cromwell or a jousting
companion such as Suffolk might be consulted, a nobleman
currently at court could have his say, noblemen in the country
could write; and rulers like Henry VIII were capable of making
decisions themselves.

Men in search of preferment in early Tudor England used all
possible avenues: there was a plurality of approaches.
Advancement was not found in the privy chamber alone. Great
noblemen might, if they chose, become resident at court for a
period and they assumed the principal offices at the most

important ceremonial occasions. The fourth earl of Shrewsbury
was lord steward of the household from 1502 to his death in 1538.
In many respects this was a sinecure but it was a useful position to
hold in case the court had become more important, if, for
example, any early Tudor king had had a scandalous favourite
such as a Gaveston or a Buckingham. The basic function of a
court should not be overlooked. Courts were coeval with
kingship: kings must live somewhere and they must be served. A
vast entourage of servants was required: kitchen staff,
laundrymen, craftsmen, physicians, tutors, entertainers,
chaplains. Most of those employed at court simply carried out
standard menial tasks. The provision of clean bedding for the
king was not an inherently political activity. It is questionable
that there was any political significance in the fluctuations in the
administrative organisation of the court. How far, however,
could this be seen of the greatest importance because Henry VIII
was a weak man, often the plaything of factions whose arena was
the court? Should the fall of Wolsey, the fall of Anne Boleyn, the
fall of Cromwell be seen as the work of court faction? But Wolsey
was very much the king's servant who fell not because of any
politicking against him but because he had let the king down
over the divorce and because his dismissal in 1529 was a skilful
way of threatening both the pope and church in England.
Cromwell fell because the king was horrified by his dangerous
dabbling in heresy. It may be rather that Henry VIII was far
more in control than factional explanations would suggest.[188]

Royal government could then be considerable and it could
become ever more effective. But it was to some extent a matter of
bluff. Strong government in one year, or in one period, did not
mean that royal power had been established for ever. Sudden
death could wreck the system. In summing up Henry VII's reign
M.M. Condon has noted 'a certain superficiality of achievement
despite all the auguries of change: an impermanence, a fragility
caused in part by the tensions which Henry himself created',[189]
that is, by the methods with which he governed. Moreover even a
strong king remained dependent upon his nobility in two
important aspects. First, the early Tudor crown lacked an army
and so was dependent on individual magnates to raise forces
whether under contract or as commissioners. This weakened the
crown as often as it was necessary to put down rebellion—in

1497, 1525, 1536, 1549, 1554—and (but to a lesser extent if all went well) to mount foreign expeditions or to defend the borders—in 1492, 1512-13, 1522-3, 1542-50, 1557-8. There were no significant changes that lessened crown dependence on its leading subjects here. Nor was there any 'Tudor revolution' in military affairs that radically improved the efficiency of military organisation. If some kings and ministers did make brief efforts to control noble retaining, it would be wrong to take the language of statutes and proclamations at face value. It is doubtful whether any Tudor government wanted or expected retaining to cease. Prohibitions were intended rather to be used selectively against notorious offenders,[190] for example Sir William Bulmer who in 1519 was fined for wearing the livery of the duke of Buckingham while serving in the king's household. Lord Bergavenny, fined for retaining in 1507, served with 984 men in 1513, a neat illustration of how dependent the crown was on noble retinues. Still in 1642 the crown relied on greater landowners for soldiers.[191] Secondly, the crown remained dependent on the nobility for general supervision of their localities, a dependence that tended to increase in the sixteenth century as governments attempted to impose different versions of religious uniformity and to deal with the growing social problems of poverty and vagabondage. Of course it is misleading to see crown and noble interests as opposed. In a society in which the steady returns of agricultural production were the chief source of wealth, kings and noblemen had an immense and shared interest in maintaining the political stability and social tranquillity that ensured the continuance of their privileged position at the apex of an hierarchical society. That points to a further sense in which royal power was dependent on the nobility. There was in early Tudor England an acceptance that government was properly the king's and a consequent acquiescence in, or at most a subtle criticism of, royal policy. But there were limits which a monarch would hesitate before crossing. Henry VIII knew how to secure his divorce without the pope at an earlier point than is generally thought, but he hesitated long before taking action, consulting several times with his leading subjects whom he was careful not to provoke.[192] Mary found that she could not secure the restoration of church lands and she did not dare to put her desires to see Philip crowned and Elizabeth excluded from the throne to parliament.[193] Between crown and ruling class there was in early Tudor England an unwritten consensus.

There was in that society no single source of power but rather a complex interaction between individuals, groups of men, communities and institutions. But the importance of the power of noblemen and of the nobility as a whole is clear. In war, in the fomentation and repression of rebellion, in ceremonial, in counsel in the major political issues, in the rule of the localities, in the aspirations of non-nobles, the nobility was still the most powerful and most influential segment of society.

Notes

1 M. Dewar, ed., *A Discourse of the Commonweal of this Realm of England, attrib. Thomas Smith* (Virginia, 1969), p. 80.
2 *See above*, pp. 143-4.
3 J.M.W. Bean, *The Estates of the Percy Family 1461-1537* (Oxford, 1958), p. 140.
4 R. Virgoe, 'The recovery of the Howards in East Anglia, 1485-1529', in E.W. Ives, R.J. Knecht and J.J. Scarisbrick, eds, *Wealth and Power in Tudor England: Essays Presented to S.T. Bindoff* (1978), p. 18.
5 L. Stone, *Family and Fortune: Studies in Aristocratic Finance in the Sixteenth and Seventeenth Centuries* (Oxford, 1973), p. 167.
6 BL Harleian MS 309 fo. 75.
7 B.F. Harvey, *Westminster Abbey and Its Estates in the Middle Ages* (Oxford, 1977), pp. 62-3.
8 C.C. Dyer, *Lords and Peasants in a Changing Society: the Estates of the Bishopric of Worcester 680-1540* (Cambridge, 1980), p. 177.
9 C.S.L. Davies, *Peace, Print and Protestantism 1450-1558* (1976), p. 319.
10 M. Airs, *The Making of the English Country House 1500-1640* (1975), p. 187.
11 Cf. H. Miller, 'The early Tudor peerage 1485-1547', University of London M.A. thesis, 1950, p. 151.
12 Stone, *Family and Fortune*, p. 167.
13 *LP*, III i 1285 (5, 31): C. Rawcliffe, *The Staffords, Earls of Stafford and Dukes of Buckingham 1394-1521* (Cambridge, 1978), pp. 140-3.
14 Miller, thesis cit., pp. 140-1.
15 Talbot Papers P 341; PRO E/315/29/fo. 51; *see above* p. 150.
16 B. Coward, 'A "crisis of the aristocracy" in the sixteenth and early seventeenth centuries? The case of the Stanleys, earls of Derby, 1504-1642', *Northern History*, xviii (1982), p. 62; D. Cannadine, 'Aristocratic indebtedness in the nineteenth century: the case re-opened', *Economic History Review*, 2nd series, xxx (1977), p. 649.
17 K.B. McFarlane, *The Nobility of Later Medieval England* (Oxford, 1973), pp. 223-6.

18 M.E. James, 'The first earl of Cumberland (1493-1542) and the decline of northern feudalism', *Northern History*, i (1966), pp. 53-7, modified by R.W. Hoyle, 'A northern peer reassessed: the first earl of Cumberland', paper read at the Institute of Historical Research, University of London, 6 February 1984.

19 E. Kerridge, 'The movement of rent 1540-1640', *Economic History Review*, 2nd series, vi (1953-4), pp. 17, 24-5, 28.

20 *See above*, pp. 143-4, cf. F. Heal, *Of Princes and Prelates: a Study of the Economic and Social Position of the Tudor Episcopate* (Cambridge, 1980), p. 49.

21 Stone, *Family and Fortune*, p. 244.

22 McFarlane, *The nobility of Later Medieval England*, p. 146.

23 C.S.L. Davies, 'Landed society: the upper classes', paper read at Exeter College, Oxford, Michaelmas Term, 1973; P.J. Bowden, 'Agricultural prices, farm profits and rents', in J. Thirsk, ed., *Agrarian History of England and Wales: vol. iv. 1500-1640* (Cambridge, 1967) pp. 593-695, esp. pp. 674-95.

24 Cited by J. Bossy, *The English Catholic Community 1570-1850* (1976 for 1975), pp. 174-5.

25 P. Williams, *The Tudor Regime* (Oxford, 1979), p. 430.

26 Cf. Miller, thesis, p. 151.

27 *See above*, pp. 140-1, 151-2.

28 M. Girouard, *Life in the English Country House: a Social and Architectural History* (1978), chs i and ii; *LP*, XII ii 548.

29 J. Smyth, *The Lives of the Berkeleys* (Gloucester, 3 vols, 1883-5), ii 225.

30 *See above*, pp. 141-3.

31 C.D. Ross, *Edward IV* (1975 for 1974), p. 334; D.A.L. Morgan, 'The king's affinity in the polity of Yorkist England', *Transactions of the Royal Historical Society*, 5th series, xxiii (1973), pp. 18-19.

32 W.R.B. Robinson, 'The earls of Worcester and their estates 1526-1642', University of Oxford B.Litt. thesis, 1958, pp. 14-15; cf. G. Williams, Glamorgan Society, 1536-1642', *Glamorgan County History vol. iv. Early Modern Glamorgan* (Cardiff, 1974), p. 99.

33 G.W. Bernard, 'The rise of Sir William Compton, early Tudor courtier', *English Historical Review*, xcvi (1981), pp. 754-77.

34 J.A. Youings, ed., *Devon Monastic Lands, Devon and Cornwall Record Society*, new series, i (1955), pp. 4-7; *LP*, XIV i 1354 (12, 13); D. Willen, *John Russell, First Earl of Bedford: One of the King's Men* (1981), pp. 30-1, 62-6.

35 P. Williams, 'The political and administrative history of Glamorgan 1536-1642', in *Glamorgan County History*, iv. esp. 161-3; Stone, *Family and Fortune*, pp. 209-11; R.E. Brock, 'The courtier in early Tudor society: illustrated from select examples', University of London Ph.D. thesis, 1964, p. 222.

36 Cf. Miller, thesis cit., p. 151.

37 Haynes, *State Papers*, p. 105; PRO SP10/6/13 (5, 6, 7).

38 *Historical Manuscripts Commission, Rutland*, i. 32-3.

39 Cf. for c.1500, Williams, *Tudor Regime*, p. 429.

40 Cited by J.R. Lander, *Crown and Nobility 1450-1509* (1976), p. 13.

41 *See above*, p. 146.

42 *See above*, p. 146.
43 Williams, *Tudor Regime*, pp. 407-18, esp. 409.
44 Talbot Papers B 9, N 1; C. Haigh, *Reformation and resistance in Tudor Lancashire*, (Cambridge, 1975), p. 140; cf. P.L. Hughes and J.F. Larkin, *Tudor Royal Proclamations* (3 vols, 1964-9), i. 441; Miller, thesis cit., p. 170; B. Coward, *The Stanleys, Lords Stanley and Earls of Derby, 1385-1672*, Chetham Society, xxx (1983), pp. 151-4.
45 J. Nichols, ed., *The Diary of Henry Machyn*, Camden Society, 1st series, xlii (1948), pp. 6, 74-6.
46 *LP*, I ii 2053 (i).
47 PRO SP1/110/fos. 73-6 (*LP*, XI 930).
48 Talbot Papers D 202.
49 Williams, *Tudor Regime*, pp. 4-5.
50 Cf. J.A. Bergin, 'The Guises and their benefices', *English Historical Review*, xcix (1984), pp. 34-58, esp. pp. 57-8; 'The decline and fall of the house of Guise as an ecclesiastical dynasty', *Historical Journal*, xxv (1982), 781-803, esp. 781-2, 791, 803. On the late medieval church see C. Haigh, 'Anticlericalism and the English reformation', *History*, lxviii (1983), pp. 391-407; J.J. Scarisbrick, *The Reformation and the English People* (Oxford, 1984). I hope to prepare a social history of late medieval churchbuilding and of attitudes to churches in the sixteenth century. Much criticism of the late medieval church has rested on an unquestioning acceptance of John Foxe: my graduate student Mr S.J. Smart is preparing a study of Foxe as a source for heresy and protestantism in the early sixteenth century.
51 J.P. Cooper, 'The social distribution of land and men in England 1436-1700', *Economic History Review*, 2nd series, xx (1967), pp. 434-45, reprinted in *Land, Men and Beliefs: Studies in Early Modern History* (1984 for 1983), pp. 17-42.
52 *See above*, pp. 38-42.
53 E. Hall, *Chronicle* (1809 ed.), pp. 699-700. I am completing a study of the Amicable Grant.
54 M.E. James, 'The concept of order and the northern rising, 1569', *Past and Present*, lx (1973), pp. 70-1; 'The northern rising, 1569', paper read at St John's College, Oxford, Hilary Term 1972.
55 C. Richmond, 'After McFarlane', *History*, lxviii (1983), p. 58.
56 *Pace* James, 'Concept of order', pp. 72-5; 'English politics and the concept of honour', *Past and Present supplement*, iii (1979).
57 M. Weiss, 'A power in the north? The Percies in the fifteenth century', *Historical Journal*, xix (1976), pp. 501-9; M.A. Hicks, 'Dynastic change and northern society: the career of the fourth earl of Northumberland 1470-89', *Northern History*, xiv (1978), pp. 101-2.
58 S.K. Walker, 'Power in the provinces: the example of John of Gaunt', paper read at Pembroke College, Oxford, 21 November 1983.
59 B. Coward, 'The case of the Stanleys', p. 62.
60 Richmond, 'After McFarlane', p. 59 (more convincing than his claim for the greater importance of the gentry).
61 S. Anglo, *Spectacle, Pageantry and early Tudor policy* (Oxford, 1969); Davies, *Peace, Print and Protestantism*, p. 238; Williams, *Tudor Regime*, pp. 359-67; D.

Cressy, 'Apollo and Solomon', *History Today*, xxxii (Oct. 1982), pp. 16–22.
62 *See above,* pp. 24–5.
63 Cf. H. Miller, 'Henry VIII's unwritten will: grants of lands and honours in 1547', in E.W. Ives, R.J. Knecht and J.J. Scarisbrick, eds, *Wealth and Power in Tudor England: Essays Presented to S.T. Bindoff* (1978), pp. 87–105.
64 McFarlane, *Nobility of Later Medieval England*, p. 120.
65 C.S.R. Russell, 'John Pym out of parliament', paper read to the Stubbs society, Oxford, Michaelmas Term, 1970; 'Introduction', in *The Origins of the English Civil War* (1973), pp. 1–31.
66 Cf. arguments of G.L. Harriss, 'Medieval doctrines in the debates on supply 1610–29', in K.M. Sharpe, ed., *Faction and Parliament: Essays on Early Stuart History* (Oxford, 1978), pp. 73–104.
67 S.B. Chrimes, *Henry VII* (1972), pp. 141–4; Vergil, *Anglica Historia*, p. 133.
68 E. Herbert of Cherbury, *The Life and Reigne of Henry VIII* (1649), pp. 303–6.
69 *Cal. S.P., Spanish,* xi. 169, 428; *Cal. S.P., Venetian,* vi (i) 227; Loach, 'Opposition to the crown', p. 282.
70 *Pace* D.R. Starkey, 'Reform in theory and in practice 1450–1540', paper read at the Institute of Historical Research, University of London, 5 March 1984.
71 C.S.R. Russell, *Parliaments and English Politics 1621–1629* (Oxford, 1979); Loach, 'Opposition to the crown'.
72 PRO SP10/6/7 (10, 11); SP10/6/11; BL Harl. MS 249 fos. 29–29v, 34 (5); BL Add. MS 48023 fo. 350v; Haynes, *State Papers,* pp. 74–6, 85; *Lords Journals,* pp. 295–9, 307, 313; *Commons Journals,* p. 2; J. Loach, 'Conservatism and consent in parliament, 1547–59', in J. Loach and R. Tittler, eds, *The Mid-Tudor Polity c.1540–1560* (1980), p. 17; R.J.W. Swales, 'The Howard interest in Sussex elections, 1529–1558', *Sussex Archaeological Collections,* cxiv (1976), pp. 49–60. (I am preparing a study of the fall of Sir Thomas Seymour.)
73 *See above,* pp. 84–5.
74 J. Fitzherbert, *Surveyinge* (1539), fo. 2.
75 Cf. M.E. James, 'The concept of order', p. 82.
76 S. Reynolds, *An Introduction to the History of English Medieval Towns* (Oxford, 1977), p. 138.
77 Staffordshire Record Office, D (W) 1721/1/10, after p. 434.
78 K.M. Sharpe, 'The earl of Arundel, his circle and the opposition to the duke of Buckingham, 1618–28', in idem, *Faction and Parliament: essays on early Stuart history* (Oxford, 1978), pp. 209–45.
79 I have not read everything but I have attempted to make a fair sample. I have not mentioned Erasmus and More: the originality and richness of their thought makes them inappropriate for a study of typical attitudes. Here commonplaces are more relevant. It does not therefore affect the argument if I have inadvertently attributed to an early Tudor writer an aphorism from the Bible or classical literature. It is not my purpose, and there would be little reliable evidence, to attempt an analysis of the intellectual development of any individual writers cited, or of the inconsistencies within their works. Nor is my purpose to present an analysis of the development, if any, of political thought in general in this period. I hope I

have avoided the distortion of 'source mining' arising from my taking quotations on the same theme from different writers. As writers did not distinguish noblemen and gentlemen, I have followed them. Much political thought was a response to a particular event rather a carefully elaborated philosophy—for example, the tirades against rebels—but it is still worthwhile to look at the precise nature of such a reaction and to ask why one rationalisation rather than another was chosen.

80 *Historical Manuscripts Commission, Marquess of Bath*, iv. 109.
81 D.M. Brodie, ed., *The Tree of Commonwealth: a Treatise Written by Edmund Dudley* (Cambridge, 1948), pp. 88–92; cf. T. Starkey, *Exhortation to Unitie and Obedience* (rept. Amsterdam, 1973), fo. 23v.
82 L. Humfrey, *The Nobles or of Nobilitye* (1563), sig. B vi–viv.
83 O.H. hufton, 'Attitudes towards authority in eighteenth-century Languedoc', *Social History*, iii (1978), pp. 281–302.
84 Cf. G.E. Aylmer, 'Caste, ordre (ou statut) et classe dans les premiers temps de l'Angleterre moderne', in R. Mousnier, ed., *Problèmes de stratification sociale* (Paris, 1968), p. 142; S. Anglo, 'The courtier: the renaissance and changing ideals', in A.G. Dickens, ed., *The Courts of Europe: Politics, Patronage and Royalty 1400–1800* (1977), pp. 34–53, esp. pp. 37–8; C.C. Willard, 'The concept of true nobility at the Burgundian court', *Studies in the Renaissance*, xiv (1967), pp. 33–48.
85 Humfrey, *Of Nobilitye*, dedication.
86 *The Booke of Noblenes*, trans. J. Larke (?1550), sign. A vi (but cf. sig. A iiv and A iii).
87 T. Eylot, *The Boke named the Gouernour*, ed. H.H.S. Croft, (2 vols, 1880), book i esp. chs xiii–xxiii.
88 J. Rastell, *Of Gentylnes and Nobylyte* (repr. Oxford, 1950 for 1949), sig. A viv; B i.
89 Dudley, *Tree of Commonwealth*, pp. 81, 88–9.
90 *The Booke of Noblenes*, sig. B i.
91 Humfrey, *Of Nobilitye*, sig. K viiiv; L i.
92 A. Murray, *Reason and Society in the Middle Ages* (Oxford, 1978), pp. 328–9.
93 Dudley, *Tree of Commonwealth*, pp. 81–4.
94 Rastell, *Of Gentylnes*, sig. B i.
95 *The Booke of Noblenes*, sig. B iiiv; cf. Dudley, *Tree of Commonwealth*, pp. 81–4; *The Courtyer of Count Baldessar Castilio*, trans. T. Hoby (1561), sig. C. iiiv; Humfrey, *Of Nobilitye*, sig. R vv.
96 Humfrey, *Of Nobilitye*, sig. B i–iiv.
97 Davies, *Peace, Print and Protestantism*, pp. 32–33; Humfrey, *Of Nobilitye*, sig. A viiv–viii.
98 As claimed by Q. Skinner, *The Foundations of Modern Political Thought* (Cambridge, 2 vols, 1979), i. 236–8, 259.
99 Eg. Elyot, *Governor*, p. 14.
100 Humfrey, *Of Nobilitye*, sig. K. ivv; L iiv.
101 Cf. Murray, *Reason and Society*, pp. 274–5.
102 Humfrey, *Of Nobilitye*, sig. D iv.
103 Fitzherbert, *Surveyinge*, Prologue, fo. 1; cf. Elyot, *Governor*, i. 4–5.
104 Dudley, *Tree of Commonwealth*, pp. 90–1.

105 Rastell, *Of Gentylnes*, sig. B iv; cf. Genesis, ix. 21-7.
106 J. Cheke, *The Hurt of Sedition: how grievous it is to a common welthe* (1549: 1563 ed. cited), sig. B iii–iiiᵥ.
107 Humfrey, *Of Nobilitye*, Dedication, sig. A ivᵥ.
108 Elyot, *Governor*, ii. 120.
109 *Ibid.*, 88-9.
110 Rastell, *Of Gentylnes*, sig. A ii.
111 Cited by J. Strype, *Ecclesiastical Memorials*, ii. app. X p. 65.
112 A. Jouanna, *L'idée de race en France au XVIème siècle et au début du XVIIème siècle (1498-1618)* (Paris, 3 vols, 1976), esp. pp. 1, 19, 113-17, 287; A Devyver, *Le sang épuré: les préjugés de race chez les gentilshommes français de l'ancien régime (1560-1720)* (Brussels, 1973), esp. chs 1-3; and for an earlier period J. Martindale, 'The French aristocracy in the early middle ages: a reappraisal', *Past and Present*, lxxv (1977), pp. 4-45.
113 C. Hill, 'The Norman Yoke', in *Puritanism and Revolution* (1958), ch. 3.
114 Elyot, *Governor*, ii. 27-8 (and cf. ii. 186); cf. *The Boke of Noblenes*, sig. A vii; Rastell, *Of Gentylnes*, sig. B iᵥ.
115 Rastell, *Of Gentylnes*, sig. B iv.
116 *A Discourse*, pp. 31, 52.
117 Elyot, *Governor*, ii. 186.
118 Cheke, *Hurt of Sedition*, sig. I iᵥ; M.E. James, *Family, lineage and Civil Society: a Study of Society, Politics and Mentality in the Durham Region 1500-1640* (Oxford, 1974), p. 38.
119 *A Discourse*, p. 84; cf. Rastell, *Of Gentylnes*, sig. C iᵥ–ii; R.G.A.K. Mertes, 'The secular noble household in medieval England, 1350-1550', University of Edinburgh Ph.D. thesis, 1981, pp. 315-16.
120 Humfrey, *Of Nobilitye*, sig. F i; H i; cf. K iiiᵥ–iv.
121 *The Institucion of a gentleman*, sig. C iiii–D iᵥ.
122 N.B. Harte, 'State control of dress and social change in pre-industrial England', in D.C. Coleman and A.H. John, eds, *Trade, Government and Economy in Pre-industrial England: Essays Presented to F.J. Fisher* (1976), pp. 132-65.
123 E.g. *Tudor Royal Proclamations*, i. nos 86, 116, 118, 193, 215, 293.
124 Humfrey, *Of Nobilitye*, sig. C viiᵥ–viii; Rastell, *Of Gentylnes*, sig. C iiᵥ.
125 J.P. Cooper, 'General introduction', in *idem*, ed., *New Cambridge Modern History vol. iv. The Decline of Spain and the Thirty Years' War 1609-1648/59* (Cambridge, 1970), pp. 28-9 (reprinted in *Land, Men and Beliefs*, pp. 127-8.
126 G.W. Bernard, 'The rise of Sir William Compton, early Tudor courtier', *English Historical Review*, xcvi (1981), pp. 754-77.
127 E.W. Ives, *The Common Lawyers of Pre-Reformation England: Thomas Kebell: a Case Study* (Cambridge, 1983), pp. 16, 330-65, 380, 418.
128 F. Billaçois, 'La crise de la noblesse européene (1550-1650): une mise au point', *Revue d'Histoire Moderne et Contemporaine*, xxiii (1976), pp. 258-77, esp. 274. Cf. in a different context C.R. Lucas, 'Nobles, bourgeois and the origins of the French Revolution', *Past and Present*, lx (1973), pp. 84-126, and much other research on eighteenth-century French society. Cf. also A.J. Fletcher, *A County Community in Peace and War: Sussex 1600-1660*

(1975), p. 22.

129 M. Wiener, *English Culture and the Decline of the Industrial Spirit 1850-1980* (Cambridge, 1981); F.M.L. Thompson, 'The making of the English upper class', paper read at the Institute of Historical Research, University of London, 14 January 1983.

130 *The Institucion of a Gentleman*, sig. D viii–viiiᵥ (but note contradition with sig. F iii); cf Castliglione, *Courtier*, sig. C iv; cf. D iii; H iiiiᵥ.

131 J.G. Nichols, ed., *The Booke of Noblesse: Addressed to King Edward the Fourth on his Invasion of France in 1475, Roxburghe Club* (1860), p. 22.

132 Dudley, *Tree of Commonwealth*, pp. 50, 66, 98-9.

133 M.E. James, 'The concept of order', p. 52.

134 J.P. Cooper, 'Conceptions of gentility and status and their relation to education and social mobility in the sixteenth century', paper read to the History of the University of Oxford seminar, Trinity term 1972, and published as 'Ideas of gentility in early modern England', in *Land, Men and Beliefs*, esp. pp. 49-52; J.J. Goring, 'Social change and military decline in mid-Tudor England', *History*, lx (1975), pp. 185-97.

135 Castiglione, *Courtier*, sig. Zz iiᵥ.

136 Turner, fos. 16ᵥ-17.

137 Humfrey, *Of Nobilitye*, sig. A ii.

138 J. Lydgate, *The present Boke Called the Governaunce of Kynges* (1511), sig. C iᵥ-ii.

139 *The Institucion of a Gentleman*, sig. F vi.

140 Rastell, *Of Gentylnes*, sig. A iiiᵥ.

141 *The Institucion of a Gentleman*, sig. D iiii–iiiiᵥ; G i–iᵥ.

142 *The Boke of Noblesse*, pp. 77-9; Elyot, *Governor, passim*.

143 Dudley, *Tree of Commonweealth*, p. 45.

144 Turner, fo. 46.

145 Humfrey, *Of Nobilitye*, sig. X iiᵥ; cf. Elyot, *Governor*, book i. chs. xiii-xxiii.

146 Sharpe, 'The earl of Arundel', p. 239.

147 McFarlane, *Nobility of Later Medieval England*, ch. vi; Cooper, 'Ideas of gentility', pp. 42-6.

148 G. Kipling, *The Triumph of Honour: Burgundian Origins of the Elizabethan Renaissance* (Leiden, 1977), esp. pp. 13, 30.

149 E.g. J.R. Maddicott, 'The county community and the making of public opinion in fourteenth-century England', *Transactions of the Royal Historical Society*, 5th series, xxviii (1978), pp. 27-43; 'Magna carta and the local community 1215-1259', *Past and Present*, cii (1984), pp. 25-65.

150 E. Russell, 'The influx of commoners into the University of Oxford before 1581: an optical illusion?', *English Historical Review*, xcii (1977), pp. 721-45.

151 Turner, fos. 1ᵥ-10ᵥ.

152 Humfrey, *Of Nobilitye*, sig. M iii; vii.

153 Dudley, *Tree of Commonwealth*, p. 98.

154 Elyot, *Governor*, ii. 118.

155 *The Institucion of a Gentleman*, sig. G iiᵥ-iii.

156 Humfrey, *Of Nobilitye*, sig. M vii.

157 Fitzherbert, *Surveyinge*, fo. 3.

158 Humfrey, *Of Nobilitye*, sig. N ii; ivᵥ-v.

159 Elyot, *Governor*, i. 42.
160 *The Institucion of a gentleman*, sig. G iii~v~–iiii; vii.
161 Jouanna, *L'idée de race*, pp. 195, 199.
162 *Calendar of State Papers, Spanish*, iv (ii) no. 739 p. 176.
163 M. Greengrass, *France in the age of Henri IV* (1984), pp. xi–xii.
164 Cf. C.J. Harrison, 'The petition of Edmund Dudley', *English Historical Review*, lxxxvii (1972), pp. 82–99; B. Bradshaw, review of J.G. Bellamy, *The Tudor Law of Treason* (1979), *Journal of Ecclesiastical History*, xxxi (1980), pp. 361–5; J. Hurstfield, review of G.R. Elton, *Policy and Police* (1972), *The Times*, 16 Mar. 1972; and (extravagantly) D. Fenlon, 'Thomas More and tyranny', *Journal of Ecclesiastical History*, xxxii (1981), pp. 453–76.
165 I am most grateful to Mr P.J. Gwyn for showing me his unpublished paper 'Wolsey and the nobility' which argues this case, especially the importance of the timing, in depth; his conclusions were largely, and independently, confirmed by T.R. Gordon, 'The fall of Edward Stafford, duke of Buckingham', University of Southampton B.A. dissertation, 1983. See also B.J. Harris, 'The trial of the duke of Buckingham—a revisionist view', *American Journal of Legal History*, xx (1976), pp. 15–26. The quotation from More is in W.E. Campbell and A.W. Reed, eds, *The English Works of Sir Thomas More* (2 vols, 1931), i. 482–3.
166 James, 'A Tudor magnate', pp. 28–30.
167 Hoyle, "A northern peer reassessed'.
168 P.J. Gwyn, 'Wolsey and the north' (unpublished paper).
169 G.W. Bernard, 'The fortunes of the Greys, earls of Kent, in the early sixteenth century, *Historical Journal*, xxv (1982), pp. 671–85.
170 A. Cameron, 'The giving of livery and retaining in Henry VII's reign', *Renaissance and Modern Studies*, xviii (1974), p. 19.
171 *Historical Manuscripts Commission, Rutland*, i. 63.
172 Cf. P. Maddern, 'Law and violence in fifteenth century East Anglia', paper read at Pembroke College, Oxford, 31 October 1983; G.L. Harriss, 'Introduction', in K.B. McFarlane, *England in the fifteenth century* (1981), pp. xix–xxi.
173 I am most grateful to Dr C.W. Brooks, to whom I owe many of these points, for discussing these themes with me.
174 E. Powell, 'Arbitration and the law in England in the late middle ages', *Transactions of the Royal Historical Society*, 5th series, xxxiii (1983), pp. 49–68; R.A. Griffiths, 'Public and private bureaucracies in England and Wales in the fifteenth century', *Transactions of the Royal Historical Society*, 5th series, xxx (1980), pp. 128–9; I. Rowney, 'Arbitration in gentry disputes in the later middle ages', *History*, lxvii (1982), pp. 367–76; C. Rawcliffe, 'Great lords as peacekeepers: arbitration in the fifteenth and early sixteenth centuries', paper read at the Institute of Historical Research, London, 24 May 1982; cf. J.M. Brown, 'Bonds of manrent in Scotland before 1603', University of Glasgow Ph.D. thesis, 1973, esp. pp. 221–60.
175 Bernard, 'The rise of Sir William Compton', p. 769.
176 Williams, *Tudor Regime*, p. 236.
177 W.T. MacCaffrey, 'Talbot and Stanhope: an episode in Elizabethan politics', *Bulletin of the Institute of Historical Research*, xxxiii (1960), pp. 73–85.

178 Williams, *Tudor Regime*, pp. 237–8.
179 P.W. Lock, 'Officeholders and officeholding in early Tudor England c.1520–1540', University of Exeter Ph.D. thesis, 1976, pp. 49, 95, 98, 212, 260.
180 D.R. Starkey, 'Representation through intimacy: a study in the symbolism of monarchy and court office in early modern England', in I.M. Lewis, ed., *Symbols and Sentiments* (1977), p. 195.
181 Williams, *Tudor Regime*, p. 45; J.J. Scarisbrick, 'Cardinal Wolsey and the common weal', in E.W. Ives, R.J. Knecht and J.J. Scarisbrick, eds, *Wealth and Power in Tudor England: essays presented to S.T. Bindoff* (1978), pp. 45–67.
182 C.S.L. Davies, 'Provisions for armies 1509–1550: a study in the effectiveness of early Tudor government', *Economic History Review*, 2nd series, xvii (1964–5), pp. 234–48.
183 G.R. Elton, *Policy and Police* (Cambridge, 1972); cf. review by J. Catto, *Sunday Times*, May 1972.
184 B.W. Beckingsale, 'The characteristics of the Tudor north', *Northern History*, iv (1969), pp. 67–83.
185 C. Haigh, *Reformation and Resistance in Tudor Lancashire* (Cambridge, 1975), pp. 103–4.
186 Chatsworth, N. Johnston MS Life of Francis, fifth earl of Shrewsbury, pp. 257–66 (document printed in N. Pocock, *Burnet's History of the Reformation* (Oxford, rev. ed., 7 vols, 1865), v. 330–41.
187 Bernard, 'The rise of Sir William Compton', pp. 754–77.
188 On the court *see* D.R. Starkey, 'The king's privy chamber 1485–1547', University of Cambridge Ph.D. thesis, 1973; 'Representation through intimacy'; 'From feud to faction: English politics c.1450–1550', *History Today* (Nov. 1982), pp. 16–22; 'Ightham Mote: politics and architecture in early Tudor England', *Archaeologia*, cvii (1982), pp. 153–63; E.W. Ives, *Faction in Tudor England* (1979); *Letters and Accounts of Sir William Brereton of Malpas, The Record Society of Lancashire and Cheshire*, cxvi (1976); 'Court and county palatine in the reign of Henry VIII: the career of William Brereton of Malpas', *Transactions of the Historic Society of Lancashire and Cheshire*, cxxiii (1971), pp. 1–35; R.M. Jeffs, 'The later medieval sheriff and the royal household: a study in administrative change and political control 1437–1547', University of Oxford D.Phil. thesis, 1960, pp. 239–40; G.R. Elton, 'Tudor Government: the points of contact. III The Court', *Transactions of the Royal Historical Society*, 5th series, xxvi (1976), pp. 211–28; R.F. Green, *Poets and Princepleasers: Literature and the English Court in the Late Middle Ages* (Toronto, 1982), chs 1 and 2; Bernard, 'The rise of Sir William Compton'. I have benefited from many discussions on this subject with Mr P.J. Gwyn and Mr S.J. Gunn (to whom I am grateful for showing me his unpublished paper 'Charles Brandon, duke of Suffolk: a magnate among mignons?'). I hope to explore this further elsewhere.
189 M.M. Condon, 'Ruling elites in the reign of Henry VII', in C. Ross, ed., *Patronage, Pedigree and Power in Later Medieval England* (Gloucester, 1979), p. 134.
190 I have adopted the comments, on different subjects, by J. Loach, *English Historical Review*, xcvi (1981), p. 867.

191 J.P. Cooper, 'Retainers in Tudor England', in *Land, Men and Beliefs*, pp. 78–96.
192 G.W. Bernard, 'The pardon of the clergy reconsidered' *Journal of Ecclesiastical History* (forthcoming, 1985).
193 *See above*, pp. 81–8.

Note on Sources

The family papers of the Talbots, earls of Shrewsbury, were rescued from deterioration under the onslaught of rats and damp by the antiquarian Nathaniel Johnston between 1671 and 1677. They had been neglected after the failure of the family in the male line in the early seventeenth century and the destruction of Sheffield Castle during the civil war. Under Johnston's direction, many papers were bound in fifteen volumes and deposited in the College of Arms; others found their way, then or later, to Lambeth Palace, Arundel Castle, Sheffield City Libraries and the Bodleian Library. The papers deposited in the College of Arms have usually been referred to as the 'Talbot Papers' and have been cited thus in this book, using the letter of the volume and the number of the piece. (I have used volumes A, B, C, D, E, O and P). In 1983 the Talbot Papers were sold by the College of Arms to Lambeth Palace Library where they joined another part of the family papers which have been cited in this book by their Lambeth Palace Library call numbers. (I have used volumes 695-8, 700, 704-5, 707, 709-710). These manuscripts were listed in *A Calendar of the Shrewsbury and Talbot Papers, vol. i. Shrewsbury MSS in Lambeth Palace Library*, ed. C. Jamison and E.G.W. Bill (1966) and *vol. ii. Talbot Papers in the College of Arms*, ed. G.R. Batho (1971). A selection of letters from the collection in the College of Arms was published by E. Lodge, *Illustrations of British History* (3 vols., 1791, rev. ed. 1838). Those papers at Arundel were calendared by F.W. Steer, *Arundel Castle Archives*, i. (Chichester, 1968), pp. 197-202; those at Sheffield by R. Meredith, *Catalogue of the Arundel Castle Manuscripts [in Sheffield City Libraries] with an appendix consisting of a Calendar of Talbot Papers part of the Bacon-Frank Collection* (Sheffield, 1965), esp. pp. 181-222. While working through these records Nathaniel

Johnston prepared a series of lives of the lords of Sheffield, including accounts of the fourth and fifth earls of Shrewsbury: they are in Sheffield City Library, with fair copies at Chatsworth and Longleat. These lives, which were completed between 1692 and 1694, were never published: the then earl of Shrewsbury was not interested and the marquess of Halifax died in 1695 shortly after apparently showing enthusiasm for them. (J.D. Martin, 'The antiquarian collections of Nathaniel Johnston', University of Oxford B.Litt. thesis, 1956, pp. 22-23, 62-63, 329). They consist mostly of transcripts of letters, briefly introduced, and supplemented by long passages from chroniclers such as Holinshed. The Bridgewater Papers at the Shropshire Record Office contain accounts of the estates of the earls in Shropshire: see *A Guide to the Shropshire Records* (1952), esp. pp. 85-96. I have also searched through various classes of manuscripts in the Public Record Office and the British Library.

Index

221

Marney, Henry, lord 21
Mary, Queen 1, 33, 62, 68-9,
    73-90, 92-3, 106, 154, 160, 175-6,
    184-5, 207
Mary, queen of Scots, 121, 128
Mason, Sir John, 76, 78
Maximilian, Holy Roman Emperor,
    109
Melbourne, 51, 180
Melrose abbey, 122-3
Miller, Thomas, Lancaster Herald,
    34, 41, 53
Montagu, Sir Edward, chief justice,
    74
More, Thomas 22, 200
Moreton, Charles, 160
Moreton, John, 150, 158
Mountgrace, prior of, 17
Musselborough, 127

Needwood Chase, 51, 146
Neville, George, lord
    Bergavenny, 20-1, 207
Neville, Henry, fifth earl of
    Westmorland, 72, 77, 85, 128-9,
    155, 181-2, 195, 201
Neville, Ralph, fourth earl of
    Westmorland, 42
Nevilles, earls of Westmorland, 113,
    178
Newark, 36, 41
Newcastle-on-Tyne, 114
Newcastle-under-Lyme, 51, 146, 180
Noailles, French ambassador, 80-2
nobility: attitudes to law, 201-3;
    counsellors to crown, 2-3, 24-6,
    59-60, 88, 183-5, 194-5; decline,
    alleged, 1-4, 59-60, 182-3;
    definition, 176-7; households and
    hospitality, 173, 177, 196; incomes
    and wealth, 173-7; learning and
    literacy, 194-5; military service
    105-7, 129, 193, 206-7;
    parliament, 184-5; privileges, 40,
    185-91; rebellion, 39-41, 61;
    recruitment, 176, 178-9, 191-3,
    205; relations with gentry, 107,
    162, 177, 183; relations with

tenants, 4, 39-41, 61, 107, 175,
    182, 186; retinues, 20, 107, 180-1,
    206-7; supervision of localities, 3,
    11, 15, 24-6, 43-4, 112-14,
    177-80, 194, 203-5, 207
Norham, 118, 122
Northampton, marquess of, *see* Parr
Northumberland, duke of, *see* Dudley
Northumberland, earl of, *see* Percy
Nottingham, 32-4, 36, 120

Ogle, Lord 115
Ossory, bishop of, 140

Paget, William, lord, 62, 65, 70,
    78-85, 88, 185
Palmer, Sir Thomas, 67, 80, 125
Parker, John, 145
parliaments, 59, 60, 65-6, 70, 72,
    79, 81-7, 89-92, 158, 160-2, 176
    184-5
Parr, William, marquess of
    Northampton, 70, 77, 183
Partridge, Sir Miles, 70
Paulet, William, earl of Wiltshire,
    marquess of Winchester, 62, 70,
    74, 77, 83, 173
Pease, the, 127
Pembroke, earl of, *see* Herbert
Pentriche, Derbyshire, 142
Percies, earls of Northumberland,
    112-13, 178, 182
Percy, Henry, fourth earl of
    Northumberland, 182
Percy, Henry, fifth earl of
    Northumberland, 11-16, 20, 25-6,
    112, 114, 154 173, 201
Percy, Henry, sixth earl of
    Northumberland, 11, 16, 112, 114,
    153-4, 176, 201
Percy, Sir Ingram, 176
Percy, Thomas, seventh earl of
    Northumberland, 112, 116-17,
    128-9, 180, 182
Percy, Sir Thomas, 176
Percy, Sir William, 115
Petre, William, 74, 76, 82, 88
Philip II of Spain, 79, 80, 83,